INSIDE THE EURO CRISIS

AN **EYEWITNESS** ACCOUNT

INSIDE THE EURO CRISIS

AN **EYEWITNESS** ACCOUNT

SIMEON DJANKOV

PETERSON INSTITUTE FOR INTERNATIONAL ECONOMICS
Washington, DC
June 2014

Simeon Djankov, visiting fellow at the Peterson Institute for International Economics, was deputy prime minister and minister of finance of Bulgaria from 2009 to 2013. In this capacity, he represented his country at the Ecofin meetings of finance ministers in Brussels. Prior to his cabinet appointment, Djankov was chief economist of the finance and private sector vice presidency of the World Bank. In his 14 years at the Bank, he worked on regional trade agreements in North Africa, enterprise restructuring and privatization in transition economies, corporate governance in East Asia, and regulatory reforms around the world. He is the founder of the World Bank's Doing Business project. He was also principal author of the *World Development Report 2002*.

Djankov is rector of the New Economic School in Russia and a visiting lecturer at Harvard University's Kennedy School of Government. He was associate editor of the *Journal of Comparative Economics* from 2004 to 2009 and chairman of the Board of the European Bank for Reconstruction and Development in 2012–13. He is also a member of the Knowledge and Advisory Council at the World Bank. He has published over 70 articles in professional journals. He obtained his doctorate in economics in 1997 from the University of Michigan at Ann Arbor.

Printed in the United States of America
16 15 14   5 4 3 2

Library of Congress Cataloging-in-Publication Data
Djankov, Simeon.
  Inside the euro crisis / Simeon Djankov.
    pages cm
  ISBN 978-0-88132-685-7
  1. Monetary policy—European Union countries. 2. Debts, Public—European Union countries. 3. Financial crises—European Union countries. 4. Banks and banking—European Union countries. I. Title.
  HG230.3.D583 2014
  330.94—dc23
                                    2014009203

PETERSON INSTITUTE FOR INTERNATIONAL ECONOMICS
1750 Massachusetts Avenue, NW
Washington, DC 20036-1903
(202) 328-9000   FAX: (202) 659-3225
www.piie.com

Adam S. Posen, *President*
Steven R. Weisman, *Vice President for Publications and Communications*

Cover Design by Sese-Paul Design
Cover photo by © Rao Aimin/Xinhua Press/Corbis
Printing by Versa Press, Inc.

This publication has been subjected to a prepublication peer review intended to ensure analytical quality. The views expressed are those of the author. This publication is part of the overall program of the Peterson Institute for International Economics, as endorsed by its Board of Directors, but it does not necessarily reflect the views of individual members of the Board or of the Institute's staff or management. The Peterson Institute for International Economics is a private, nonprofit institution for the rigorous, open, and intellectually honest study and discussion of international economic policy. Its purpose is to identify and analyze important issues to making globalization beneficial and sustainable for the people of the United States and the world and then to develop and communicate practical new approaches for dealing with them. Its work is made possible by financial support from a highly diverse group of philanthropic foundations, private corporations, and interested individuals, as well as by income on its capital fund. For a list of Institute supporters, please see www.piie.com/supporters.cfm.

Contents

Table

Figures

Box

Preface

The problems inherent in the partial union of the euro area were foreseen by many experts over many years. But when its sovereign debt and financial crisis engulfed the region in 2010, the policy response was often chaotic, short-sighted, and hampered by political and ideological constraints. For now, the euro area has stabilized, and it may be setting out on a new path, thankfully. But as is made clear by this unusual and perceptive book by Simeon Djankov, an insider in the decision-making process, the costs of the crisis were higher than needed, and the euro area is far from out of danger. *Inside the Euro Crisis: An Eyewitness Account* offers some important suggestions for repairing the damage and minimizing the chances of crisis in the future. More than that, it tells a dramatic story of one individual economist's experience as part of the high-level decision-making process as the crisis unfolded.

Djankov, formerly a widely cited and senior economist at the World Bank, became finance minister and deputy prime minister of Bulgaria in July 2009, without previously knowing any politicians in his native country. Indeed, as he notes wryly, his only connection with the political world was through an ancestor who served as a legislator at the end of the 19th century. While at the World Bank, Djankov had spent no time dealing with the problems of the European Union as it made its historic transition toward a single currency in the previous dozen years. Yet, suddenly he was thrust into managing not only a financial crisis in Bulgaria but also an existential crisis for Europe itself, as he participated in dozens of monthly meetings and emergency communications of Ecofin, the powerful gathering of EU finance ministers.

As Djankov notes, the crisis revived old questions about the advisability of the unified currency zone—questions that had been raised in Europe a decade earlier. "Whether our countries were in the eurozone or not, all of us in Ecofin were forced to confront issues of how to save the eurozone, establish greater powers for the European Central Bank (ECB) to prevent bank runs, undertake structural reforms, and create a European fiscal union," he writes. Djankov also discusses his painful experience to try to reform some ailing sectors of the Bulgarian economy during this tumultuous period, notably his ultimately successful experience with pension reform in 2010–11.

Djankov takes the reader inside the process to describe what ideas were considered and how they got rejected or implemented as he and other economic officials struggled to deal with problems spreading through Greece, Ireland, Portugal, Spain, and Cyprus, and as unemployment soared throughout the region. He discusses how progress was made in some areas—for example, in steps toward establishing a banking union and making constitutional amendments in several eurozone countries to institute budget rules. In other areas—for example, the establishment of a fiscal union—little was achieved. The process by which these successes and failures came about has not been the subject of previous writings, as few scholars could lift the veil on Ecofin decision making and the strong personalities of those involved, and fewer EU insiders could write with such insight and analytical clarity.

The main contribution of this book thus lies in documenting what went on behind the European Union's closed doors, before investors and the public learned of the politically made decisions. It complements an already voluminous journalistic and academic literature on whether these decisions were the right ones and how they affected the resolution of the euro area crisis. One thing the author makes very clear: European economic decision making was too slow and inhibited by poor understanding of what was going on in the markets and throughout the region. Creating a more resilient euro area requires not only reining in fiscal imbalances in some euro area countries, Djankov argues, but also a different structure of the European institutions themselves.

We at the Peterson Institute are proud to have made important ongoing contributions to the policy debate on how to resolve the euro area debt crisis. In June 2009, Nicolas Véron and I published "A Solution for Europe's Banking Problem," a Policy Brief that set out a vision for unified bank supervision and regulation in Europe, one now coming to fruition in the asset quality review and the Single Supervisory Mechanism. From 2010 through early 2014, PIIE published two dozen Policy Briefs and Working Papers on the crisis as well as a conference volume on policy options in March 2012 (*Resolving the European Debt Crisis*, Special Report 21, ed. William R. Cline and Guntram Wolff). The Institute has been the leading US forum for serious discussion of euro issues. We hosted speeches and discussions on the issues by euro area finance ministers, central bank governors and board members, EU commissioners, two ECB presidents, and three heads of state. Several senior members of the Institute staff—notably Anders Åslund, C. Fred Bergsten, William Cline, Jacob Kirkegaard, Ángel Ubide, and Nicolas Véron—have provided widely followed commentary on the crisis as it has evolved. In tandem with this book, PIIE is publishing *Managing the Euro Area Debt Crisis*, a rigorously analytical account of the crisis and its decision making by William R. Cline, our long-standing expert on sovereign debt and financial crises over many years and regions.

The Peterson Institute for International Economics is a private, nonprofit institution for rigorous, intellectually open, and honest study and discussion of international economic policy. Its purpose is to identify and analyze important issues to making globalization beneficial and sustainable for the people of the United States and the world and then to develop and communicate practical new approaches for dealing with them. The Institute is completely nonpartisan.

The Institute's work is funded by a highly diverse group of philanthropic foundations, private corporations, and interested individuals, as well as income on its capital fund. About 35 percent of the Institute's resources in our latest fiscal year were provided by contributors from outside the United States. Interested readers may access the data underlying Institute books by searching titles at http://bookstore.piie.com.

The Executive Committee of the Institute's Board of Directors bears overall responsibility for the Institute's direction, gives general guidance and approval to its research program, and evaluates its performance in pursuit of its mission. The Institute's President is responsible for the identification of topics that are likely to become important over the medium term (one to three years) that should be addressed by Institute scholars. This rolling agenda is set in close consultation with the Institute's research staff, Board of Directors, and other stakeholders.

The President makes the final decision to publish any individual Institute study, following independent internal and external review of the work.

The Institute hopes that its research and other activities will contribute to building a stronger foundation for international economic policy around the world. We invite readers of these publications to let us know how they think we can best accomplish this objective.

ADAM S. POSEN
President
May 2014

Overview of the European Union's Organizational Structure

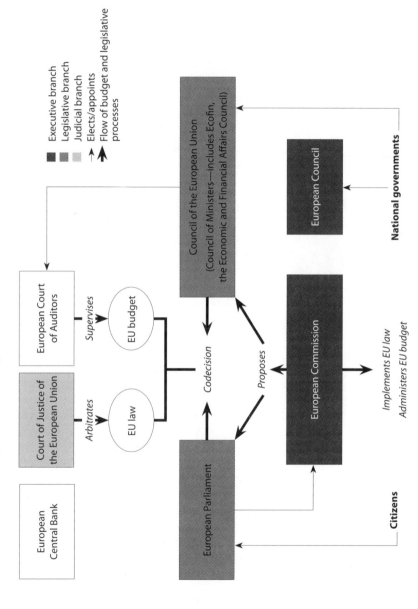

1

Introduction

In July 2009, I became the finance minister and deputy prime minister of Bulgaria. I had left Bulgaria nearly 20 years earlier and had spent my entire adult life in the United States, first studying international economics and then joining the World Bank to work on corporate and bank restructuring, regulatory reform, and financial crises. I travelled widely while at the Bank and advised many governments, but had not worked in Bulgaria. As a result, I did not know any Bulgarian politicians. The only politician in my family was my great-great-great-grandfather, who was a member of four consecutive parliaments in the 1880s and 1890s.

Nor had I spent any time dealing with the problems of the European Union, which over the last dozen years had undertaken a transition to a single currency and the establishment of the European Central Bank (ECB). As I arrived at the finance ministry in Sofia, this unprecedented effort at European integration was facing an existential crisis that would require my full attention as a member of the Economic and Financial Affairs Council of the European Union (Ecofin), the monthly gathering of EU finance ministers. Bulgaria had become a member of the European Union in 2007, and so it was still a newcomer at the tables of various European gatherings. Meanwhile, the crisis emerging in Europe was raising doubts about the ability of Greece and other countries in southern Europe to survive continued membership in the eurozone. It also was reviving old questions about the advisability of the unified currency zone—questions that had been raised in Europe a decade earlier. Whether our countries were in the eurozone or not, all of us in Ecofin were forced to confront issues of how to save the eurozone, establish greater powers for the ECB to prevent bank runs, undertake structural reforms, and create a European fiscal union. My leadership position in the Bulgarian government thus bestowed on me an active role in the historic moment unfolding in Europe—a role I had not anticipated when I accepted the job.

This book is an eyewitness account of events in Europe from July 2009 to the spring of 2013. Specifically, it is an insider's view of how some decisions were made, or not, and what thinking lay behind them. In the narrative, I also draw on my own experience in reforming some sectors in Bulgaria—for example, the painful but ultimately successful experience with pension reform in 2010-11. Meanwhile, during my term as finance minister Bulgaria was actively pursuing the idea of entering the waiting room to the eurozone, the Exchange Rate Mechanism II (ERM II), and therefore I was quite engaged in the euro crisis as it affected Bulgaria's path to entry.

This book follows chronologically the events leading to the euro crisis and the various attempts at resolving the crisis until the spring of 2013, when my term as finance minister ended. Each chapter describes the important events that shaped the agenda in Ecofin and details the main policy responses whether implemented or not. In fact, many policy prescriptions during the euro crisis were never implemented, either because they were, upon further consideration, discarded as inadequate or because they were too bold and did not have enough political support. Their description here is, in my view, one of the main contributions of this book. It reveals how much energy was spent generating and refuting ideas on resolving the crisis and the small proportion of those ideas that ever turned into concrete actions.

A caveat—upon entering the Bulgarian government, I quickly learned that every day spent out of the country brought trouble at home. For this reason, I was forced to miss some important discussions with fellow finance ministers and European Commission experts. These discussions may have changed my mind on some of the topics discussed in this book. But this was the reality not just for me—one or another finance minister was absent for long stretches of Ecofin meetings. And one did not even have to wonder why: The international media would dutifully report rifts within the particular government or difficulties in upcoming elections. Domestic politics came first. Thus the view presented here is not objective. It shows the euro crisis through my eyes, and is limited by the great difficulties I faced in participating in euro crisis discussions while surviving Bulgarian's rough and tumble politics.

How the Crisis Unfolded: Seven Tipping Points

Before describing my own involvement in the unfolding of the euro crisis, I briefly describe in this section the chronology of the crisis itself by framing it in seven tipping points that determined how it progressed.

Tipping Point 1. The first came on October 23, 2009, when Greek prime minister Georgios Papandreou admitted that Greece had lied about its budget deficits and debt for over a decade, and that the country's public deficit would exceed 12 percent of GDP, or twice the level announced by the Greek government just a month earlier. Financial markets responded strongly to the admission of false statistics by demanding much higher rates on Greek bonds. Soon, the situation spread to three other countries with high government debt ratios and wobbly banking systems—Italy, Portugal, and Spain.

Tipping Point 2. This tipping point also came in October, but in 2010, when German chancellor Angela Merkel and French president Nicolas Sarkozy met in Deauville, France, and declared that the establishment of a permanent crisis management mechanism, to take over the temporary European Financial Stability Facility (EFSF) in 2013, was conditioned on amending the EU treaty to provide for the participation of private creditors. Introducing this idea publicly in the midst of a volatile market and without detailing how it would work was a mistake. Ecofin was blindsided—it did not have such a discussion in September. After Deauville, the crisis in Ireland spread outside the banking sector.

Tipping Point 3. A year later, on October 13, 2011, Slovakia became the 17th and final country to approve the expansion of the eurozone's rescue fund, two days after its parliament rejected the plan. Legislators in Bratislava ratified expansion of funding for the EFSF to €440 billion ($610 billion). Ratification came at a high cost, however—the conservative government of Iveta Radičová fell as a result, less than a year into its term. But the eurozone now had a powerful instrument for acting quickly in case trouble befell another one of its members.

Tipping Point 4. The same month, on October 31, 2011, in a move that caught people by surprise, Greek prime minister Papandreou, announced plans for a referendum on the new bailout plan. Even his finance minister, Evangelos Venizelos, was unaware of this plan in advance. The eurozone leaders were seething. All the work in past months to show European resolve in dealing with the Greek crisis was put in jeopardy. Public opinion in Greece was clearly against the proposed conditions of the bailout, and the referendum would probably result in a rejection of these terms. But where to go from there? A suspension of aid to Greece and a subsequent default and exit from the euro seemed the most likely route.

Tipping Point 5. The fifth and most positive tipping point arrived on July 26, 2012. By then, the crisis was getting out of control, and so ECB president Mario Draghi announced that the bank would do "whatever it takes" to keep the eurozone together. The markets were relieved, and yields in the troubled European countries fell sharply. Responding to Draghi's statement, investors became more comfortable buying bonds of the region's southern rim governments. This was the single key decision that saved the eurozone and changed the course of the crisis. Draghi's determination made everyone more confident that the remaining issues would be resolved with time.

Tipping Point 6. Another tipping point was the decision by Ecofin on December 14, 2012, to adhere to a single banking supervisor. Ecofin's decision was confirmed by the heads of state the following day. This decision wiped out any remaining questions about whether European politicians were united in strengthening the euro. The reform required governments to yield control over the supervision of national banks to the ECB in November 2014.

Tipping Point 7. The seventh and final tipping point came on March 25, 2013, when the Eurogroup, European Commission, ECB, and International Monetary Fund (IMF) agreed on a €10 billion ($14 billion) bailout for Cyprus. It safeguarded small savers, but inflicted heavy losses on uninsured depositors, including wealthy Russians. The European Union was moving toward putting more burdens on bondholders and fewer on taxpayers. That approach was directed as much at Cyprus as at Slovenia, Spain, and other countries that might fall into further difficulties. The remedy in Ireland was quite different— the taxpayers footed the whole bill.

My First Impressions from Ecofin

How did these events look from my seat in Ecofin? Before providing these impressions, I will fill in the backdrop. In addition to the euro crisis, my team at the finance ministry had to deal with several other international issues. Relations with Russia on various energy projects occupied the top spot. In the course of my term in government, we cancelled a deal to build a second nuclear power station with Russian technology and terminated a project to build an oil pipeline transporting Russian oil to the Greek coast of the Adriatic. The second issue was one of continuous worry about the Bulgarian subsidiaries of several Greek banks. Analysts and investors feared that these subsidiaries would bring down the Bulgarian banking system, and we spent a lot of time arguing otherwise. Third was the euro crisis. I rank these issues to make the point that the euro crisis was not my foremost concern while in government, but it had an effect on most other decisions.

Ten days after my inauguration in July 2009, I went to my first Ecofin meeting in Brussels. Two things made an immediate impression. First, few of my colleagues had a formal education in economics or finance—5 of the other 26 finance ministers to be exact. Second, there was little urgency. We had to work around the expansive holiday schedules in Europe, and so my second Ecofin was in late September. By then, the Greek government had become mired in corruption scandals, and a week later, on October 4, 2009, Prime Minister Konstantinos Karamanlis resigned halfway through his second term.

During the next four years, Ecofin met over 40 times, and so I had plenty of opportunities to consider the main topic of the moment: the euro crisis. There was a constant focus on keeping Greece afloat and building a common fiscal policy to save the eurozone. In late 2011, the idea of a banking union surfaced and gathered speed the following autumn. The remaining agenda varied: saving Hungary, saving Ireland, saving Portugal, punishing Hungary, becoming worried about Spain, becoming worried about Italy, wondering when France would face up to its banking problems. By the time Cyprus blew up, we had been in the saving business for too long, and this is why Cyprus got the short stick.

There were moments of joy such as Estonia adopting the euro in January 2011. "A political decision," the Estonians would say. "We want to be as far from Russia as possible." During my last Ecofin, Latvia applied as well and was given the go-ahead to join the eurozone in January 2014. Latvia fully deserved it. It had suffered an 18 percent drop in output, accompanied by a rise in unemployment in 2009 and further fiscal tightening in 2010 and 2011, to maintain its version of a currency board.

There was success at home as well. After recording a 4.4 percent budget deficit in 2009 because of the previous government's preelection spending spree, Bulgaria reduced its deficit to 2 percent in 2011 and 0.5 percent in 2012 and exited the excess deficit procedure at the same time as Germany. That put Bulgaria in the small group of fiscally responsible countries. Moody's raised Bulgaria's credit rating to BB+, the only rating increase in Europe between 2009 and 2012, before Estonia and then Latvia received upgrades. The ECB's *Convergence Report* in 2012 noted that Bulgaria met all the quantitative Maastricht criteria, one of only three EU countries to do so. The remaining step was entry into ERM II. But I decided that this step had to wait until it was clear what the evolving eurozone rules and institutions would be. Over time, Bulgarians' views on the euro darkened, as elsewhere in Europe, and fewer and fewer of them thought we should adopt the euro. But today I think we should, now that the worst of the euro crisis is over.

The most memorable moment of my work in Brussels was in mid-December 2012, when Ecofin agreed to move toward a single banking supervision authority for the European Union. This was the third meeting called in a span of 10 days; the previous one had been cancelled because the positions were too far apart, and the first meeting, in November, had ended in an impasse. As one minister later remarked, "It was the most relaxed Ecofin meeting ever. The differences in opinion were so large, that there was no point arguing." Indeed, the third time was a charm—perhaps because of the coming Christmas holidays and because the meeting of heads of state was scheduled for the next day. The functioning of the single supervisor was hotly debated and then agreed on. By that time, it was early morning, and the heads of state were flying in.

But in April 2013, there was a change of view. The German finance minister, Wolfgang Schäuble, and the head of the Bundesbank, Jens Weidmann, suggested that the single banking supervisor agreement was illegal under the Lisbon Treaty and thus necessitated a treaty change. Perhaps upcoming elections for the Bundestag had something to do with their concerns—and their fears that regional German banks, the Landesbanken, would be harshly supervised. In truth, Schäuble had made this point several times during Ecofin discussions. But he had not made it so forcefully and certainly not during the December 2012 meeting at which the agreement was reached. Schäuble was a thoughtful person and took advice from his staff well. I had on several occasions—including visits to Berlin—witnessed his willingness to alter his views in light of additional analysis. So it is possible that his legal advisors had convinced him of the impossibility of rapid progress on the banking union.

This was, moreover, typical of decision making in Europe during the crisis. An issue would be discussed intensely for a while, but then it would be dropped suddenly for a newer idea. The issue would have arisen from a bilateral meeting between France and Germany ahead of Ecofin gatherings. The newer idea would suffer the same fate a few months later. In a span of three years, the euro-strengthening exercise went through six variations—the Euro Pact, the Euro Plus Pact, the Fiscal Compact, the financial transactions tax, the fiscal union, and the banking union. With the exception of one idea—the Fiscal Compact, which translated the Maastricht criteria into national legislation—all others had small immediate value added. The banking union would take a decade to be properly implemented. Its first feature—the single banking supervisor—was postponed until October 2014 after it had been initially agreed to start in March 2013. And the discussions on a common guarantee fund and restructuring facility started only in July 2013, after I had left the Bulgarian government.

Another feature was the constant repositioning because of upcoming elections. "We can't deal with troubled Greek banks before the French elections [in May 2012]," European Commission bureaucrats would say. Indeed, French banks had a lot to lose if the IMF and the ECB insisted that private creditors share the burden of writeoffs. The result was significant foot-dragging, to the detriment of the restructuring program in Greece. Another example was the parliamentary elections in Finland and the Netherlands, when the Ecofin discussion on bailouts became more extreme in favor of kicking Greece out of the eurozone to suit the ruling parties in their final weeks of campaigning. And yet another example was Cyprus, where the problems with troubled banks had been known and discussed at Ecofin in early 2012. But the European Commission waited until after the presidential elections in Cyprus in February 2013 to agree with the new president, Nicos Anastasiades, on the bailout package. It was too late, however, and the additional loss of value in the banking sector was in the billions, leaving the Cypriot government with a bigger hole to fill.

Throughout my experience in Ecofin, I was constantly reminded of what Daniel Ellsberg wrote about the indecisive approach taken by the Johnson and Nixon administrations to the Vietnam War: "At every juncture [policymakers] made the minimum commitments necessary to avoid imminent disaster—offering optimistic rhetoric, but never taking the steps that even they believed could offer the prospect of decisive victory. They were tragically caught in a kind of no-man's-land—unable to reverse a course to which they had committed so much, but also unable to generate the political will to take forward steps that gave any realistic prospect of success" (Ellsberg 1972, 7). This was how Ecofin felt to me for a long time. For that reason, I hesitated about going to every meeting—there was so much work at home that each day away was costly. In the end, though, I participated in most of the Ecofin meetings because they were the main opportunity I had to learn how other countries were dealing with the crisis. Before each Ecofin meeting, I spoke to Jürgen Ligi, the Estonian finance minister, to Anders Borg, the Swedish finance minister, and to Jyrki Katainen, the Finnish finance minister for most of my term. I had chosen these countries as a comparator group both for their known fiscal discipline and economic success and for their similar country size.

At some point in 2011, the eurozone members became agitated over the remarks of some noneurozone ministers, among them UK chancellor of the exchequer George Osborne and Swedish finance minister Borg, who expressed their views on the slow pace of decisions and on the missing growth plan for Europe. Thus eurozone members' discussions of bailouts moved to the eurozone dinner held the evening before the Ecofin meeting—eurozone members only. At the initiative of Borg and Margrethe Vestager, the finance minister of Denmark, we began to hold a noneurozone dinner to discuss how the European Union could advance beyond the current crisis. (These were among the few gatherings I attended in which the growth prospects for the European Union were considered. It helped that noneurozone countries were in better fiscal and economic shape than the eurozone ones—and that there were not any immediate bailout issues to discuss.)

The Ecofin meeting the next day started with an extensive summary of the eurozone group dinner and again discussions on the various bailout programs. Take pity on the finance ministers of the bailout countries—they had to sit through this grilling twice! And a grilling it was. First, Dutch finance minister Jan Kees de Jager questioned the commitment to belt-tightening and structural reforms in Greece, and later Portugal and Spain. Then Finnish finance minister Katainen, later Finland's prime minister, took the floor with similar remarks, followed by Austrian finance minister Josef Proell (and after the fall of 2011 his successor, Maria Fekter). On their heels was Anders Borg. When one of the southern rim ministers took the floor and explained that in the north things might work differently, I took the floor and listed what Bulgaria had achieved in a short period of time and then what Estonia and Latvia had accomplished in a much more trying situation. That did not win me any favors from the southern rim ministers.

During my term in office, parties belonging to the European People's Party (EPP) Group, made up of center-right parties across Europe, governed 20 of the 27 EU countries. The ministers from these governments met at breakfast the day of Ecofin, often together with the EU commissioners belonging to the EPP parties (Michel Barnier, Algirdas Šemeta, and Janusz Lewandowski). The commissioners informed us of their work, and we updated each other on how the crisis was developing in our countries. At these breakfasts, I would listen to German finance minister Schäuble, Luxembourg's prime minister, Jean-Claude Juncker, and Anders Borg and think Europe was in safe hands. The EPP Group breakfasts had one prominent feature: Common positions would be discussed on the main issues of the day. Although it was never explicit, the breakfasts helped those of us attending prepare the tactics for the subsequent discussions at Ecofin. Because the majority of noneurozone members had center-right governments, Austria, Finland, Germany, and the Netherlands could find significant support for their tougher stance on Greece and other bailout countries—and on the general view that Europe needed more fiscal responsibility.

As the crisis continued, center-left governments tended to be replaced by center-right governments, with their greater expertise and understanding of the demands of markets, deficits, and budgets. At first, none of the ministers from bailout countries were from EPP Group parties; rather, all were from the Party of European Socialists. But by 2013, they were all EPP—the elections had brought in center-right governments. The quality of the debate then shot up because the new ministers had finance backgrounds, unlike their predecessors. Vítor Gaspar, the Portuguese minister, Yannis Stournaras, the Greek minister, and Spaniard Luis de Guindos all had impressive resumés and were straight talkers. This was thankfully a feature of crises: competence in finding solutions was urgently needed, and able professionals had come to the fore.

One could argue that I was as unqualified as many of the other finance ministers because of my lack of experience in Western Europe. After all, the onset of the euro crisis caught up with me while I was serving as chief economist of the finance and private sector vice presidency of the World Bank Group. The crisis took us as much by surprise as anyone else. The problems in the summer of 2008 with subprime mortgages and the subsequent drying up of trade credit globally seemed like isolated problems, far from the eurozone. When Iceland's banking sector collapsed in October, however, it suddenly became a euro problem as well because some continental European investors had much to lose. And they did lose. I had done some work in the Netherlands and Sweden, but it was all related to cutting the red tape for business. The World Bank had not worked in other reform areas in West European countries for 20 years.

My boss at the time, Michael Klein, vice president for finance and private sector at the World Bank, had a great deal of experience in crisis management. From his work at Shell, he had learned that crises quickly become unpredictable. We put together a crisis group from across the World Bank—finance experts, trade economists, small business developers, political scientists—that developed the four scenarios that might unfold (Djankov et al. 2009). The most likely scenario? It was that Greece would collapse and split the eurozone into northern and southern blocs, with the north maintaining a common currency. The south would be pulled in different directions, some countries toward Russia and some toward Turkey and the Middle East. In the fall of 2008, this analysis seemed like science fiction, capturing extreme possibilities. But the work on the scenarios did uncover a fundamental weakness in Europe—the stability of the euro.

The Euro and Its Weaknesses

In its conception, the euro has a flaw: It locks in countries on the periphery of Europe in an exchange rate they can ill afford to maintain unless they undertake structural reforms. Put simply, right at the start when Germany and Portugal adopted a single currency, it was obvious that Portugal would not be able to compete in the fixed exchange rate regime unless it reformed its labor market and business regulations. Because its currency would be overvalued, Portugal could not export the goods and services it produced at prices that were competitive on the global market. But in fact it was Germany that adjusted some of its labor regulations and pension rules under Chancellor Gerhard Schröder, while Portugal waited until well into the crisis to do so. And yet even Germany did not make it easy for businesses to start operations or to build investor protections, according to the 2013 *Doing Business* report of the World Bank (2013).

The same applied to France, Greece, Malta, and Spain—the whole southern rim of the eurozone. They were unwilling to adjust their labor markets, and their export-oriented sectors suffered as a result. The external trade data say it all. In 2012 France ran a current account deficit of €82 billion ($114 billion), Greece €20 billion ($28 billion), Portugal €11 billion ($15 billion), and Spain €32 billion ($44 billion). However, depressed consumption and higher taxes reduced the trade deficits in 2013. In May 2013, Spain had its first quarterly current account surplus in 50 years (figure 1.1). This was to a large extent due to a surplus in services, thanks to the tourism sector.

Some supporters of the euro say the original design needs strengthening with a common fiscal policy, a single banking supervisor, and a vetting mechanism for national budgets whereby structural reforms are undertaken to increase competitiveness. For example, if the southern rim countries had undertaken the labor reforms made by Germany under Gerhard Schröder, they would be in much better shape. Youth unemployment, in particular, would be lower. So the main culprit was the regulatory burden on business. And the supporters are right, to a degree. According to World Bank data, it takes 11 procedures and €9,000 ($12,500) to open a small business in Athens. It takes 735 days and 43 procedures to resolve a simple commercial dispute in Larnaca, Cyprus. And it takes 59 days and visits to eight different offices to register a small piece of property in Paris. It is cheaper and faster to do all this in Berlin. But operating in a fixed exchange rate regime probably trumps these concerns as a constraint. Good economists such as Vítor Gaspar, the Portuguese minister, and Yannis Stournaras, his Greek colleague, agreed.

The most ardent supporters of the euro say it is simply experiencing growing pains, and that it is a political project that cannot be judged in terms of optimal currency areas and the like. As the former president of the European Commission Jacques Delors remarked, "Obsession about budgetary constraints means that the people forget too often about the political objectives of European construction. The argument in favor of the single currency

Figure 1.1 Current account balances in the eurozone's southern rim, 2011–13

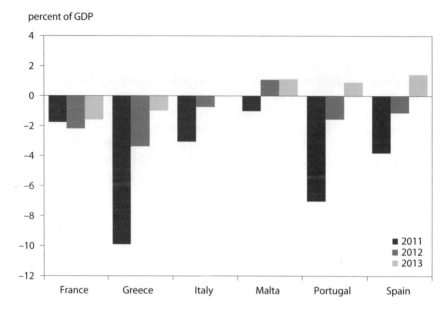

percent of GDP

Source: IMF, *World Economic Outlook*, October 2013, www.imf.org/external/pubs/ft/weo/2013/02/weodata/index.aspx (accessed on February 27, 2014).

should be based on the desire to live together in peace" (Eichengreen 2010, 56). The euro gives Europe's citizens a symbol of their European identity. For this reason, no country could exit the eurozone. This is the view that was often stated to me by both Jean-Claude Juncker, Luxembourg's prime minister and until January 2013 head of the eurozone, and Schäuble, the German finance minister. I gradually came to see it that way as well, although at the beginning of my career as finance minister I was far from this view.

This group of so-called integrationists was quite large both in Ecofin and among the longer-serving heads of state. It included Mario Monti, Italy's technocratic prime minister, and Herman Van Rompuy, the president of the European Council. They firmly believed that any step that brought European countries closer together was a good one. I also shared this view. Bulgaria had greatly benefited from becoming part of the European Union in terms of both its national psyche and the influx of cohesion funds. But once the topic of fiscal union, and the accompanying tax harmonization, came up in late 2011, I adjusted my views. Most integration was good. Some was bad. European countries differed in their economic development, and it would be a mistake to impose the same tax structure on all of them.

On the euro, I continue to subscribe to the optimistic view that the euro should remain a strong currency with some significant reforms both at home and in Brussels. Some of these reforms were in the making during the crisis years—the common fiscal policy and the banking union. And both were in the beginning stages when I left the Bulgarian government in March 2013. Their completion would be a decade-long process, and perhaps even longer for the fiscal union. I think this is the right pace—no reason to rush into ill-conceived adventures. The entry of the East European countries in the eurozone, Bulgaria included, will strengthen the eurozone further. Whatever misgivings economists had at the start of the euro project because of obvious optimal currency area reasons are irrelevant now. The euro is good for Europe, and dismantling it would be a cure worse than the illness. I also support the completion of the banking union in the eurozone: On balance, it also benefits Europe.

One euro-related task remained unresolved in all my Ecofin work. How could Brussels entice governments to undertake the structural reforms needed to maintain the euro? It had failed to come up with the recipe. A new idea that emerged in 2011 was to link structural reforms to the allotments of structural funds: Whoever did not reform would not get money from the European Union's structural funds after 2013. This sounded fine in theory and was even attempted once—on Hungary in 2011. But that attempt failed, and subsequent attempts are likely to fail, too. Imagine Brussels telling France that it would be withholding funds for its farmers until the French government implemented labor reforms. Manuel Barroso, president of the European Commission, would be subjected to vociferous criticism by the French government and the French media.

In fact, President Barroso does not take criticism well, and perhaps that is why he was largely absent during the resolution of the euro crisis. For this reason, he is also absent from this book. He simply was not around when the important issues were being discussed. And not once did he attend Ecofin. I often wondered why. It was equivalent to my prime minister, Boyko Borisov, not participating in discussions on the budget situation in Bulgaria, or on how to resolve the difficulties we experienced in dealing with the revenue shortfall early in our government. Prime Minister Borisov, to his credit, participated in all of these discussions, often staying late at night or over the weekend. I would have expected the president of the European Commission to do the same when the future of the eurozone was at stake.

When in 2011 the European Commission decided to pick on Hungary for being consistently derelict in following the Stability and Growth Pact rules, the Hungarian finance minister, Gyorgy Matolcsy, came to me for advice. Later elected to head up the Hungarian Central Bank, he was new to his post as finance minister and came into office just as Hungary was being singled out as the country to penalize. It was no matter that there were many countries to choose from in the penalty giving, France and Italy included. "Delay," I advised. "Another crisis will come and you will be forgotten." I even helped in Ecofin by insisting in the spring of 2011 that the European Commission produce an extensive analysis of how various EU members had performed in following the rules. Sure enough, the Commission experts took several months to produce the analysis, and by then Italy was getting into trouble and Hungary was quickly forgotten. I soon received a case of Tokaji wine from Hungary's ambassador in Sofia.

Lessons from the Euro Crisis

Perhaps the most important lesson I learned while participating in Ecofin meetings was that the EU institutions were not equipped to make decisions on how to tackle the eurozone crisis, and instead they spent considerable time in delaying tactics, hoping that the problem would resolve itself. When this did not happen, there was a further delay, finger-pointing at various culprits for the crisis—US bankers, credit rating agencies, politicians in southern Europe. It took three years—to the fall of 2011—to get to work.

The second lesson I learned was that a united Europe did not mean a Europe of equals. Germany led all discussions on eurozone issues, sometimes showing token respect for France's views. Germany's main allies—Finland and the Netherlands—played important but secondary roles. No one else mattered much, or at least mattered consistently. This attitude was on view, for example, during adoption of the European Stability Mechanism, the vehicle through which eurozone countries could receive bailout assistance. The process was amateurish and led, as noted, to the fall of the Slovak government. Foreseeing the dangers in the Slovak Parliament, European leaders should have given much more support to Prime Minister Radičová, much like the support that was extended to Finnish finance minister Jyrki Katainen during his election campaign. At the time, Ecofin ministers and heads of state were working hard to find ways to alleviate concerns in Finland over the Greek and other bailouts. Another example was the collapse of Cyprus. It was avoidable. That mishap was due in part to the change at the helm of the eurozone—Jean-Claude Juncker, the previous head of the eurozone, would have handled it smoothly. But what also underlay this disaster was the anger of many European politicians at Greece—and they found a victim in Cyprus. Some eurozone members wanted the Cyprus resolution to be noisy and calamitous to appease their audiences at home.

Today, I am a firm believer in the bright future of the European Union and the eurozone; it is in the interest of the world. Otherwise, Europe starts looking inward and neglects its responsibilities on global issues. But, based on my experience and lessons learned, four things must happen for a strong euro:

1. All eurozone countries have to abide by the fiscal rules. Fiscal profligacy is contagious, and if one country drags its feet, others follow. This is especially true of the larger eurozone countries such as France, which was often negligent in adhering to the Maastricht rules. Historically, however, Germany was the first country to flout the Maastricht rules. Lack of fiscal discipline is what landed many eurozone countries in this protracted crisis.

2. Structural reforms are needed in public administration and in pensions and labor markets. The euro crisis helped with these, but the European Commission's analysis and recommendations remain weak.

3. European governments need to cut the red tape for business. European Council president Van Rompuy made attempts to address this issue in 2011, but otherwise Brussels has remained uninterested in the long-term growth prospects of the European Union. This requires change.

4. Most important, the path for adopting the euro must be part of entry into European Union, not an afterthought. On this point, I had discussions with the integrationists in Ecofin, and by early 2013 the idea was receiving support. Latvia's entry into the eurozone in January 2014 provided further momentum. I admit that the United Kingdom's euro future is beyond my comprehension.

And yet I believe Europe is not ready yet for a fiscal union in which government expenditures are decided in Brussels. This will take time to develop for three reasons. First, no national parliament is ready to hand decision making on budgetary issues to the European Commission. Second, such a move would endanger democracy in the budgetary process by significantly removing the decision making from those who elected the government on whether to pursue certain economic and social policies. And, third, in my work with the European Commission I could compare the quality of bureaucrats in Brussels and in Sofia. The Bulgarian bureaucracy, at least the one dealing with fiscal and tax issues, was significantly better prepared in its specific expertise as well as in its general administrative quality. Until Brussels has fiscal experts at least as well prepared as Bulgaria's, I would not support giving more powers to EU authorities.

The last point is important because it raises questions about how far the European project can advance in its integration. If I were asked to summarize the main conclusion from my years of work on the euro crisis, I would begin by pointing to the difficulty of providing an adequate answer to the question of how Portugal and Germany can compete globally in a single currency. Yes, in the United States Alabama and Massachusetts compete, each using the dollar. But there is a big difference: Unlike in Europe, there is capital and labor mobility in the United States as well as significant federal transfers. Twenty-nine percent of Americans live and work outside the state in which they were born. Only 3 percent of Europeans live in another EU country. Although officially there are few constraints to such mobility in Europe, languages play a big role, as do the inability of Europeans to transfer pension and health care benefits from one country to another and the policies of nationalist parties in countries such as the Netherlands.

In the absence of such mobility, the Europe Union came up with a mechanism of transfers as a way of inducing people to stay put. Each year, in addition to structural funds, the poorer members of the European Union receive cohesion funds, which together are equivalent to about 6 percent of their GDP.

The idea is to create conditions for better life and work in each country so that people do not have to move. So far so good, except that these funds are sometimes wasted: They are viewed as "free" and spent on glossy promotions of luxury resorts such as in Cyprus. Or, worse yet, they fall into the pockets of government officials, as was recorded in Bulgaria, Greece, Italy, Poland, and Romania. Funds were then stopped and the national budgets repaid. These countries ended up worse off.

Bulgaria's cohesion funds stopped flowing in 2008, just a year after it entered the European Union and saw the funds tap open. Much of the money was supposed to go toward road construction. Money was spent, but no new roads were built by the then-Socialist government. It turned out that the head of the road construction agency had contracted with his brother's company (he really did!) to build the roads. The case was referred to the Bulgarian courts, which after three years exonerated both brothers. The same case was also tried in German courts because some German advisors had participated in the embezzlement schemes. They were sentenced to three years in prison. Meanwhile, the Germans were fuming at the inability of the Bulgarian judiciary to defend the EU funds.

From that episode came this joke. A Bulgarian EU funds bureaucrat visited his Romanian colleague. He was surprised to see his big new house and Audi in the driveway. "How can you afford these?" he asked. The Romanian bureaucrat led him to a nearby road. "See this highway?" he asked. "No, I just see a two-lane road," said the Bulgarian. "Well, this is how I can afford a nice house and car," his colleague responded. A year later, the Romanian visited Bulgaria and was stunned to see his friend's mansion and Maserati. "How can you afford these?" he asked. The Bulgarian bureaucrat brought him to a field. "See this highway?" he asked. "No, I don't see anything," said the Romanian. "This is how," the Bulgarian responded proudly. Unfortunately, this is not a thing of the past. In November 2013, Bulgaria saw its flow of funds for environmental development stop.

Even in the absence of corruption, however, transfers are small relative to the issues they are supposed to address. A comparison with the United States is useful. In 2008 during Hurricane Katrina, the federal government made transfers to Louisiana in the form of direct assistance, Social Security, and Medicaid benefits that totaled nearly 30 percent of the state's GDP. This amount is three times higher than the average EU transfer to poorer countries in Europe. And it does not include bank programs organized by the US Federal Reserve System to create cheap credit for reconstruction in the affected areas.

And yet I do not believe that larger transfers are needed for European integration. What is most needed is a long-term view of European competitiveness, combined with instruments for strict fiscal discipline. When reading an earlier draft of this book, well-known economist John Williamson remarked that on the issue of fiscal discipline I was too pessimistic in my views. Brussels could take over from parliaments the powers of designing national budgets for those countries that had breached the Maastricht criteria. Otherwise, the national parliaments would remain in charge. This seems like a reasonable compromise, and I am ready to subscribe to it. But this is not how it was presented by Commissioner Olli Rehn in various Ecofin meetings. So, understandably, he got a lot of pushback.

Tax harmonization in the European Union is as unnecessary as a larger transfer system. In the minds of French, Spanish, and Italian authorities, fiscal centralization comes in a bundle with tax harmonization—at least this is what French finance ministers Christine Lagarde and then Pierre Moscovici, Italian finance ministers Giulio Tremonti and then Mario Monti, and Spanish finance ministers Elena Salgado and then Luis de Guindos argued when the topic came up. The German position varied over time, with German finance minister Schäuble sympathetic to the tax harmonization view. My view is the opposite: Tax harmonization is harmful to the convergence of the poorer members of the European Union.

About the Book

This book comes in an expanding field. Thomas Mayer, a former IMF economist and Deutsche Bank manager, has studied the euro crisis from a historical perspective (Mayer 2012). What is his main point? The euro was "an ambitious political project pursued in reckless negligence of economics." He also suggests that the fall of the Berlin Wall distracted Germany, and so the euro came into being despite Germany's doubts. Another book, by Johan van Overtveldt, editor of the Belgian weekly *Trends*, argues that Greece and Portugal were too sneaky to be trusted, and that the political goal of their "crises" was to put an end to the euro and Germany's membership in the European Union (van Overtveldt 2011). McKinsey & Co.'s *The Future of the Euro* (2012), a study frequently cited by both Mario Draghi and Chancellor Angela Merkel, compares the increases in unit labor costs across the eurozone. It found that while German labor costs barely budged during 2001–10, they increased by 25 percent in Greece, and 28 percent in Portugal (figure 1.2). It is no wonder, then, that these countries experienced a loss in competitiveness. McKinsey & Co. also calculates the annual benefits of the euro to be €330 billion ($460 billion), of which about half goes to Germany.

Alberto Alesina, an economics professor at Harvard, was the only academic economist invited by Ecofin to present his views on the euro crisis during my term as finance minister. Perhaps it was because he wrote about Europe's euro troubles before other authors did and painted a rather compelling picture. With his colleague Francesco Giavazzi from Bocconi University, he argued in *The Future of Europe: Reform or Decline* (2006) that a major European decline was coming. Europe emerged from World War II with a per capita income level of less than half (42 percent) that of the United States. But it gradually caught up, to about 80 percent of US GDP per capita in the 1980s. After that, the catching up reversed, and by 2005 the European Union was at less than 70 percent of US GDP because of the lack of structural reforms and the general complacency of Europeans that the dolce vita would continue forever.

Figure 1.2   Nominal unit labor costs in Germany, Greece, and Portugal, 2001–10

index, 2005 = 100

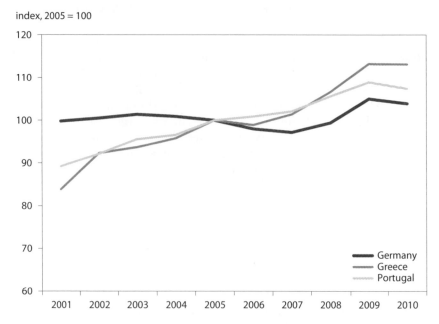

Source: Eurostat, http://epp.eurostat.ec.europa.eu/portal/page/portal/statistics/search_database (accessed on February 27, 2014).

In their follow-up book, *Europe and the Euro* (2010), professors Alesina and Giavazzi compiled a collection of essays on the reasons for the euro crisis. They focused on the question of whether euro entry was good for structural reforms and found that belonging to the eurozone accelerated the reform process in the product market—particularly in the transportation and telecommunication sectors—but had no effect on the labor market. The logic was that countries became unable to use their monetary policy to accommodate negative shocks. This created incentives to liberalize product markets in order to rely more heavily on market-based adjustments. Also, the euro increased price transparency and therefore facilitated trade. A larger European market increased competition and made it more difficult for domestic monopolists to protect their rents. Labor reforms, on the other hand, were blocked by all-European labor unions.

An important feature of this book is that it tells the story of my involvement in policy reforms in Bulgaria prior to the main story of wrestling with the euro crisis. I chose to tell this story because the euro crisis significantly affected my work as finance minister in a noneurozone country, just as it affected the work of my fellow ministers from other noneurozone countries. And although the focus of scholars of the eurozone will no doubt be the political decisions that took place in Frankfurt, Brussels, Athens, Dublin, and Lisbon, all of us in the European Union were victims of the same crisis and faced similar problems. Moreover, noneurozone policymakers had an important voice in many decisions about the future of the eurozone—for example, in the set-up of the fiscal and banking unions. If scholars want to know how decisions on the eurozone were made, they can benefit from knowledge of how noneurozone countries acted during this difficult period.

This book is organized chronologically, highlighting the main events in the unfolding of the euro crisis. A list of these events also appears in the chronology at the end of the book, along with a glossary that describes many of the institutions and terms used. Chapter 2 focuses on my work in Bulgaria, including some of the reforms undertaken to keep the public finances in order and not succumb to large deficit spending as did most of our neighbors in Europe. Chapter 3 describes the onset of the euro crisis with Icelandic banking troubles, and the origins of the euro, both in Robert Mundell's economic theory and in practice. Chapter 4 details past attempts to form a fiscal union in Europe, and also analyzes the beginning of banking troubles in Ireland. Chapter 5 documents the first Greek bailout, and describes the first tipping point in the euro crisis, Prime Minister Papandreou's admission that Greece had consistently manipulated national statistics to meet the Maastricht criteria. It also reflects on the pros and cons of a proposed solution to the euro—letting troubled countries take euro holidays. Chapter 6 covers the second tipping point in the euro crisis: the Sarkozy-Merkel introduction of "private sector participation" in bailout packages. Doing so publicly in the midst of a volatile market and without detailing how it would work was a mistake. It rattled investors and undermined confidence in the ability of European institutions to undertake crisis management. The chapter also presents the theoretical basis for creating a northern euro as a way to eliminate the long-term weaknesses in the design of the eurozone.

Chapter 7 presents the crisis developments that led to Portugal's request for a bailout package. In doing so, it describes the third tipping point in the crisis—approval of the expansion of the European Financial Stability Facility at the cost of the fall of the government in Slovakia. The chapter also goes into the notion of issuing eurobonds as a way to support failing economies.

Chapter 8 documents the events surrounding Prime Minister Papandreou's announcement on October 31, 2011, of a surprise referendum on the second bailout package. This was the fourth tipping point in the euro crisis: Greece decided to test the resolve of eurozone leaders. On November 2, 2011, EU leaders cut off aid payments to Greece and said it must decide whether it wanted to stay with the euro. The chapter also describes Italian prime minister Silvio Berlusconi's decision to resign, as well as the popular debate about euro devaluation that took place among economic theorists in late 2011.

As described in chapter 9, by July 26, 2012, the euro crisis was getting out of control. In response, ECB president Mario Draghi announced that the ECB would do "whatever it takes" to keep the eurozone together. This was the fifth tipping point in the crisis—and this one was for the better. Following on this resolute ECB action, Ecofin advanced significantly in working out the details of both a banking union and a fiscal union.

Chapter 10 documents the steps taken toward creating the single banking supervisor in the eurozone, as agreed at the Ecofin gathering on December 14, 2012, and confirmed by the heads of state immediately. The sixth tipping point in the euro crisis, it wiped out any remaining doubts that European politicians were united in strengthening the euro. The reform required governments to yield control over the supervision of national banks to the ECB in October 2014.

Chapter 11 focuses on the seventh and final tipping point in the euro crisis. As noted, it came on March 25, 2013, when the Eurogroup, European Commission, ECB, and IMF agreed on a €10 billion bailout ($14 billion) for Cyprus. Slovenia soon ran into troubles of its own. The troubles of Cyprus and Slovenia prompted Leszek Balcerowicz, the most accomplished European economic reformer, to call for structural reforms in the eurozone of the same magnitude as the ones taken in some East European countries during their transition from communism.

The concluding chapter enumerates the successes and failures in decision making and how my views evolved on some key issues.

Disclaimer

Bulgaria is not yet a eurozone country, but it is not a bailout country either. As noted earlier, during my tenure as finance minister Bulgaria was actively pursuing the notion of entering the eurozone, and therefore I was quite engaged in the euro crisis because it affected Bulgaria's path to entry. But the finance ministers from eurozone bailout countries would likely have a very different read on the events and decisions described here. In fact, several of these ministers are academic economists, such as former Portuguese finance minister Vítor Gaspar, and so they are likely at some point to pick up their pens.

During my tenure as deputy prime minister and finance minister, I worked alongside integration believers such as the prime minister of Luxembourg and head of the eurozone Jean-Claude Juncker, Italian prime minister Mario Monti, and German finance minister Wolfgang Schäuble. I also had many thought-provoking discussions with the doubters such as British chancellor of the exchequer George Osborne, Swedish finance minister Anders Borg, German deputy finance minister and later member of the ECB's Executive Board Jörg Asmussen, and Thomas Wieser, head of the Eurogroup Working Group. The interactions with them generated some of the ideas presented in this book.

2

My Work in Bulgaria

My involvement in the euro crisis began with my first encounter with the future prime minister of Bulgaria, Boyko Borisov, in Washington in December 2008. As the leader of Bulgaria's largest opposition party and as mayor of the capital city, Sofia, Borisov was visiting the World Bank and the International Monetary Fund (IMF) to discuss the election platform of his party, GERB (Citizens for European Development of Bulgaria), for the upcoming parliamentary elections. I was invited to the meeting at the IMF as the chief economist for the finance and private sector vice presidency at the World Bank.

A former firefighter, a black belt in karate, and an avid soccer player, Borisov had already enjoyed a stellar career, running Bulgaria's police force for four years and then winning two elections for mayor of Sofia. And all this even before he founded GERB so that he and others could participate in the July 2009 parliamentary elections. Because GERB had a lead in the opinion polls half a year before the elections, World Bank and IMF officials had agreed to meet him and his team.

Mayor Borisov was flanked by two other Bulgarians. One led the discussions because the mayor did not speak English fluently, and the other served as the mayor's interpreter when there were questions or comments. Toward the end of the discussion, the moderator asked for the "World Bank opinion." "The platform won't work," I said, and suddenly the expression on Mayor Borisov's face changed from daydreaming to fight mode.

His platform was a combination of tax cuts and preferences for certain sectors. At a time of a rapidly evolving global financial crisis and dwindling tax revenues, it could have bankrupted Bulgaria quickly. I suggested instead making immediate expenditure cuts, keeping the tax system intact, and determining whether some infrastructure projects could be financed to keep the construction sector going. Construction had been the fastest-expanding sector in Bulgaria over the previous five years, but it was rapidly imploding because of the dearth of financing at the start of the financial crisis. The latter point registered with Borisov. When the meeting ended, he asked me how other European countries were dealing with the crisis. He seemed genuinely interested in learning more. On the way to the elevators, I explained what I knew, gave my card to his advisors, and left.

About two months after this episode, one of Borisov's advisors called me and asked me to look at the economics and finance sections of Borisov's election platform. We began revising it, talking over Skype almost daily. Soon, another advisor joined us—Roumiana Bachvarova, who would become Prime Minister Borisov's chief of staff. Over the course of five to six weeks, we rewrote most of the platform, not just the economics part. Borisov joined in two of these discussions as well.

By then it was mid-May. Borisov called me one day to ask whether I could visit Bulgaria for a few weeks and help GERB's economic team through the elections. I accepted the invitation on the spot and then arranged for unpaid leave from the World Bank. On May 30, 2009, I landed at Sofia's airport. From the airport, we drove straight to Borisov's house in the outskirts of Sofia. When we arrived, Borisov hugged me as though we were old friends and put me in charge of GERB's economics team. With that, I was in campaign mode.

The campaign lasted five weeks. Every day I met scores of new people, and I travelled around the country. Frequently, I spent the evenings at Borisov's home, where, after the long days, I often had dinner with him and his daughter, who also lived in the United States. She had just received her undergraduate degree from the University of California at Los Angeles (UCLA), but had come home to support her dad during the campaign. The schedule was frenzied—literally from dawn to dusk. One morning, Borisov called and asked me to visit him at the soccer field where he played. At half-time, he came off the field and said, "If we win, you will be the minister of economy." "Finance," I responded. "In a crisis finance matters more." "We'll see," he said, and went back to the game.

In the elections, the voters gave Borisov a resounding victory: a near full majority in the parliament. Three days after the elections, he invited me to his home for morning coffee and offered me the Finance Ministry. I was thankful but said I would need to tell my family before any announcement. "Do so," he said. But it was not to be. In the taxi on my way back to the city, I heard on the news that the first minister in the new government had been selected—the portfolio: finance. I vividly remember the moment because the taxi driver said, "I hope this guy is better than the previous ones. But I doubt it. They're all the same."

Forming the Government

Two of the most hectic weeks in my life followed. We had to build a government. During the election campaign, I had met many of the GERB experts in various fields and felt empowered to suggest future ministers. Fortunately,

Borisov agreed with me more often than not, so I managed to nominate the minister of ecology, the minister of infrastructure (Rosen Plevneliev, who in 2011 was elected president of Bulgaria and who was also nominated by several business associations and the Chamber of Builders), and the minister of economy (Traicho Traikov). My initial choice for the Ministry of Economy was Biser Boev, who actively participated in the election campaign, but his candidacy was not approved by Borisov because of his previous work in the media. I then approached Traicho Traikov, whom I had briefly met at the university before I left to study abroad. Traicho was a top manager of one of the largest energy companies in Bulgaria, and he had also worked in Europe. We went together to Borisov's office. In his first remark to Traicho, Borisov said, "I see you have an expensive suit. That's good. It means you have enough money so that you won't steal when in government."

My attempts to nominate the minister of transport failed. Eventually, my suggested candidate would become the minister, but not before two wasted years without reforms in that sector. Instead, the ministry went to someone Borisov had worked with in the Sofia municipality. I also tried to support a candidate for the Ministry of Agriculture and almost succeeded. A bright woman with experience in the sector was first selected and announced, only to be withdrawn after a vicious media attack financed by her opponents within the party.

I did not have enough knowledge in the other ministerial portfolios and did not suggest names. Still, I was present when most were announced. One of the more memorable was the minister of sport: His selection was made public at a swimming pool. Prime minister–elect Borisov called and asked me to show up at a pool and meet the proposed minister. I had witnessed important decisions at soccer fields before, but not at pools. When I came in, several famous sports personalities were drinking beer by the pool. There was a brief discussion of the merits of potential candidates, and then it was announced that Svilen Neikov had won the nomination because he had a PhD in sports management. Svilen, the coach of a Bulgarian Olympic champion in single scull, turned out to be one of our best ministers.

The list of ministers was ready two days before the deadline. On the last day, Borisov nominated two deputy prime ministers as an indication of the two main directions in which the government was headed: (1) financial stability and infrastructure development and (2) the fight against crime and corruption. I became the deputy prime minister in charge of the first effort. Tzvetan Tzvetanov, Borisov's most trusted party lieutenant, took over the second one.

Once in the government, I began to select the team at the Finance Ministry. I followed a simple rule: All top appointments would be people from within the ministry. My two deputy ministers were former ministry section chiefs. My chief of staff had managed the department on state enterprises. The ministry's secretary general had been the director of human resources. They knew each other well, and the team's chemistry was instant.

Now I had to appoint the head of customs. The one I inherited had run the service twice in the previous decade. Under him, customs operated as if it were a unit of the Interior Ministry—probably because one needed the cooperation of both the border police and customs officers to smuggle illegal goods into the country. Moreover, there were many stories about how former interior ministers had enriched themselves by turning a blind eye to the contraband trade. I knew I needed someone tough enough to stand up to the Interior Ministry but also to cooperate with it when needed. Borisov offered a solution. Vanyo Tanov, a former general in the police, had resigned three years earlier as head of the elite police forces after exposing his minister for having ties with organized crime groups. The minister had to resign amid much acrimony.

I met General Tanov at Borisov's suggestion and liked him at once. A towering figure with a booming voice, he was the opposite of me in physical appearance. And with 25 years of service under his belt in the police, he knew more about police practices than any interior minister. Under his leadership, the customs office quickly cast off the influence of the Interior Ministry and conducted many successful operations against smuggling. However, the interior minister, Tzvetan Tzvetanov, took a dislike to Tanov because of his popularity among the police, and so I had to spend the better part of my first year in office fighting to keep General Tanov in place.

As deputy prime minister, I was also responsible for nine other ministries and for 17 intragovernmental commissions—for example, the Atomic Power Safety Commission and the Commission on People with Disabilities—as well as for the tripartite dialogue with the labor unions and business associations. In dealing with these responsibilities I was assisted by my team, who also served as the brain trust for the various reforms. My team consisted of two lawyers to assist with legislative initiatives, two experts versed in communications and the media, and two members of GERB's youth organization to help in our work with the parliament and regional and municipal authorities. It was run by Irina Velkova, my trusted chief of staff. The team was very young—27 years old on average. No one had worked in the public sector before. This was a lesson I had learned from Polish economist and Polish deputy prime minister Leszek Balcerowicz when I had asked him several years earlier how he selected his team. He advised: "All young people straight out of the university. So they don't have any biases."

With my team in place, I turned to cost-cutting. The first decree of the new government called for a 15 percent across-the-board cut in administrative expenditures. While the other ministers were still celebrating their appointments, the Ministry of Finance prepared this decree. We also proposed the dissolution of two ministries: the Ministry for Emergencies and the Ministry for Administrative Reform. The latter had become infamous for spending more EU funds on the travel of its bureaucrats to Paris and Rome than on actual reform initiatives. By the time the bureaucrats from these ministries went on strike to prevent their closure, it was too late.

Bulgaria's Euro Ambitions

In one of my first actions in late 2009, I declared I would visit most eurozone capitals and convince my colleagues there that Bulgaria was ready to adopt the euro. In the days before the euro crisis, the previous Bulgarian government had twice approached the European Central Bank (ECB) and the European Union with informal requests to start the entry process—once in 2007 and a second time in late 2008, just as the crisis was about to erupt. On both occasions, my predecessor and the head of the Bulgarian Central Bank had been warned that it was too early for Bulgaria to be considered, despite its good macroeconomic and fiscal record. The second time had ended with a miscue. The news had leaked that Finance Minister Plamen Oresharski was engaging in informal talks on eurozone entry in Brussels. As he left the Ecofin meeting, an international journalist asked him when Bulgaria would apply to join the eurozone. My predecessor, who was not known for his command of the English language, said, "Next time, next time," which in Bulgarian means "Don't bother me now." The next day, several European papers ran headlines that said in effect, "Bulgaria to Join the Eurozone Next Month."

It was obvious that, despite its good macroeconomic and fiscal performance, Bulgaria was not a trusted candidate for the eurozone. More specifically, the experience of the previous government made it clear that eurozone members had to be convinced that once in the eurozone Bulgaria would maintain fiscal responsibility. That was what I set out to tell eurozone finance ministers in 2009 as I visited 12 capitals in October and November. Then the Greek crisis erupted and made the point moot. I initially thought the issue could be revisited in two years, in 2011. But by then the economic situation in Europe had worsened substantially, and we had to wait longer.

I still think Bulgaria should enter the eurozone as soon as possible—now that the worst of the euro crisis is over. In early 2013, I had several discussions on the topic of euro entry with Prime Minister Borisov. We agreed that the topic was especially delicate in view of the elections later in the year. A cautious approach, then, would be to ask the ECB and the Economic and Financial Committee of the European Union for their informal views and design a gradual path to entry. During the February 2013 Ecofin meeting, I started such informal talks. The preliminary view was that Bulgaria needed to prove stability in policy decisions over time in order to convince the eurozone that it would not be just another country that fulfilled the Maastricht criteria only temporarily while adopting the euro. On the phone from Brussels, I reported these early conversations to Prime Minister Borisov. But it was not to be; the government resigned several days later.

Greece: Our Difficult Neighbor

The Greek crisis was already brewing when we took office. Bulgaria had strong ties to Greece through its banking sector and tourism industry. In the summer of 2009, we had already noticed a new trend in which Greek citizens were

Figure 2.1   Greek and Bulgarian five-year credit default swap rates, 2009–11

US dollars

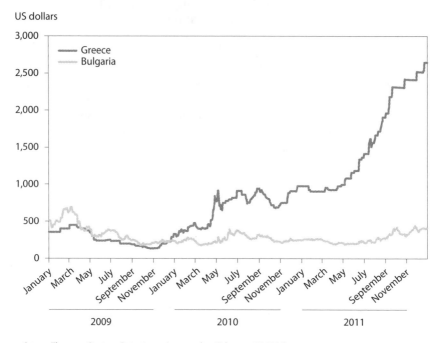

Source: Thomson Reuters, Datastream (accessed on February 26, 2014).

moving money to Bulgarian banks—a strange phenomenon considering the relative sizes of the banking sectors. We also noticed that Greeks were crossing the border and shopping in Bulgaria: The uncertainty in income was forcing some Greeks to look for cheaper goods.

In the meantime, because Greek prime minister Konstantino Karamanlis's New Democracy Party was a member of the European People's Party, a sister party to GERB, my prime minister's party, I spoke to Greek finance minister Yannis Papathanasiou several times about the crisis in our region. The main fear was that some of the Greek banks had suffered in the subprime mortgage crisis, and that the problem would spread to their subsidiaries in Bulgaria.

But the extent of the Greek problems became known only when the government of Georgios Papandreou entered office after Karamanlis resigned halfway through his second term. It made my time as finance minister hell. What would have been a difficult term in office became a daily struggle. Having the crisis epicenter next door worsened Bulgaria's economic growth prospects and made balancing the national budget almost impossible. In November 2009, international markets began raising the risk of Bulgaria's default on its debt (figure 2.1). The credit default swap (CDS) spread increased from a 12 percent probability of default to 34 percent in just two weeks. The fact that the country operated a currency board and had to keep a large amount of euros to back the Bulgarian currency (the lev) was especially risky—any run on the lev would quickly deplete the foreign reserves because the central bank would have to sell euros to prop up the lev. The investment bank briefs focused on the likelihood of such an event. The link through the banking systems with the sinking fortunes of Greece was too heavy a burden.

We needed to signal our determination to separate Bulgaria from Greece's troubles. After some discussions with Prime Minister Borisov, I proposed that we prepare a balanced budget for 2010 and announce it in parliament. I knew it was impossible to achieve, but thought that providing a zero-deficit benchmark would calm things externally and also move the domestic budget debates away from populist demands. The strategy worked. By December, international analysts were beginning to differentiate Bulgaria not only from Greece but also from the two other currency board countries experiencing budgetary issues, Latvia and Lithuania. Bulgaria's probability of default fell to under 20 percent, while Greece's continued to rise.

But as more troubling facts about the Greek banking system came out in early 2010, Bulgaria's risk of default started climbing again. On February 21, 2010, the CDS reached a 35 percent probability of default. But the balanced budget had already been approved by parliament, and the January data showed a significant reduction in the deficit relative to the previous year. I kept repeating in the international media that Bulgaria had traditionally stuck to conservative fiscal policies and would do so again. The prime minister also supported this view, and the markets were gradually placated. Politically, though, this cost me dearly. In three months, I lost half of my public support. And it would come to haunt me two months later when the significant additional expenses of the previous government came to light. Meanwhile, the immediate perceived danger of default had been eliminated.

The Most Difficult Times

March 2010 was the most difficult month of my term in government. Just after we dealt with the intense pressure from the international financial markets, another problem arose. One evening, the director of budget planning came to my office after work, wearing a worried expression. She was straightforward: "The budget deficit for 2009 is higher than we have reported." "How much higher?" I asked. "A lot higher." I remember sitting for a few minutes and not asking any questions. Then I called my deputy ministers, the chief of staff, and the deputy governor of the central bank so we could hear this together.

It turned out that in mid-2009, just before the parliamentary elections, the previous government had allowed ministries to overspend their budgets for the year, and it had instructed them to report the expenditures only in their annual reports. At the time, the budget law did not require ministries to report monthly their current expenditures (I changed the law the following year to prevent this from happening again). Therefore, when we were closing the books for 2009, the ministries reported only what they were supposed to spend, not actual expenditures. This was the report we sent to parliament and to the European Commission, showing a budget deficit of 2.8 percent of GDP—among the lowest in the European Union. With the larger actual expenditures, the budget deficit jumped to 4.4 percent of GDP and automatically subjected Bulgaria to the excess deficit procedure of the European Commission.

March 2010 was the most difficult month for me for another reason as well. I had a very serious public altercation with Bulgaria's president, Georgi Parvanov, a former member of the security police who had long denied he had belonged to the repressive arm of the communist regime. The conflict flared up after my appearance on a talk show, where I was asked to confirm claims that the president was a "young billionaire." I expressed doubts about these claims, but I quipped that Parvanov, who was 52 at the time, was "definitely not young." The next day, President Parvanov called for my resignation. At the insistence of Prime Minister Borisov, I agreed to apologize to President Parvanov in person.

I went to see the president alone, and I was met by a team of five presidential aides and the president himself. In what appeared to be a carefully orchestrated scenario, they dominated various parts of the conversation so that the president would not have to say much. I explained that I had exercised poor judgment in making the quip, but that was all. The president, however, did not seem to be interested in an apology. Instead, he used the meeting to attack the fiscal responsibility policies I was championing. I answered back: The public finances were my portfolio, not his.

An hour after the meeting, a bombshell exploded. The president released publicly the taped conversation without asking for my permission. The Bulgarian Constitution is very clear that people cannot be taped without their prior consent. In response to the situation, the parliament immediately initiated an impeachment proceeding against Parvanov. The first vote mustered enough support—162 of 240 members of parliament voted to impeach President Parvanov. However, a second vote several days later was five members short, and so he remained in his position. But his image never recovered.

I learned a lot from this experience. The main reason Bulgaria had not undergone the type of economic and political transition pursued by most other former socialist countries in Eastern Europe was that the former secret police were never removed from the political and economic life of the country. The people who had repressed freedoms during communist times continued to be among the country's elite. And they used the intimidation techniques that I thought were a thing of the past: wiretapping and spreading false information through media channels that they or their partners controlled. I faced this kind of harassment over and over during my career in the Bulgarian government. It was the heaviest burden of all, and I was totally unprepared for it.

Reform Momentum

By the summer of 2010, the budget situation was improving and the economy had begun to pick up. The forecast was for 2 percent economic growth for the year, a stark improvement from the previous year's decline of 5.5 percent. And even though my public approval rating had already fallen to 15 percent, from a high of 43 percent at the start of my term, my success at handling the pressure on the currency and cutting the budget deficit had won me some respect in parliament. It was time to push for reforms.

I used the summer to seek Prime Minister Borisov's agreement on several legislative reforms. At the World Bank I had worked with reformers in many countries on proposing legislative changes to cut the red tape for business. I had appeared in several parliaments when these changes were debated. And I had learned a lesson: Never focus on just one reform. It might be held up in parliament for one reason or another. Instead, simultaneously attack on several reform fronts, hoping to succeed on some.

With this in mind, I directed my team to pursue reforms in four areas. First, we sought to change the constitution and the organic budget law, the main fiscal law of the country, to include an explicit benchmark for the fiscal deficit and the national debt. In particular, we proposed a 2 percent deficit to GDP ceiling and a 40 percent debt-to-GDP ratio. In the event these were breached, parliament would trigger a no-confidence vote in the government. The rationale for this change was to preempt future governments from running higher deficits and increasing the debt burden.

I spent the better part of October and November 2010 convincing the leaders of the political parties in parliament why this would be another important signal to foreign investors that Bulgaria would always follow a conservative fiscal policy, thereby avoiding financial meltdowns. In the end, I could not muster enough votes to change the constitution—160 votes in the 240-member parliament were needed. But enough votes did emerge to change the organic budget law and employ the deficit and debt ceilings. This was a major victory— my most significant legislative success while in office.

The ceilings were significantly lower than the ones in effect for the eurozone countries as part of the Maastricht criteria. During the next Ecofin meeting, several finance ministers from the eurozone congratulated me on the new legislation. Europe had taken notice. On December 1, 2010, the credit rating agency Standard and Poor's changed Bulgaria's investment perspective from "negative" to "stable" in acknowledgment of the 2 percent deficit limit rule.

The second area for reform was university education. Borisov had chosen a reform-minded minister of education who had run the largest private university in Bulgaria and had overseen a significant improvement in its international ranking. Together, we proposed three reforms: first, to link the government subsidy for universities to the quality of education they offered, not just the number of students; second, to decentralize decisions on doctoral degrees;

and, third, to ensure that research and education were more tightly linked by shifting government subsidies from the Bulgarian Academy of Science to the universities. We succeeded in passage of two of them. First, parliament approved a scheme that each year ranked university departments on their relative strength. This ranking determined a share of their universities' budgets, with this share increasing every year until it reached 25 percent. In other words, quality would account for a quarter of the budget financing for universities.

Second, we disbanded the Higher Academic Committee, which was responsible for awarding academic degrees to all university faculty. The committee was composed predominantly of academicians and professors who were members of the former secret police, well past retirement age. As a result, a focus on modern research methods was discouraged, and the average age of new PhDs was 48. Under the reform, each university had the right to design internal procedures for awarding academic degrees. There was an outcry that such a step would flood the academic market with new professors. And it did the first year, when many unsuccessful applicants to the Higher Academic Committee received degrees from their universities. But by 2013 the new system was functioning smoothly. The media were complimentary: "Democratization in Academia."

By early 2011, after almost two years in the government, I was learning to be patient in pursuing reforms in the two problematic sectors: pensions and health care. The pension system was running large deficits, almost €1 billion ($1.4 billion) a year. Yet the mandatory retirement age was 60 for women and 63 for men, among the lowest in Europe. In early 2010, I had proposed increasing the retirement age to 65 years for both men and women. It would take place gradually, by adding four months each subsequent year. For men, the new age would be reached in 6 years, for women in 15 years. I also wanted to eliminate the provisions that allowed members of the police and the military to retire after just 15 years of service. After two months of hard work, I convinced enough members of parliament to make this reform happen. But the prime minister wavered under pressure from the labor unions, and the reform died. In early 2011, an identical proposal for pension reform passed parliament. The deteriorating social climate in Europe and similar reforms in other European countries had convinced the prime minister of the need for change.

As for the health care sector, previous governments had failed miserably to institute reforms. The budget for health care had doubled in real terms over the previous decade, and yet the health profile of the population was not improving. We had tried in both 2009 and 2010 to come up with a reform plan. But one health minister after another had failed to garner enough support from the medical community, and they all left the ministry embittered. Each of them had a good plan, and both the prime minister and I spent countless hours fleshing them out and discussing them with health care professionals. At first, all the discussions were positive, but ultimately it became clear that budgets would have to be redistributed to the better-functioning hospitals, and so that was the end of it. "Just give us more money and the problems would be resolved," the health care professionals would argue.

By the spring of 2011, we were on our third minister; he had worked abroad and had good ideas on what to reform. His basic plan was to concentrate most of the medical services in a dozen high-technology state hospitals and create a supporting system of polyclinics that would take care of the minor medical issues. A nationwide system for medical emergencies would also be devised. The plan was simple and embraced by health care experts. But the mayors of smaller towns and members of parliament from these regions cried foul. "Every citizen has the right to high-quality health care," they reasoned, "and it has to be provided in their local hospital." We thus failed for a third time, and the minister resigned shortly thereafter. In the end, we did what others had done before: gave hospitals more money and left the reforms for another time.

July 22, 2011, was one of my happiest days in the Bulgarian government. Bulgaria received a rating increase from Moody's. I was in London, giving a lecture at the London School of Economics. My phone rang. It was the head of Moody's European service informing me of the upgrade, to Baa2 from Baa3, just before Moody's made the news public. I called Prime Minister Borisov. "Come quickly," he said. "You need to explain what this means for Bulgarian businesses." By the time I landed in Sofia the next day, the news had already hit the front pages, and the prime minister had explained on television that improved credit ratings meant cheaper loans for businesses. He was much better than me at communicating news to the public.

Mid-Term Elections

As the summer of 2011 moved into fall, Bulgarian politicians were busy with something else: the mid-term elections. As a deputy prime minister, I was charged with administering the elections. At first, I was apprehensive: What did it mean to administer democratic elections? Then it became clear that I had to propose how they would be organized and funded. Because both municipal and presidential elections were forthcoming, I proposed holding them at the same time to save money. The date was set: October 23, 2011. The elections would cost around €20 million ($28 million).

In postcommunist Bulgaria, the ruling party had never won the municipal elections, and only once had it won the presidential elections. Understandably, the efforts of all opposition politicians were focused on showing that Borisov and GERB could be defeated. Despite the difficult economic situation, the prime minister enjoyed a high approval rating, around 40 percent, which was significantly higher than that of any other politician. As noted earlier, before becoming prime minister, Borisov had been mayor of the capital city, Sofia, and so he knew all the other mayors. He came up with a simple electoral strategy: Focus on young candidates and show the party's support for their policies. For president, GERB nominated our minister for infrastructure, Rosen Plevneliev. Rosen was a member of my team of reformers. He had come to the government after a successful career in the construction business, and he had spent a decade working in Germany. He was the right face of change, especially in

Figure 2.2   Bulgarian and EU exports of goods and services, 2009–12

percent change

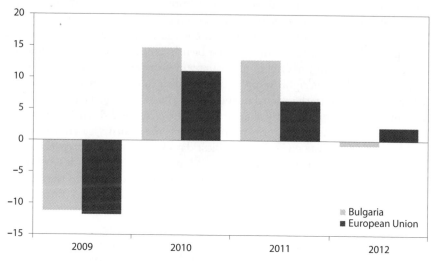

Source: World Bank, *World Development Indicators*, http://databank.worldbank.org/data/home.aspx (accessed on February 27, 2014).

view of the incumbent's secret police past. And Rosen was energetic and full of ideas.

On election night, I called Borisov to see how he was doing. "Come at once," he said. I spent the next six hours nervously waiting with him for election results. No one else from the party was there, just a few personal friends. Borisov was constantly on the phone once the first results started coming in. My first call was from Ivailovgrad, a small town on the Turkish border: GERB's candidate had won. Then there was a call from Aprilzi, a small municipality in northern Bulgaria where I have family roots. GERB had won that as well. And then the good news started pouring in. By the end of the night, GERB had won 90 municipalities, including 9 of the 10 largest. It was a huge win. Our presidential candidate had also won the most votes, but not enough to avoid a runoff against the socialist party candidate. Rosen Plevneliev comfortably won the runoff for the presidency the following week. For me, this was especially sweet because the previous president, Georgi Parvanov, embodied all the characteristics I disliked about Bulgaria's communist past.

Restarting the Economy

After the elections, I focused on ways to revive the economy. The year 2010 had ended with growth of just under 2 percent, among Europe's best. This outcome was mostly due to rapidly rising exports: Export growth was over 30 percent relative to that of the previous year (figure 2.2). Trade was reoriented, with new flows to the Middle East, Russia, and Ukraine. In 2011 exports again rose quickly—by another 33 percent—but the rest of the economy was stagnant. This sluggishness brought renewed calls from politicians to increase the budget deficit and finance a stimulus package. But we had already increased the infrastructure budget by 15 percent from the previous year, so it was not obvious to me where additional public money could spur the economy. And because of the poor record of transparent public procurement, a fiscal stimulus might have simply increased corruption. For this reason, I drafted the 2012 budget with the goal of reducing the deficit to less than 1 percent of GDP. Fiscal responsibility would then translate into higher credit ratings and in turn cheaper access to credit for Bulgarian businesses. This indirect channel for growth, I reasoned, was more sustainable than pouring public money into a stimulus package.

To this day, some politicians and citizens of Bulgaria continue to argue that I should have increased the deficit in 2011 and 2012. But I am still convinced that the money would have gone to waste. In fact, this view has been vindicated: When a socialist-led coalition formed the next government in May 2013, they did not follow through on the election promise for a large fiscal stimulus. The new prime minister, my predecessor as finance minister, knew what would happen. Fiscal stimulus does not work in countries with an abundance of corrupt politicians.

Falling Out of Favor

The year 2012 ended on a sour note for me. In November, Interior Minister Tzvetanov asked for additional money for his ministry, around €14 million ($20 million). This had become an annual routine. The Interior Ministry would overspend and then at the end of the year lobby the prime minister for additional resources. Because of the close relationship between the two, there would be significant pressure to yield. And I had done so in 2010 and 2011. But this time I stood firm: The police should not be treated differently from other sectors. There was no extra money for others, and there would be no extra money for the police.

The issue was compounded by the demands from another lobbying group, the so-called Bentley mafia. The Bentley mafia is made up of the largest Bulgarian agricultural producers, mostly specializing in grains. Bulgaria's grain producers were receiving large amounts of aid from the European Union—over €1 billion ($1.4 billion) a year. They had grown into a powerful lobbying group, and they mercilessly pushed for subsidies from the national budget as well. Their name, the Bentley mafia, originated in their apparent weakness for Bentley cars. It was not unusual to see several Bentleys in a row parked in front of the Finance Ministry when they were organizing a strike to demand more subsidies.

In October 2012 the Bentley mafia paid hundreds of agricultural workers to lay siege to parliament, all of which received daily national news coverage for almost three weeks. I was burned in effigy amid calls for my resignation. For a while, it looked as though this time the prime minister would yield. And then the Bentley mafia made a mistake: One day they burned Prime Minister Borisov in effigy as well. That did it—no yielding. But it was just temporarily, as it turned out.

March 13, 2013, was my last day as the finance minister of Bulgaria. The past few weeks had been difficult. On January 16, the residents of several of the larger cities had received much higher electricity bills than in previous months. That was odd because the weather had been mild. A week later, spontaneous strikes broke out, first in Sofia and then around the country. The three energy distribution companies, which in Bulgaria are owned and operated by large EU utilities, had no response to the situation. The minister of economy and I held several emergency meetings with their bosses, trying to understand what was going on. They swore the electricity bills were accurate. Finally, we uncovered the reason for the higher bills: The December bills had not been sent out, and so in effect the new bills covered a longer period. Why that had happened remained a mystery. Was it staged? It seemed unlikely that the electricity companies forgot to ask for their money.

Whatever the reason, the effect was disastrous. Tensions mounted, and quickly the strikers were joined by lobbying groups who hoped the government would cave in to their demands for fear of continuing disorder. The grain producers, the Bentley mafia, were among the first to announce they would join the strikes unless the government handed over €400 million ($560 million) in additional agricultural subsidies.

I went to the regular Ecofin meeting in Brussels on February 12, 2013, and from there to Washington and Boston to give lectures on the euro crisis. I spoke with Prime Minister Borisov from Brussels, and we agreed that additional presentations on the reasons for the strikes in Bulgaria would be useful in Washington. But by the time I landed in the United States, the prime minister had changed his mind on the grain subsidies and ordered that the money be paid. There was nothing left for me to do. I flew back to Bulgaria and cleared off my desk. February 20, 2013, came with a surprise: Prime Minister Borisov announced that the whole government would resign.

When I saw the prime minister for the first time after the resignation, he was friendly. "You started all this," he said jokingly, implying that my departure had influenced his decision. I told him I would have done the same if I had been him—better to yield than to govern when public opinion turned against you.

Next Parliamentary Elections

On May 12, 2013, Bulgaria held snap parliamentary elections. Borisov's party, GERB, won the most seats but could not form a government. Only three other parties entered parliament: the socialists; their sister party, the DPS (Movement for Rights and Freedoms); and the nationalists. The three formed an unsteady alliance and elected the new government. My predecessor as finance minister, Plamen Oresharski, became the new prime minister. The government's program was a hodgepodge of promises that would bankrupt the country if fulfilled. And this was precisely how things began. But three weeks into its term, the government was forced into a defensive mode.

On June 13, 2013, members of parliament approved a new head of the Bulgarian intelligence services. The new head, however, was a reviled figure in Bulgarian politics.[1] He ran a large media empire that switched allegiance from one party to another, depending on who was in power. Within hours, over 20,000 people had gathered in front of the parliament to protest the appointment.

At first, the government did not react. But strikes sprang up in other Bulgarian cities as well, and in the evening of June 14 parliament voided its decision. But by then it was too late; the following weekend over 100,000 people went on strike across Bulgaria. It was not about this single appointment anymore; it was about corruption in the Bulgarian political system. The strike would turn out to be the longest in Bulgarian history—over seven months. It would block any further policy initiatives by the government. Ministers would simply be afraid to show up in public places because signs calling for their resignation would follow them everywhere.

As for me, leaving the government left me numb for a while. After a hectic work schedule of long days and nights, I was suddenly faced with peace and quiet, and it was unnerving. It took me several months to adjust to my new lifestyle.

---

1. Matthew Brunwasser, "After Political Appointment in Bulgaria, Rage Boils Over," *New York Times*, June 28, 2013.

3

Birth of the Euro

At the onset of the euro crisis in 2008, I was still at the World Bank in Washington. I followed through the media the collapse of the US financial services firm Lehman Brothers on September 15. At the time, I was working mostly on regulatory reform in Egypt and Colombia, and the fall of Lehman Brothers did not appear to hold much importance for the rest of the world. Soon, however, Iceland's banks collapsed. In late September, the Icelandic government assumed a 75 percent stake in the country's third largest bank, Glitnir. A week later, the same thing happened to the second largest bank, Landsbanki. And yet these events seemed to be connected to the subprime crisis in the United States, with hardly any relevance for Europe.

On September 22, 2008, the ministers of finance and central bank governors of the G-7 countries vowed to protect the global financial system. Their declaration read: "We reaffirm our strong and shared commitment to protect the integrity of the international financial system and facilitate liquid, smooth functioning markets, which are essential for supporting the health of the world economy." They went on to say, "We are ready to take whatever actions may be necessary, individually and collectively, to ensure the stability of the international financial system."

Apparently, though, such a declaration was not enough. Trade credit rapidly dried up, and international trade drew to a halt. On September 26, 2008, the US Federal Reserve, the Bank of England, the European Central Bank (ECB), and the Swiss National Bank announced the introduction of operations to provide US dollar liquidity with a one-week maturity. The ECB also provided US dollar one-week funding to Eurosystem counterparties against Eurosystem-eligible collateral, with an initial volume of $35 billion.

On September 29, the ECB conducted a special-term refinancing operation in order to improve the overall liquidity position of the eurozone banking system. The same day, in response to continued strains in short-term funding markets, the Federal Reserve and the ECB doubled their reciprocal currency arrangements (swap lines) from $120 billion to $240 billion. These larger facilities expanded the provision of US dollar liquidity in the eurozone.

The Euro Crisis Starts in Iceland

On October 8, 2008, Iceland seized control of its biggest bank, Kaupthing. This takeover was in response to the decision by British prime minister Gordon Brown to use antiterrorism legislation to freeze the bank's UK-based assets. The liquidity squeeze in European banks then worsened. The ECB decided to carry out weekly refinancing operations with a fixed-rate tender procedure with full allotment, which meant that the interest rate was set in advance and the ECB provided as much liquidity as the banks requested.

On the same day, the ECB lowered its lending rates by 50 basis points. It also reduced the difference between interest rates on marginal lending and on deposit facilities from 200 to 100 basis points. But the financial markets found the measure insufficient, and trade continued to suffer. Noneurozone countries such as Denmark and Sweden had special troubles because they were not benefitting from the ECB actions. To the contrary, the assistance that the eurozone banks were receiving was making liquidity a bigger problem in Denmark and Sweden, and they had to resort to raising interest rates. This in turn affected the three Baltic countries negatively because the banking systems in Estonia, Latvia, and Lithuania were dominated by Swedish banks.

On October 15, 2008, the European Commission proposed increasing the minimum protection for bank deposits to €100,000 ($140,000) to maintain the confidence of all depositors in the financial safety net. This had a calming effect on small depositors until March 2013, when the Cypriot government decided to impose losses in Cyprus on these depositors as well.

The collapse of the Icelandic banks and the ensuing financial crisis became the first serious test of the eurozone. Prior to that it had enjoyed a decade of stability. At its inception in 1999, the euro traded at $1.174. It then fell to $0.825 in October 2000, and gradually appreciated to $1.567 in July 2008, just prior to the crisis (figure 3.1). Adoption of the euro was accompanied by promises of structural reforms and increased competitiveness.

Early Skeptics of the Euro

After entry into the euro area, the Bank of Greece will be implementing the single monetary policy decided by the Governing Council of the European Central Bank and it will certainly be impossible to improve the economy's international competitiveness by changing the exchange rate of our new currency, the euro. The objectives of higher employment and output growth will therefore have to be pursued through structural reforms and fiscal measures aimed at enhancing international competitiveness by increasing productivity, improving the quality of Greek goods and services and securing price stability.

**Figure 3.1   Euro-dollar foreign exchange spot rate, January 1999–
January 2014**

US dollars per euro

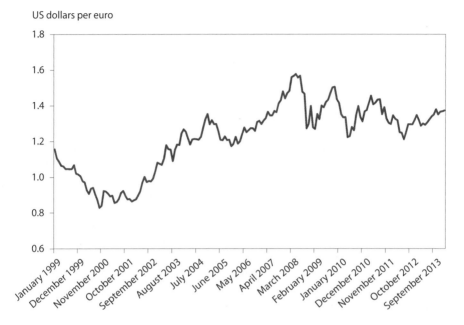

Source: WM/Reuters, Datastream (accessed on February 27, 2014).

These are the words of Lucas Papademos, Greece's central bank governor, spoken at the ceremony commemorating the introduction of the euro to Greece in 2001. Ten years later, Papademos would become the prime minister of a caretaker government charged with preventing Greece from having to exit the eurozone.

From the very start, many economists were skeptical about the euro. Their main concern was the lack of flexibility in the economies of potential members and, as a consequence, in the future monetary union. On February 9, 1998, 155 German academic economists published an open letter entitled "The Euro Is Coming Too Early." In it, they cited the lack of reforms in labor markets and insufficient progress in consolidating public finance for many would-be members of the eurozone (Issing 2008). In 2013 some of these academics would start a new political party, Alternative für Deutschland, which would barely miss the 5 percent target for entering the German Parliament. The party's main platform was stopping bailout support for undisciplined southern eurozone members.

In the United States, economists were just as skeptical, with some such as Milton Friedman and Maurice Obstfeld predicting an ignominious end to the euro adventure. Others had their doubts as well. Initially, Sweden wanted to fix a one-to-one conversion rate of the Swedish krona to the euro and wanted to continue to use both currencies. The country would return to the national currency only in the event of an "emergency." Eventually, however, it backed out of the euro completely: In 2003 Swedish voters rejected the euro in a referendum.

When the European Economic Community (EEC) was established in 1957, its members focused on building a common market for trade. Over time, however, it became clear that a common currency would bolster the internal market, and in 1991 the Maastricht Treaty was signed, ushering in the euro. In 1999 the euro was introduced for accounting and settlement purposes. In January 2002, euro banknotes and coins entered circulation in 12 European countries: Austria, Belgium, Finland, France, Germany, Greece, Ireland, Italy, Luxembourg, the Netherlands, Portugal, and Spain. A year earlier, in 2001, Greece had entered the eurozone so that it could be among the first wave of countries adopting the euro banknotes and coins. It was joined in 2007 by Slovenia, followed by Cyprus and Malta in 2008, Slovakia in 2009, Estonia in 2011, and Latvia in 2014.

This movement was a gradual one. Things deteriorated, however, when private capital flows from the core to the periphery came to a sudden stop in 2008. This development left the southern rim economies with prices and unit labor costs that were well out of line with those in the core. For example, in early 2013 the ECB published a survey on new wealth in the eurozone. The main finding was that net wealth was much lower in northern Europe relative to the southern rim. The average German family had net assets of under €200,000 ($277,000), while Spanish families had net assets of €300,000 ($416,000) on average, and those in Cyprus €670,000 ($929,000). Why? Because since the launch of the eurozone wages and consumer prices in Germany had stayed roughly constant. But in Greece, Italy, and Spain they had increased tremendously (figure 3.2). The result was that an apartment in Milan or Larnaka was much more expensive than one in Munich or Hamburg. Matching housing prices with the incomes of households in southern Europe would require another decade of declining values.

This was the problem that Milton Friedman had warned about earlier, and it would be very difficult to solve without a currency devaluation. Restoring competitiveness through wage cuts was proving extremely hard, even in countries with flexible labor markets such as Ireland. Hourly labor costs in the Irish business sector recorded a measly 2 percent decline between 2008 and 2011—and this was despite rapidly rising unemployment. In Greece, nominal wages have fallen by 20 percent so far, but it has taken six years, five finance ministers, and three prime ministers to get here. And there is a still a long way to go. Latvia, by contrast, did it in three years after the onset of the crisis, and by 2012 it was enjoying rising employment (Åslund 2010).

During an informal Ecofin meeting in Nicosia in September 2012, there was a discussion about whether the euro could have been conceived differently. And whether, in particular, southern rim countries could have waited to enter it. "No" was the answer by policymakers such as Luxembourg prime minister Jean-Claude Juncker who were involved in the birth of the euro: "European

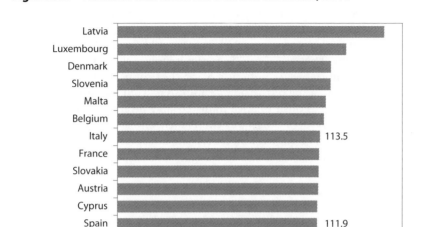

Figure 3.2   Nominal unit labor costs in the eurozone, 2011

Latvia
Luxembourg
Denmark
Slovenia
Malta
Belgium
Italy — 113.5
France
Slovakia
Austria
Cyprus
Spain — 111.9
Netherlands
Greece — 111.0
Portugal — 106.5
Germany — 105.0
Ireland
Eurozone average (17)

0   20   40   60   80   100   120   140   160

index, 2005 = 100

Source: Eurostat, http://epp.eurostat.ec.europa.eu/portal/page/portal/statistics/search_database (accessed on February 27, 2014).

integration was the main motivation, and it was felt that whatever difficulties emerged would be dealt with in transit." In all likelihood, though, expectations did not include anything on the scale of the 2008 crisis. I hasten to note, however, that even in the most trying periods of the euro crisis, such as in the fall of 2011, Juncker remained confident the eurozone would leave these troubles behind and be stronger for it.

Origins of the Euro

Difficult decisions—that was what I expected coming into my first Ecofin meetings. At the time, no one expected the crisis to last long. The European Commission was forecasting an economic recovery by late 2011. But the more seasoned politicians were cautioning against such forecasts. As Jean-Claude Juncker observed when we first met in October 2009, "Finance ministers are always reviled for not giving enough money. But your time in government will be especially difficult." In retrospect, this statement defined my government career in Bulgaria. There was never enough money, and I was always blamed for it. The euro crisis affected Bulgaria through falling investments and trade with Europe and troubles with Greek banks. But it also affected me by turning nearly everyone against the finance minister. Few of my fellow ministers understood the situation, but they helped me as much as they could. So did the prime minister, most of the time. That said, I could count my supporters on two hands.

To feel comfortable in the discussions in the Ecofin, I had to meet the main characters. I knew some of the finance ministers from my time at the World Bank—for example, Polish finance minister Jan Vincent-Rostowski, Swedish finance minister Anders Borg, and the French minister, Christine Lagarde. And I had read a lot about the longest-serving European prime minister, Jean-Claude Juncker. At the first Ecofin meeting, he was the person I wanted to meet the most. I asked him how best to understand the current troubles in the eurozone. "Read about Jean Monnet" was his answer. In other words, to understand the creation of the eurozone, one had to understand how the EEC came about. And, indeed, history is perhaps best understood from the insider's point of view. Although Monnet never occupied public office, in 1955 he founded the Action Committee for the United States of Europe to encourage European integration. The Action Committee brought political parties and European trade unions together and laid the foundation for the EEC, later to become the European Union. After Jean Monnet's memoirs, I delved into Pierre Werner's and Jacques Delors's writings. Werner was prime minister of Luxembourg from 1959 to 1974 and from 1979 to 1984. In 1970 he was given the mandate by the heads of the EEC governments to draft a plan for an economic and monetary union within the Community. The "Werner Plan" was later extended by Jacques Delors, a French socialist who served as the eighth president of the European Commission from January 1985 to December 1994. Together, these men contributed the most to what is now the eurozone.

The road to the eurozone can be divided into three steps. The first was the creation of the European Monetary Mechanism in 1979. Its origin lies in the turmoil in the international currency markets in 1968–69 that threatened the common agricultural policy, a main pillar of the EEC. In response, Europe's leaders set up a group led by Pierre Werner, prime minister and finance minister of Luxembourg at the time, to propose how a monetary union could be achieved by 1980.

The Werner group developed a process to create a monetary union within 10 years, including the possibility of a single currency. An agreement was signed in 1971, and member states began to narrow the fluctuations between their currencies. When in the late 1970s the United States went on an inflation binge under President Jimmy Carter, German chancellor Helmut Schmidt and French president Valéry Giscard d'Estaing pushed for the creation of the European Monetary System. Schmidt was concerned that the German mark would appreciate against the dollar and some other European currencies and would hurt German exports. Giscard d'Estaing did not want France to rejoin the "currency snake" because it functioned asymmetrically.

After tough negotiations between France and Germany, and over the strong objections of Denmark and the United Kingdom, the Bremen summit in July 1978 accepted the idea of a "zone of monetary stability" (Ludlow 1982). In 1979 it became a reality. It was advocated as a more flexible version of the Bretton Woods system that had governed global foreign exchange arrangements until 1973. This comparison is increasingly used by academics in proposing solutions for the euro ills. Polish economist Leszek Balcerowicz made the point the most clearly: The euro should be viewed as a successor of other fixed exchange rate regimes such as the gold standard—with all their downsides.

With the blossoming of Reaganomics and with the soaring US dollar in the early 1980s, enthusiasm for exchange rate stability subsided. But with German unification and the weak dollar in the late 1980s, it gathered speed again. And from it arose the Maastricht Treaty, which represents the second step toward the eurozone. This new Treaty on European Union, which contained the provisions needed to implement the monetary union, was approved at the meeting of the European Council held in Maastricht, the Netherlands, in December 1991. The Council also agreed on the five Maastricht convergence criteria that each member state would have to meet to participate in the eurozone:

1. HICP (Harmonized Index of Consumer Prices) inflation (12-month average of yearly rates) must be no more than 1.5 percent higher than the arithmetic average of the HICP inflation rates in the three EU member states with the lowest HICP inflation. EU member states with an HICP rate significantly below the comparable rates in other member states do not qualify as a benchmark country for the reference value and are ignored.

2. The ratio of the annual general government deficit to GDP at market prices must not exceed 3 percent. Deficits "slightly above the limit" are not accepted unless it can be established that either the deficit ratio has declined substantially and continuously before reaching the level close to the 3 percent limit or the small deficit ratio excess above the 3 percent limit was caused by exceptional circumstances and is temporary in nature.

3. The ratio of gross government debt relative to GDP at market prices must not exceed 60 percent. Or if the debt-to-GDP ratio exceeds the 60 percent limit, the ratio shall at least be found to have sufficiently diminished and be approaching the reference value at a satisfactory pace.

4. Countries must have joined Exchange Rate Mechanism II (ERM II) under the European Monetary System for two consecutive years.

5. Long-term interest rates (average yields for 10-year government bonds in the past year) must be no more than 2 percent higher than the arithmetic average of the similar 10-year government bond yields in the three EU member states with the lowest HICP inflation. If any of the three EU member states of concern are suffering from interest rates significantly higher than the GDP-weighted eurozone average interest rate, then such a country will not qualify as a benchmark country for the reference value.

The Stability and Growth Pact in which these rules were laid out imposed financial fines for breaches of the criteria. It was hoped, however, that these sanctions would never be used. And yet in 2002 the excessive deficit procedure had already been initiated for France, Germany, and Portugal. This was at the insistence of Dutch finance minister Gerrit Zalm, who wanted the largest eurozone countries to be penalized just as small ones had been. After that, Germany ceased to be a strong backer of the Stability and Growth Pact, and its position changed only after the current crisis began.

A significant point of contention was the circumstances under which a deficit above 3 percent was not considered excessive. After several Ecofins devoted to this issue, a compromise was reached on December 13, 1996, in parallel sessions of Ecofin and the European Council in Dublin. It stated that a recession of less than 0.75 percent "as a rule" did not qualify as exceptional, whereas a recession of over 2 percent automatically did. If the recession was in between these two figures, Ecofin would determine whether the recession was exceptional. The result was a rule that could be overturned by an Ecofin minority of at least 26 out of 87 weighted votes or covering at least six member states if they refused to label a budgetary deficit of over 3 percent as "excessive."

The third step was the euro launch on January 1, 1999. At the same time, the eurozone came into operation, and monetary policy passed to the ECB, which had been established a few months earlier—June 1, 1998—in preparation for the third stage of the monetary union. After three years of working with the euro as "book money" alongside national currencies, the ECB placed euro banknotes and coins in circulation on January 1, 2002.

Early Troubles

Yves Thibault de Silguy, who was Europe's monetary affairs commissioner in 1998, argued in a 2012 interview that "without the euro at that time, the common market would have been finished. Without the euro tomorrow the common market will disappear rapidly."[1] Many disagreed, however.

Documents from 1994 to 1998 on the introduction of the euro suggest that the German government had deep misgivings about the date of the euro launch and especially about including Italy in it.[2] According to these documents, which were featured in a May 2012 article in the German newspaper *Der Spiegel*, the decision to invite Italy was based exclusively on political considerations. It also created a precedent for a similar decision two years later: to accept Greece into the eurozone. Instead of waiting until the economic requirements for a common currency were met, Chancellor Helmut Kohl wanted to demonstrate that Germany, even after its reunification, had a European orientation.

1. James Melik, "Euro in Crisis: Founders Reflect on Its Origins," BBC, June 13, 2012.

2. Sven Böll, Christian Reiermann, Michael Sauga, and Klaus Wiegrefe, "Operation Self-Deceit: New Documents Shine Light on Euro Birth Defects," *Der Spiegel*, May 8, 2012.

Although Kohl pushed through the common currency, Gerhard Schröder, the center-left Social Democratic Party candidate for the Chancellery at the time, was skeptical.

In February 1997, following a German-Italian summit, one German ministry of finance official noted that the government in Rome had suddenly claimed that its budget deficit was smaller than indicated by the International Monetary Fund. A few months later, Jürgen Stark, then state secretary in the German finance ministry, reported that the governments of Italy and Belgium had exerted pressure on their central bank heads. The top bankers were supposed to ensure that budget auditors would "not take such a critical approach" to the debt levels of the two countries. In early 1998, the Italian treasury published surprisingly positive figures on the country's financial development.

A bigger problem was neglected as well. In Maastricht, European leaders had agreed that the total debt of a euro candidate could be no more than 60 percent of its annual economic output, unless the ratio was declining sufficiently and rapidly approaching the reference value. Italy's debt level was twice that percentage, and between 1994 and 1997 its debt ratio declined by only 3 percentage points. "A debt level of 120 percent meant that this convergence criterion could not be satisfied," said Jürgen Stark in 2012. "But the politically relevant question was: Can founding members of the European Economic Community be left out?"

Government experts had known the answer for a long time. "Until well into 1997, we at the Finance Ministry did not believe that Italy would be able to satisfy the convergence criteria," said Klaus Regling, who at the time was the director for European and International Financial Relations at the German finance ministry. Regling now is the chief executive of the euro bailout fund, the European Stability Mechanism (ESM).

That skepticism is reflected in the German documents. On February 3, 1997, the German finance ministry noted that in Rome "important structural cost-saving measures were almost completely omitted, out of consideration for the social consensus." On April 22, speaker's notes for the chancellor stated that there was "almost no chance that Italy will fulfill the criteria." And on June 5, the economics department of the Chancellery reported that Italy's growth outlook was moderate and that progress on consolidation was overrated.[3]

Helmut Kohl was determined to finalize the monetary union before the 1998 parliamentary elections. But Germany had a problem of its own. The country's sovereign debt level was above the 60 percent mark. Even worse, Germany's total debt was not declining as the treaty required, but growing. Chancellor Kohl was aware of the problem. "In contrast to Belgium and Italy, the German debt level has risen since 1994," his staff wrote in a March 24, 1998, memo. "In our view, there is a legal problem in Germany's case, because the

---

3. Ibid.

Maastricht Treaty only provides for an exception if the debt level is declining," the memo continues.

Kohl and his finance minister, Theo Waigel, claimed mitigating circumstances. Without German reunification, they argued, the debt ratio would only be 45 percent. The reasoning was accepted by both the European Commission and partner countries. Kurt Biedenkopf, who was at the time prime minister of the state of Saxony, was the only member of the Bundesrat, the legislative body that represents the German states, to vote against the monetary union. "Europe wasn't ready for that epochal step," said Biedenkopf to *Der Spiegel*. "Most politicians in Germany thought that the euro would function even without common institutions and without financial transfers. That was naïve."[4]

Danish citizens thought so, too. Denmark is the only country to twice reject euro entry: first in 1992 when Denmark voted in a referendum on the Maastricht Treaty, and second in 2000 when a referendum on introducing the euro yielded 46.8 percent voting yes and 53.2 percent voting no. In 2008 the newly elected government again raised the prospect of a euro referendum, but the ensuing financial crisis got in the way.[5]

The biggest skeptics about the euro have been the British (Begg 2009). In 1997 the UK government announced that any move toward the euro would depend on meeting five economic tests:

1. *Convergence of business cycles.* Business cycles in the eurozone and the United Kingdom must be compatible. The assessment depends on indicators such as inflation, interest rates, the output gap, and the real effective exchange rate with a view toward long-term convergence.

2. *Flexibility.* The UK economy must be flexible enough to ensure that any asymmetrical shocks can be absorbed by, for example, labor market flexibility and mobility and fiscal policy.

3. *Investment.* UK participation in the single currency must promote investment (foreign or domestic) in the long term.

4. *Financial services.* The eurozone must improve the competitive position of the United Kingdom's financial services industry, particularly in London.

5. *Growth, stability, and jobs.* Entry into the eurozone must have positive effects on employment and growth, measured by the impact on UK foreign trade, price differentials, and macroeconomic stability.

A first assessment of the tests by the treasury was carried out in June 2003. It found that the Chancellor of the Exchequer could not definitively conclude that convergence would be sustainable and that the economy was flexible

---

4. Ibid.

5. Marcus Walker, "Denmark Pushes for Vote to Adopt the Euro," *Financial Times*, November 5, 2008.

enough to cope with any difficulties with the eurozone. Therefore, a decision to adopt the euro was not in the national interest of the United Kingdom.

Even where the euro was welcome, it did not produce the expected result. A case in point was Portugal. It saw a sharp increase in capital inflows from 2000 on, but, whereas these led to a boom elsewhere, in Portugal they triggered a slump. Two factors were at work. First, underdeveloped credit markets in Portugal implied that most of the capital inflows went to fund the nontradable sectors—for example, the construction of municipal roads. As a result, productivity fell and the real exchange rate appreciated. Meanwhile, resources were taken away from the tradable sectors. Second, because of generous past promises on old-age pensions, the Portuguese government continually raised taxes between 2000 and 2007. The tax hikes discouraged work and, combined with the misallocation of resources, produced a slump. Some of the capital was used to sustain an increase in consumption over output. Productivity in the tradable sectors then suffered because of reduced learning by doing (more and more low-cost goods were being imported from low-wage countries such as China).

It was not surprising, then, that in June 2013 a book calling for withdrawal from the euro and a return to the escudo topped the bestseller list in Portugal. *Porque Debemos Sair do Euro* (*Why We Should Leave the Euro*) was written by Professor João Ferreira do Amaral from the Insituto Superior de Economia e Gestão. He began by saying, "In 1581 Portugal surrendered to Spain. In 1992 it laid itself at the feet of a European Commission increasingly answering to Germany's tune. There was no referendum, the voters were never consulted. The Portuguese elites, who hoped to benefit richly from European Structural Funds, cavalierly handed over our currency—and with it our monetary sovereignty. The rest is history" (p. 7).

Theory behind the Euro

The supporters of the euro had misgivings, too. The best description of these misgivings was voiced by Mario Draghi, president of the ECB: "The euro is like a bumblebee. This is a mystery of nature because it shouldn't fly but instead it does. So the euro was a bumblebee that flew very well for several years. And now—and I think people ask 'how come?'—probably there was something in the atmosphere, in the air, that made the bumblebee fly. Now something must have changed in the air, and we know what after the financial crisis. The bumblebee would have to graduate to a real bee. And that's what it's doing."[6]

The creation of the euro was based on economic theory—that of the optimal currency area. An optimal currency area is the geographic area in which a single currency would create the largest economic benefit. Work by Robert Mundell in the 1960s suggested that countries that share strong economic ties might benefit from a common currency. It would facilitate trade and allow for closer integration of capital markets.

---

6. Introductory remarks by Mario Draghi, president of the European Central Bank, at the Global Investment Conference, London, July 26, 2012.

Proponents pointed to the economies of scale in the creation of a currency area. First, there would be an economy in policymaking. When a small country fixes its currency to that of a larger country, it sets the course for the rest of its macroeconomic policies. Thus when in the 1970s Milton Friedman advised Yugoslavia to fix its dinar to the German mark, he based his advice on the argument that Germany had a better monetary policy than Yugoslavia. Second, a currency area is better insurance against external shocks. The more countries join a currency area, the smaller the proportion of any external disturbance to their output.

Much of the economics profession disagreed with Mundell's theory. James Meade, Mundell's teacher at the London School of Economics, was a strong believer in flexible exchange rates. He had suggested that the signers of the Treaty of Rome achieve balance of payments equilibrium by letting exchange rates float. Milton Friedman, like Meade, championed flexible exchange rates, but for different reasons. Meade saw flexible exchange rates as a tool for achieving external balance while freeing policy options for the implementation of national growth policies. Friedman, by contrast, saw flexible exchange rates as a way of getting rid of exchange and trade controls. Both economists saw flexible exchange rates as a means of altering real wages when wage rigidities would otherwise cause unemployment.

To his credit, Mundell also thought currency areas were not for everyone, and in a 1968 article he listed the reasons why a country might not join a currency area (Mundell 1968). Among these reasons were the following: if a country wants a rate of inflation different from the currency area inflation rate; if a country wants to use the exchange rate as an instrument of employment policy to lower or raise wages; if a country wants to use seigniorage as a source of hidden or off-budget funding for personal use by members of a corrupt dictatorship or naïve democratic government; if the political authorities cannot achieve a balanced budget or establish confidence in the permanence of budgetary equilibrium or the viability of fixed exchange rates; and if a country does not want to accept the degree of integration implied by joining, such as common standards or immigration, labor, or tax legislation.[7]

The European countries were a good match with Mundell's criteria for an optimal currency area (Mundell 1960, 227–57; 1961c, 509–17). In 1998–99, statistical work by Professor Andrew Rose at the University of California at Berkeley suggested that a common European currency might produce an increase in intra-European trade, perhaps as much as three times the previous trade volumes (Rose 2000, 9–45). That "fact" was critical in convincing politicians of the virtue of the euro. However, it turned out to be wrong, or at least significantly exaggerated. But European politicians wanted to believe it, and it continues to be used in policy discussions today, even though a large empirical literature points to much smaller effects.

---

7. Robert Mundell, "A Plan for a World Currency," Joint Economic Committee, Hearings before [Reuss] Subcommittee on International Exchange and Payments, September 9, 1968.

How the Facts Differed from Theory

Since the creation of the eurozone, the statistical data accumulated have revealed rather modest gains in trade. Researchers have found that trade between pairs of the original 12 eurozone members increased by 15 percent from 1999 to 2002 beyond what could be explained by other factors. The estimates of the euro effect in a larger set of 22 industrialized countries ranged from 6 to 26 percent for the same period, depending on the type of estimation. More recently, Jeffrey Frankel analyzed different samples and found a similar effect: The euro led to a 15 percent increase in bilateral trade over the decade after its introduction (Frankel 2009). Another study found that countries sharing the euro experienced a boost in bilateral trade of between 9 and 14 percent over the period 1998–2005, depending on country size because smaller countries gain more (Chintrakarn 2008, 186–98). But all was far from the original promise.

At the very outset of the creation of the eurozone, two conditions were described as necessary for its success. First, there should be labor mobility so that workers can move from adversely affected areas to ones enjoying economic growth. This was already acknowledged by Mundell as a major condition for an optimal currency area (Mundell 1961a, 509–17; 1961b, 154–72).

Second, as advocated by US economist Peter Kenen, spending at the country or within-country regional level should have a large federal component to help in dealing with asymmetric shocks (Kenen 1969, 1995). Only a large enough transfer would keep people in the poorer regions from flocking to the richer ones. Such a mechanism was indeed created, the so-called structural funds. But because the European Union's budget is less than 1 percent of Europe's GDP, it would prove insufficient. The US federal budget is, by contrast, 24 percent of GDP.

Even without these two necessary conditions, entering the eurozone is problematic. But even with them, problems exist. The main disadvantage of entering the eurozone is the loss of flexibility. Changes in relative prices and wages are easily implemented through currency depreciation. It is a lot more difficult to do so by negotiating with labor unions or renegotiating individual contracts. Most European constitutions prohibit reductions in social guarantees.

In early 2010, in a single effort Iceland achieved a 30 percent fall in wages relative to the European core by depreciating the krona. Latvia and Romania tried to induce reductions in the pensions of public servants, only to see these policies reversed by the constitutional court. They then had to resort to steep cuts in the public administration and in public sector salaries. Cyprus, Greece, and Spain need at least a comparable adjustment. But it requires several years of wage reductions in the face of high unemployment. Greece is a testimony to this gradual approach. In Portugal, the constitutional court made it illegal to reduce the salaries of public officials. The government of Pedro Passos Coelho was then left scrambling to find a further €4 billion ($5.5 billion) in budget cuts to keep the 2013 budget on track. The result was the resignation two months later of the able finance minister, Vítor Gaspar.

4

Search for Fiscal Discipline as Crisis Mounts

In 2008 financial crisis management was a large part of my job at the World Bank, and so I was technically equipped for my upcoming work in Bulgaria and in Ecofin. In early 2008 at the Bank, we were building the access of small firms and poorer households to finance. We had just recruited a new director for finance, the former deputy central bank governor of Rwanda, and were working with the Bill and Melinda Gates Foundation to establish ways to reach those in middle-income countries who had no access to banks. The coming crisis changed this focus. By midyear, it had become clear that we should shift our attention to developed markets. We hired several experts from the Federal Reserve Board in Washington and from European central banks. By the time Lehman Brothers collapsed in September 2008, my boss, Michael Klein, vice president for finance and the private sector at the World Bank, had put together a crisis response team. As a member of it, I participated in daily meetings on how the crisis might develop and how the Bank could cooperate with other institutions to assist client countries.

From my perch in Washington, it was unclear why Europe did not take more decisive action to alleviate the crisis. In the international meetings on crisis management that became a weekly occurrence in late 2008 and early 2009, European leaders took a wait-and-see approach, hoping that the crisis would blow over and that they would not have to engage in painful restructuring and rescue efforts.

Lack of Leadership in Brussels

My views changed, however, after I became the finance minister of Bulgaria in July 2009. It had quickly become clear to me why the European Commission did not take decisive steps: It lacked leadership. The president of the Commission,

Manuel Barroso, did not actively seek solutions, either because he felt the crisis would go away on its own or because he thought this was the job of the European Central Bank (ECB). Neither of these views should have been held for long: The European Commission's own forecasts were becoming increasingly worrisome, and Jean-Claude Trichet had publicly argued that it was up to Europe's political leaders to handle the sovereign crisis in countries such as Ireland. And yet President Barroso's distant attitude remained unchanged until well into 2011.

Meanwhile, the European Commission itself was not staffed to deal with major crises. Its members were nominated by the governments of the European Union (EU) and went through some perfunctory hearings before being selected. As a result, the Commission typically ended up with many commissioners who had experience in foreign relations and few, if any, who had expertise in economic or financial issues (the EU president cannot ask member countries to nominate experts in a particular area). It is true that Bulgaria's first choice failed the hearings in late 2009, but that was a rare occurrence and had happened only twice before in the history of the Commission. In a crisis, then, Commission president Barroso could not change his "cabinet" and bring in more financial expertise. He had to work with the people nominated by the member countries. Presumably, the Commission could have done some organizational restructuring and reshaped its directorates to be more attuned to the main challenges and transferred powers from one commissioner to another. But President Barroso chose not to do that, and instead at some point he simply elevated Commissioner Olli Rehn to the position of deputy president, leaving the portfolios intact. It was no wonder, then, that the decision making was lacking. The staffing constraints did not allow much initiative.

Perhaps President Barroso was fooled into inaction by the reaction of the financial markets in the summer of 2009. In the sovereign debt market, 10-year Portuguese government bond yields actually declined, in a pattern similar to that of Spanish and Italian bonds, and the difference between Portuguese and German bonds returned to less than 100 basis points during that period. There was a lull in the policy arena as well. There was hope that the intervention by the ECB—the first of several—would be enough to calm the markets and give governments time to deal with domestic issues without resorting to all-eurozone solutions. During this period, Ecofin did not meet as regularly because finance ministers wanted the public to believe that things were under control and that such meetings were not needed. The International Monetary Fund (IMF) went along with this, even advising some countries to use more fiscal space—in other words, to run larger deficits—to jump over the hump. Meanwhile, the markets remained calm for a while.

Analyzing the crisis from Washington, I thought this action was insufficient, but it was a step in the right direction. It was insufficient because it avoided an immediate euro crisis without taking care of the indirect channels of contagion within the European Union. The extra liquidity helped the eurozone economies escape the sudden drying up of liquidity that the collapse of Lehman Brothers had caused elsewhere. But that helping hand was not offered to noneurozone countries such as Estonia, Hungary, Latvia, Lithuania, and Romania. These countries had no resort to ECB funds and fell into severe recessions. This was especially true of the Baltic countries because their governments had to defend their currency boards or pegged exchange rate arrangements. The result was a steep decline in GDP and a jump in unemployment. These outcomes in turn had a negative effect on Sweden, whose banks dominated the financial sector in the Baltics, and on Austria and Italy, whose banks had significant market shares in Hungary and Romania.

Because of the small size of the noneurozone banking sector in the European Union, except the United Kingdom, I thought the ECB would have been much better off creating a mechanism for supporting these banks with the type of instruments available through the Eurosystem. The European Commission also should have supported a broader approach. Its lackluster behavior was interpreted as an absence of solidarity and soon gave rise to euroskeptic leaders such as Viktor Orbán in Hungary.

The reason the European Commission did not act in these ways was the consistent lack of initiative from Brussels. This lack of initiative had developed historically from overdependence on the largest member states, mostly Germany. In truth, Brussels followed, did not lead, decision making in Berlin. Indeed, what I learned from discussions on the fiscal union in Brussels was that the process through which the European Union had evolved made it impossible to take a big step forward. Neither President Barroso nor President Herman Van Rompuy nor Commissioner Rehn was empowered to propose a plan. In the past, big decisions had always been proposed by Germany or Germany plus France, or some high-level working group outside the Commission. This was what President Barroso was waiting for.

Irish Worries

Fearing runs on banks in Ireland in the aftermath of the fall of Lehman Brothers, G-20 leaders met in Washington on November 15, 2008, to discuss efforts to revive economic growth. World Bank president Robert Zoellick was also a participant in the meeting. Our team prepared the background materials for him and met the expert teams attending the forum to draft the joint declaration. Even though a cloud of uncertainty over what course to take in limiting the crisis hung over the meeting, many leaders, mostly Europeans, actually perceived the crisis to be an American problem. It started in the United States, and so it should be solved primarily by the United States. In a series of interviews in the week leading up to the Washington meeting, French president Nicolas Sarkozy blamed American greed for the crisis.[1] So did the Italian finance min-

---

1. Bruno Waterfield, "Europeans Signal Clash with US over Global Capitalism," *Telegraph*, October 19, 2008; Mark Landler, "Sarkozy's Fiscal Meeting Raises Diplomatic Hackles," *New York Times*, November 19, 2008.

ister, Giulio Tremonti.[2] Some European politicians felt vindicated in their mistrust of markets. This finger-pointing continued well into early 2009. The troubles in Iceland and Ireland, however, soon made the problem European.

Four days after the G-20 meeting, the International Monetary Fund announced that Iceland would receive a package totaling €1.52 billion ($2.1 billion) under the IMF's fast-track emergency financing mechanism. The IMF's Executive Board approved the two-year Stand-By Arrangement for Iceland on November 19, and made €600 million ($827 million) immediately available to the country.

Soon after, Ireland became the first eurozone country to fall into recession. On January 15, 2009, Irish finance minister Brian Lenihan nationalized the Anglo Irish Bank. The main reason for the collapse of Irish banking was the devastating boom-bust cycle in the Irish property market. Because the property boom prior to 2008 was financed through aggressive lending by the Irish banks, the decline in property prices and the collapse in construction activity had resulted in severe losses in the banking sector. These losses contributed in turn to the economic crisis through a credit squeeze and to a fiscal crisis, directly through the staggering costs of recapitalizing the banking system and indirectly through the loss of asset-driven revenues. Leaked records of conversations among Irish private bankers suggested that the recapitalization might have been done with the blessing of the ECB.

On the same day, the ECB cut the interest rate on the main refinancing operations to 2 percent. It also lowered the interest rate on the marginal lending facility to 3 percent and on the deposit facility to 1 percent. This move added liquidity to the banking systems of the eurozone countries, but added to the difficulties of Denmark and Sweden and of the three Baltic countries. This was the main reason Estonia and then Latvia quickly took the path to eurozone entry.

The developments in Iceland and Ireland were still viewed by many analysts as specific to those countries, linked to unreasonable investments by greedy bankers. But by the end of January 2009, the sentiment had changed. Indeed, from this point on bad news broke almost daily. Hungary, Latvia, Romania, and Ukraine all succumbed to full-blown crises. But because none of these countries were in the eurozone, their fiscal and economic struggles remained beyond the attention of Brussels. Or perhaps it was becoming increasingly clear that the worst was yet to come for the eurozone.

At the beginning of February 2009, the new prime minister of Iceland, Jóhanna Sigurðardóttir, presented her government's plan to rescue Iceland from financial ruin. She replaced the central bank board, which had failed to prevent the collapse of the banking system, and she asked a parliamentary committee to prepare a plan for joining the European Union.

On February 25, the de Larosière Group, charged with making recommendations to the European Commission on strengthening financial super-

2. "Lessons from a Crisis," *Economist*, October 2, 2008.

Figure 4.1 Ireland's budget deficit, 2006–13

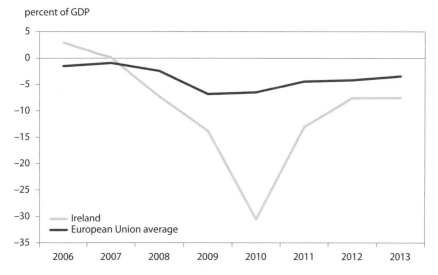

percent of GDP

Source: IMF, *World Economic Outlook*, January 2014, www.imf.org/external/pubs/ft/weo/2013/02/weodata/index.aspx (accessed on February 27, 2014).

vision in the European Union, published its report. In addition to Jacques de Larosière, former president of the European Bank for Reconstruction and Development, the group comprised Polish economist Leszek Balcerowicz; Otmar Issing, former chief economist of the ECB; Onno Ruding, former executive director of the International Monetary Fund; and several other financial heavyweights. Among its recommendations, the group was cautious in recommending the creation of a single banking supervisor for the eurozone. It did not recommend rapid action on the issue. In June 2013, I spoke to Balcerowicz about the de Larosière Group. His views had not changed. The banking union might take more than a decade to emerge. And even then, national banking authorities would be in a better position to undertake the supervision.

In March 2009, Ireland lost its AAA debt rating as its public finances deteriorated further (figure 4.1). The government of Brian Cowen, which took over just before the crisis erupted, unveiled its second budget in six months to deal with a rapidly contracting economy. The new fiscal deficit goal was 10.75 percent, at the time the highest in the European Union.

The rapid fall of Ireland's fortunes was not simply a banking and financial disaster; it was also a big blow to the growth model of Europe. Before the crisis, Ireland was always cited as an example of a small European country that was conducting smart regulatory policies to attract foreign investment, maintaining low tax rates, and creating opportunities for new technologies that could be produced rapidly. At the time, if you had asked development economists how the small East European countries should develop, they would surely have pointed to Ireland. It was the inspiration, for example, for the low corporate tax introduced in Bulgaria in 2007. I had visited Ireland twice between 2005 and 2008 to study its business-friendly regulations and had featured them as examples in the World Bank's *Doing Business* report. Ireland's downfall created a big void in the development model for small European states.

Spurred by the active role of the Federal Reserve in the United States in dealing with banking crises, the ECB became more aggressive in taking action. On June 4, 2009, the bank decided that the Eurosystem would purchase euro-denominated covered bonds issued in the eurozone. The goal was to encourage banks to expand their lending to the economy and to ease funding conditions for banks and enterprises. Under this program, the Eurosystem purchased €60 billion ($83 billion) in covered bonds over the 12-month period to the end of June 2010, when the program was completed. A total of 422 different bonds were purchased, 27 percent in the primary market and the remainder in the secondary market, with an average duration of 4.12 years (Beirne et al. 2011).

But the European Commission continued to act indecisively and, on advice from the International Monetary Fund, even urged countries with some budgetary space to expand their fiscal stimulus as a way to alleviate the recession. This had a negative side effect. Deficit consolidation efforts in many countries came to a halt. In Portugal, for example, the deficit increased from 2.7 percent of GDP in 2008 to 9.3 percent of GDP in 2009. Portugal had run deficits even in the precrisis years, and had already breached the 60 percent debt-to-GDP target in 2004 (figure 4.2). Growth was minuscule in the decade leading up to the crisis, resulting in further deterioration of debt levels. The crisis simply pushed Portugal's public finances over the edge.

Limitations of the Stability and Growth Pact

Portugal's crisis was precisely what the Stability and Growth Pact, the basis for the eurozone's fiscal stability, was supposed to avoid. It was clear that if a country ran consistent deficits and had virtually no growth, the stability of its public finances was in danger. But the pact had failed to limit deficit spending. Even though all eurozone entrants had subscribed to the pact's rules, few countries bothered to follow them. At first, I could not understand why something so central to the concept of the eurozone was so blatantly disregarded. But over time I figured it out: The large countries disregarded it—some such as Italy and France from the start—and so everyone else had the incentive to do so as well. To his credit, Dutch finance minister Jan Kees de Jager brought it up several times in discussions at Ecofin. I also remember the Finnish finance minister, Jyrki Katainen, raising this issue at Ecofin meetings in early 2010. But their concerns fell on deaf ears.

So, eurozone members did not abide by their own rules—and indeed resistance to common fiscal rules was evident from the birth of the eurozone. "What you are proposing is a computer that takes the decisions. Policy by software." In October 1996, that was how the French finance minister, Jean Arthuis, had

Figure 4.2 Portugal's public debt, 2004–12

percent of GDP

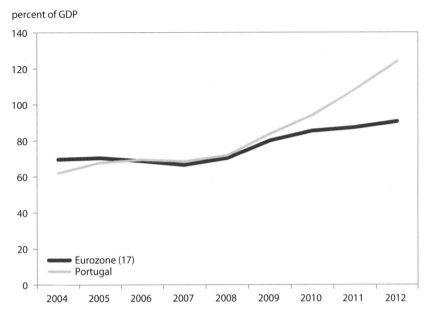

Source: Eurostat, http://epp.eurostat.ec.europa.eu/portal/page/portal/statistics/search_database (accessed on February 28, 2014).

described Germany's idea of creating a basis for common fiscal rules in the eurozone. The following January, the European Council implemented the Stability and Growth Pact at the suggestion of German finance minister Theo Waigel. Waigel first presented his proposal at the Ecofin gathering in Brussels on November 27, 1995. But the intergovernmental agreement as originally envisaged by Waigel and his state secretary, Jürgen Stark, was shunned by other European monetary union members. The European Council then suggested a solution within the existing EU legal framework. But this solution did not include automatic fines and reduced the sanctions to a discretionary measure of Ecofin. Thus the ministers themselves had to judge each other (Begg 2002).

Waigel had originally proposed a Stability Pact, but by 1997 it had been renamed the Stability and Growth Pact at the insistence of France. Unemployment had become a big issue for the Juppé government, and the French finance ministry thought that adding "Growth" to the name of the pact would signal a desire to tackle employment issues as well (Heipertz and Verdun 2004). But, because France was perennially in breach of the pact, the rules were loosened in 2005 under pressure from Paris but also from Berlin and Rome. And if the two main eurozone members did not follow the rules, understandably other members followed suit.

When asked in 2010 whether the Stability and Growth Pact had failed

Europe in the current crisis, Waigel answered no. "Greece fiddled with the numbers, which is quite a nasty trick. However, the European Commission and the other institutions should have questioned Greece's budget figures much sooner. The country should not have joined the euro zone under such circumstances."[3] Perhaps, but the eurozone itself had failed by not implementing its own rules. This often led to awkward situations at Ecofin, where the Dutch minister would reprimand Greece or Spain for not tightening its fiscal policy, and they would respond, "Well, you don't exactly meet the Maastricht criteria either." It was hard to argue with that.

Still, Waigel's pact became the basis for a common fiscal policy in the European Union. Thus a fiscal union in which budgets and taxes were decided centrally was considered in conjunction with the establishment of the euro. The argument was that member states would not be able to run up unaffordable deficits. When they ran into trouble, money could be diverted from the more successful states to the ones that needed help.

Why was fiscal union stalled for so long? First, the surrender of sovereignty was too great (Debrun et al. 2008, 297–362). It was hard enough to persuade taxpayers to subsidize regions in the same country. Persuading electorates to send their taxes to a central authority, without having a say on where it would be spent, was impossible, especially for smaller countries such as Luxembourg and the Netherlands, which had few votes in the European Parliament.

In view of sovereignty issues, how would a fiscal union be enforced? "The budget law is a matter of national parliaments," said Guido Westerwelle, Germany's foreign minister, in 2012. "The European Commission doesn't determine the budget. That is the job of the German Bundestag, the national parliament."[4] In other words, there was no credible enforcement mechanism. One could submit national budgets to Brussels in advance for approval, but what happened if a budget was rejected and the national parliament agreed to it anyway? Brussels bureaucrats could complain to the European Court of Justice, but even it could only impose a penalty.

Second, the timing of the creation of such a fiscal union always seemed wrong. In times of crisis, the only thing governments provided was fiscal pain. Spending had to be cut. If the European Union took control of national budgets at such a moment, it would become unpopular. Brussels would be seen as Scrooge.

Creating a fiscal union was also difficult in boom years, when Brussels was able to hand out lots of cash to build new schools and roads. The decision would have to be made by national parliaments, who in effect would be signing away much of their discretion—and certainly the ability to provide their regions with better infrastructure and other services.

---

3. "Theo Waigel: Greek Crisis Exposed EU Weaknesses," EurActiv, September 13, 2010.

4. Quoted in Matthew Lynn, "Euro Dies Slow Death Without Common Fiscal Policy," Bloomberg News, May 18, 2010.

Third, tax policy varied widely across the eurozone and especially in the European Union. Ireland, for example, was long known as the country with low corporate tax rates (12.5 percent) that had managed to attract foreign investors. France was known as the country with the highest corporate tax rates, and with many preferences for specific companies and industries. Harmonizing taxes would be a significant problem, akin to the creation of the euro. Just as some economists had argued that a single currency helped the competitiveness of some countries (such as Germany) at the expense of others (the southern rim members), so a unified tax regime would be at the expense of the nations that were catching up economically.

I had this discussion many times with the French and German finance ministers and their staffs. "We are ready for a harmonized tax rate if Europe adopts the lowest current one—that is, Bulgaria's," I would say. "A 10 percent corporate and personal income tax would make businesses and people in your countries very happy." For obvious reasons, they were never swayed by this argument. "Who then should decide what the common tax rate would be?" I would ask. No answer.

For these reasons, fiscal policy coordination in the eurozone was limited to the package of budgetary rules (Buti, Franco, and Ongena 1998, 81–97). In 2011 the Stability and Growth Pact was supplemented with the Fiscal Compact, which prescribed automatic correction mechanisms for deficits and the introduction of national debt rules. For monitoring purposes, the European Commission adopted in December 2011 "six pack" legislation, consisting of five EU regulations and one directive. Its aim was to eliminate gaps in the Stability and Growth Pact and strengthen both its preventive arm and its corrective arm. This was one of the big successes of European Commissioner Rehn. He did manage to push this legislation through the European Parliament, where at first there was considerable disagreement.

Using the Pact to Punish Profligates

The 2012 Treaty on Stability, Coordination and Governance requires EU member countries to confine their structural deficit to a maximum of 0.5 percent of GDP, and to 1 percent for countries whose total debt falls short of 40 percent of GDP. This requirement was bolstered in early 2013 by the "two pack" legislation that called for monitoring draft budgets and greater surveillance of countries that had taken advantage of financial bailouts.

The European Commission monitors compliance with the Stability and Growth Pact by assessing countries' stability and convergence programs. Eurozone members report their compliance by submitting annual "stability programs"; noneurozone countries submit annual "convergence programs." These programs include the medium-term budgetary objectives of each country and the measures being taken to attain these objectives. The European Council, acting on Commission proposals, issues opinions to member states and, if necessary, requires them to strengthen their programs.

If the budgetary discipline in a member state worsens and its deficit exceeds the 3 percent of GDP limit, the Council launches an excessive deficit procedure against the member state, which must respond with corrective actions. If not, as a last resort, financial penalties are imposed.

This rule was not enforced until recently; in 2012 Brussels decided to punish Hungary for breaching the rules every year since its entry into the European Union in 2004. In fact, the action against Hungary was prompted by other considerations altogether. In late 2011, Viktor Orbán, Hungary's prime minister, had proposed constitutional reform that would ostensibly deprive Hungary's central bank of some of its independence. More important, the media would be required to report their true ownership and the sources of their financing, which appeared in Brussels to be an attack on media freedom. Hungary thus became the first country to be penalized, even though there were many takers. France, for example, has never met the Maastricht criteria since their adoption in 1991.

The excess deficit procedure is carried out as follows. First, twice a year, before April 1 and before October 1, member states have to send Eurostat data on their government deficit and debt, nominal GDP, and other associated variables (Eurostat is the European Union's statistical agency). After each reporting date, Eurostat examines whether the data conform with its statistical rules and, if so, validates them. Next, Ecofin formulates an opinion on the country's deficit situation. If the Commission believes that an excessive deficit exists or may occur, it addresses an opinion to the Council. Then, the Council decides whether an excessive deficit exists.

In addition to the excess deficit procedure, Ecofin designed a macroeconomic imbalance procedure, mostly in an attempt to better monitor private capital flows. Launched in early 2012, this procedure is supposed to identify potentially harmful imbalances.[5] The macro imbalance procedure is based on a scoreboard consisting of 11 indicators that cover the major sources of macroeconomic imbalances. The scoreboard is published in the Alert Mechanism Report that marks the starting point of analysis. For each indicator, alert thresholds have been defined to detect potential imbalances. The scoreboard and the thresholds are applied mechanically, without taking into account the economic and social characteristics of countries. This procedure was the subject of significant debate at Ecofin when European Commissioner Rehn first presented the methodology. Anders Borg, the Swedish finance minister, and I argued that the methodology was overzealous and that it would raise false alarms.

The indicators on external imbalances and competitiveness proposed by Commissioner Rehn included

- a three-year average of the current account balance as a percentage of GDP, with an indicative threshold of +6 percent and −4 percent of GDP;

---

5. The procedure is based on the Alert Mechanism Report, which identifies countries and issues for which a closer analysis is warranted.

- a net international investment position as a percentage of GDP, with an indicative threshold of –35 percent;
- percentage change over five years in export market shares measured in values, with an indicative threshold of –6 percent;
- percentage change over three years in nominal unit labor costs, with indicative thresholds of +9 percent for eurozone countries and +12 percent for noneurozone countries; and
- percentage change over three years in real effective exchange rates based on Harmonized Index of Consumer Prices (HICP) deflators, relative to 35 other industrial countries, with indicative thresholds of ±5 percent for eurozone countries and ±11 percent for noneurozone countries.

The indicators on internal imbalances included

- private sector debt as a percentage of GDP over 160 percent,
- private sector credit flow as a percentage of GDP over 15 percent,
- year-on-year percentage change in deflated house prices over 6 percent,
- public sector debt as a percentage of GDP over 60 percent,
- three-year average of unemployment rate over 10 percent, and
- year-on-year percentage change in total financial liabilities of the financial sector over 16.5 percent.

Not surprisingly, the first scorecard put nearly every European Union country on alert. In particular, in May 2012, 12 countries were identified as warranting further economic analysis: Belgium, Bulgaria, Cyprus, Denmark, Finland, France, Hungary, Italy, Slovenia, Spain, Sweden, and the United Kingdom.[6] The European Commission found that Spain and Cyprus were experiencing very serious imbalances, and the imbalances of France, Hungary, Italy, and Slovenia were considered serious.

In addition, the Commission found that Malta and the Netherlands warranted in-depth review. In Malta, the financial sector required closer investigation. Potential risks were the extremely large financial system and the high exposure of banks to the property markets, in combination with high private sector indebtedness. In the Netherlands, the potential risks stemmed from an elevated level of private sector debt in combination with high housing prices.

In summary, the first scorecard painted a bleak picture of Europe's macroeconomic future: 18 of 27 countries (two-thirds of the European Union) either exhibited significant weaknesses or had very serious problems.

When the first report about Bulgaria was issued, I wondered how I would explain it to the Bulgarian media. The report concluded that Bulgaria exceeded

---

6. The Alert Mechanism Report looks at all EU member states except those that are subject to enhanced surveillance under economic adjustment programs supported by official financing. In 2012 these were Greece, Ireland, Portugal, and Romania.

the criteria on the net international investment position and unit labor costs. One explanation might be that our wages were rising too fast and that Bulgarian companies were borrowing too much from abroad. The communication problem was obvious: Most people would consider higher wages and borrowing from abroad to be good things. After some thought on the plane back from Brussels, I simply announced that Bulgaria was in the same group as Austria, Finland, and Sweden. And that was that: No discussion ensued.

The next meeting of Ecofin was the scene of a lively debate on the scorecard. I asked Commissioner Rehn which textbook his experts had been reading, and whether it would be productive to invite some lecturers on macroeconomics to address the European Commission. Similar questions were raised by Luc Frieden, the finance minister of Luxembourg, and George Osborne, the British finance minister. There was no response. In general, it was fruitless, at best, to bring substantive points to Commissioner Rehn. He simply did not want to involve himself in substantive discussions.

The macroeconomic imbalance procedure also has a corrective arm: An excessive imbalance procedure can be opened for a member state. The state concerned would have to submit a corrective action plan with a clear roadmap and deadlines for implementing corrective action. As of July 2013, this mechanism had not yet been put to the test. Meanwhile, in the second installment of the macroeconomic imbalance procedure in 2013, Spain and Slovenia were identified as having very serious problems.

Attempts to Strengthen Fiscal Discipline

It remains to be seen whether with time the macroeconomic imbalance procedure will lead to more stable macroeconomic behavior (Strauch, Hallerberg, and von Hagen 2009). I think it is too cumbersome and at times contradicts basic economics. For emerging economies such as Bulgaria, economic theory would predict a large flow of capital attracted by higher returns and thus a current account deficit. But the methodology designed by Commissioner Rehn's experts disregarded such economic relations. Undoubtedly, they had reasons to worry about private capital flows, but there had to be some correction for the level of economic development a country had reached.

In the meantime, in late 2011 the president of the European Council, Van Rompuy, wrote a report proposing the creation of a fiscal capacity for the European monetary union in order to better deal with country-specific shocks (European Council 2011). Potential sources of funding included a fixed share of national taxes (e.g., the value-added tax) or a common European tax such as a financial transaction tax. The latter would have to be collected in all the euro countries, which raised objections. For this reason, the proposal did not gain supporters and was discarded in 2012.

In January 2013, the European Commission outlined a fiscal plan that contained proposals for a central budget, the issuance of common debt, and a full banking union (European Commission 2013a). In March 2013, the

Commission proposed a convergence and competitiveness instrument that could provide financial assistance for structural reforms in member states currently facing economic difficulties. This is a promising idea. But the Commission needs to secure funding for it, something that has proven difficult in the 2014–20 budget cycle.

In May 2013, French president François Hollande called for an economic government for the eurozone with its own budget, the right to borrow, an integrated tax system, and a president. It would harmonize fiscal and welfare policies and debate the main economic and political decisions taken by member states. "It is my responsibility as the leader of a founder member of the European Union . . . to pull Europe out of this torpor that has gripped it, and to reduce people's disenchantment with it. If Europe stays in the state that it is now, it could be the end of the project," President Hollande concluded.[7]

Germany is also convinced of the need for a fiscal union. "We seem to find common solutions when we are staring over the abyss," Chancellor Angela Merkel said during an April 2013 visit to Poland. "But as soon as the pressure eases, people say they want to go their own way. We need to be ready to accept that Europe has the last word in certain areas. Otherwise we won't be able to continue to build Europe."[8]

Admirable intentions—but many changes have to be made before anyone seriously considers a fiscal union, including changes in the structure of the EU institutions. For example, who would be in charge? Currently, four different commissioners are responsible for fiscal issues. In addition to Commissioner Rehn, who is in charge of financial and monetary affairs, Michel Barnier is responsible for some of the relevant legislation, Joaquín Almunia for the internal market, and Algirdas Šemeta for taxation. Their bureaucracies operate separately. Several times in Ecofin discussions, when the future architecture around the euro was broached, these commissioners would pull in different directions.

It is also not obvious whether the president of the European Council has the powers needed to shape the longer-term vision of a fiscal and banking union. On two occasions during the crisis, Van Rompuy met with us—the finance ministers—to discuss his plans for Europe's competitiveness and growth. The issue of the fiscal union was not on either agenda. But at least President Van Rompuy tried; President Barroso never initiated such a meeting.

The United States as an Example?

In 2010, when the discussion of a fiscal union first gathered speed, my staff at the Bulgarian Ministry of Finance was conducting research on the US federal

7. Hugh Carnegy and James Fontanella-Khan, "François Hollande Goes on 'Offensive' over Stalled EU Economy," *Financial Times*, May 16, 2013.

8. Noah Barkin, "Merkel Says Euro Members Must Be Prepared to Cede Sovereignty," Reuters, April 22, 2013.

government's budget. I used this analysis in several discussions at Ecofin because it showed what a long way Europe had to go to achieve a fiscal union. For one thing, the fiscal redistribution is much higher in the United States than in Europe. In the United States, the federal government collects two-thirds of revenues, the states one-fifth, and local government the rest. Because state budgets receive some direct funding from the federal government, the state and local government share of total spending is somewhat higher than 40 percent. In the European Union, member states were providing the bulk of the EU budget in the form of contributions largely related to their gross national income and value-added tax revenues. Most member states were contributing to the common budget by amounts equivalent to 0.8–0.9 percent of GDP, and were receiving EU funds in the range of 0.5–3.5 percent of GDP. Second, unemployment insurance in the United States acts as an automatic stabilizer. If a growth slump causes the unemployment rate to rise, a larger number of people receive transfer payments from the national budget. By contrast, in the eurozone the system of shock absorption through capital and labor markets was not functioning as well. Economists estimated that on average 39 percent of a state-specific shock in the United States between 1963 and 1990 was smoothed over through interregional (public and private) ownership of capital investments, with the trend steadily rising (Asdrubali, Sorensen, and Yosha 1996, 1081–110). In the 1990s, the share had already reached 55 percent compared with only 9 percent in the eurozone. Even after the monetary union was created in the eurozone only 14 percent of a regional shock was ironed out by cross-border capital investments. The reason: Investors in the eurozone had a pronounced home bias, and except in Austria over 50 percent of total equity holdings were in the hands of resident investors.

Moreover, an all-European unemployment insurance scheme does not exist. If it did, contributors from countries with structurally low unemployment such as Austria, Luxembourg, and the Netherlands would effectively subsidize countries with high unemployment such as Greece. If countries with less generous social security systems adjusted their conditions to be more generous, however, this would create negative migration incentives. This was undesirable in view of the already low level of internal mobility in the eurozone.

5

First Greek Bailout and Europe Wobbles into 2010

The first inkling that Greece was headed for major trouble came on October 23, 2009. In a televised interview, Prime Minister Georgios Papandreou announced that Greece had lied about its budget deficits and debt for over a decade. The country's public deficit would exceed 12 percent of GDP, doubling the level declared by the Karamanlis administration just a month earlier—and this for a country with a precrisis public debt level in 2007 of 105.4 percent of GDP, the highest in the European Union (figure 5.1).

This revelation set in motion a chain of events that, more than anything else, challenged the survival of the eurozone. It also changed fundamentally my term as Bulgaria's finance minister. For Bulgaria, any possibility of quick euro entry was gone. And I would spend a significant part of my time convincing investors and analysts that the Bulgarian banking system could withstand the likely collapse of Greek banks. The subsidiaries of these banks in Bulgaria accounted for over a third of the country's total banking assets. Remembering Bulgaria's banking crisis of 1996–97, the markets began to factor in a repeat. Yields on the Bulgarian foreign debt shot up.

The Greek government's admission that national statistics had been unreliable for years had a devastating effect on Europe. This was a replay of 2004 when the Greek government had conceded that the country's budget deficits had not been below the Maastricht criteria of 3 percent since 1999, not even when Greece entered the eurozone in 2001 (Brück and Stephan 2006, 3–15). This news poisoned the talks with the European Union and influenced the way in which the sovereign debt crisis was handled politically in Berlin, Brussels, the Hague, and Helsinki.

Figure 5.1   Greece's debt-to-GDP ratio, 2006–12

percent

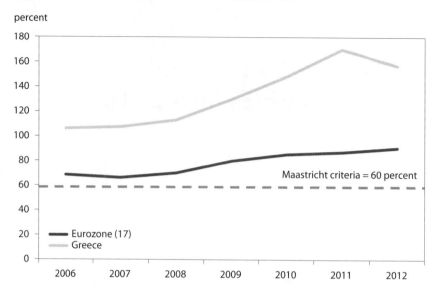

Source: Eurostat, http://epp.eurostat.ec.europa.eu/portal/page/portal/statistics/themes (accessed on February 24, 2014).

First Tipping Point

Prime Minister Papandreou's admission was met with general confusion in Europe. The previous week, Ecofin had held its monthly meeting and nothing like that had been mentioned. It appeared that the European Commission had not been informed in advance. In Bulgaria, the news coincided with the weekly cabinet meeting. I explained to the other ministers that the news meant more difficult times for Bulgaria as well. And I reminded them that a third of the Bulgarian banking sector was in the hands of Greek banks. We were also neighbors, and Greece was the third largest foreign investor in Bulgaria. These businesses depended on credits from Greek banks, so they were directly affected. This would make our governing job all the more difficult.

The next day, the financial markets responded vehemently to the admission of false statistics by demanding much higher rates on Greek bonds. Almost immediately, the demands spread to other countries with high government debt ratios and wobbly banking systems—Italy, Portugal, and Spain. What was a receding global financial crisis rapidly turned into a homegrown European crisis.

There are tipping points in any crisis, and this was the first tipping point in the euro crisis (see the chronology at the end of this volume). In hindsight, what could have been done differently? One lesson I learned from Georgios Papandreou's admission: Do not blame your predecessors for all the problems they caused. Even if true, that alerts investors to the problems before you have designed solutions. This was precisely what Papandreou did: He pointed to a large problem, but he did not spell out the solution. The markets were understandably rattled.

Indeed, it is the first instinct of any politician who comes to power to blame all problems on his or her predecessors. This was what Prime Minister Papandreou did in October 2009, and this is precisely what my government had done when it came to power a few months earlier. In ordinary times, other Europeans probably do not pay much attention. But during a crisis, everyone carefully follows the news in other EU countries. So when a new government describes the failings of the previous one, it tarnishes the whole country, not just the former ministers. Other governments take notice and bring up the subject during Ecofin discussions or in bilateral meetings. And a finance minister or prime minister cannot simply say, "That was said for local consumption only." If I ever enter public service again, I will be a lot more circumspect about the achievements and failings of my predecessors.

In this situation, Prime Minister Papandreou was not the only one to blame. Another factor contributing to the reaction of markets was the badly timed advice of the International Monetary Fund (IMF). A few weeks earlier, its experts had advised countries with remaining fiscal space—Cyprus, Slovenia, and Spain—to expand stimulus spending.[1] And so they did. But it proved contagious to other eurozone members, Greece included. In the same speech announcing the enormous deficit, Papandreou also promised greater spending on education, health care, research and development, and public investment in green energy.[2]

I could not understand the IMF's advice and had lively discussions with IMF staff when they came to Sofia in late October 2009 for the regular Article IV Mission, which studies risks in the macroeconomic environment on an annual basis. Especially because of the kinds of unpleasant surprises likely to emerge in the early stages of such a crisis, advising governments to spend their way out of the crisis seemed irresponsible. The technical answer was that IMF staff saw large multipliers in public spending, much larger than academic papers would normally suggest. And that to fight the crisis one needed fiscal expansion. Perhaps so, but there was a second reason that was not directly expressed. The managing director of IMF, Dominique Strauss-Kahn, was eyeing the French presidency in 2011, and an image as the savior of Europe would enhance his political aspirations.

The Strauss-Kahn prescription did make sense to some degree. Eurozone budget deficits and public debts had all increased. The same thing had happened to the public debt in the United States, from 63 percent of GDP in 2006 to 76 percent in 2010, and in Japan, from 167 percent of GDP in 2007 to 199.7 percent in 2010. Moreover, the European Union and the IMF had

---

1. Anders Åslund, "Think Again: Austerity," *Foreign Policy*, April 23, 2013.

2. Dina Kyriakidou, "New Greek PM Papandreou Says Economy 'Explosive,'" Reuters, October 16, 2009.

agreed on the need to increase public spending to avoid an economic depression in 2009. Even the most fiscally conservative countries in the eurozone saw their debt-to-GDP ratio jump between 2007 and 2010. In fact, by 2010 every eurozone country had been put under an excessive deficit procedure, with the exception of Luxembourg.

That strategy could have worked if the public finances of the European Union had been sound before the crisis, and if a temporary fiscal boost could have quickly returned European economies to their precrisis status. To some extent, this strategy was used successfully in dealing with the East Asian crisis, but a number of European countries, not just Greece, had consistently run budget deficits in the decade preceding the crisis. And growth was tepid even before the Lehman Brothers collapse. In such a situation, a fiscal boost only exacerbates the crisis. Interestingly, in 2009 no discussions were held in Ecofin meetings on the merits of fiscal stimulus for the European Union. And IMF managing director Strauss-Kahn did not attend Ecofin meetings, unlike his successor Christine Lagarde, who came regularly. He had either underestimated the severity of the crisis, or his personal ambitions were at odds with the long-term health of the eurozone.

Setting Up Some Missing Institutions

On December 2, 2009, at the last Ecofin meeting of the year, we finance ministers agreed to set up three new European authorities: the European Banking Authority, the European Insurance and Occupational Pensions Authority, and the European Securities and Markets Authority. Some of the financial architecture missing around the euro was finally being established. Andrea Enria, the head of banking supervision at the Bank of Italy, became the head of the European Banking Authority. He was known as a supporter of high capital requirements for banks in the eurozone as a precaution against a worsening sovereign debt crisis. His presentation to Ecofin was impressive, and once the authority began operations in 2011 he would be an important voice in our discussions, especially when the topic of the banking union heated up in 2012.

The same week, the European Central Bank (ECB) said it would continue conducting its main refinancing operations as fixed-rate tender procedures with full allotment for as long as needed. Again, however, nothing was done to help the banking systems in the noneurozone countries. This was a major weakness in the leadership of the ECB under Jean-Claude Trichet. After Iceland, he should have realized that the health of the eurozone depended on the health of the other European economies. Had support for the Baltics, Denmark, Hungary, Romania, and Sweden materialized early on in the crisis, Europe could have pulled out of the recession much earlier. Instead, the impacts of the problems in Iceland and the Baltics on Sweden and Denmark meant rising interest rates in those countries, which squeezed their banking systems and in turn had a negative impact on the Baltic economies. The downturn in the Baltics was, then, more severe than it should have been.

In November 2009, I met with Trichet on the side at the Ecofin meetings. Although Bulgaria was not as affected as the Baltics by the credit squeeze, I wanted to explain why some assistance to noneurozone countries was in the interest of the ECB. Otherwise, it would have to put up more bailout money for certain eurozone countries later on. But our views did not converge. Trichet believed Bulgaria, Estonia, Latvia, and Lithuania had chosen to tie their currencies to the euro through currency board arrangements, and there was a price to be paid for that. Reducing this price was not in the mandate of the ECB. I saw things differently. First, eurozone banks operated in all currency board countries. In Bulgaria, Greek-owned banks accounted for a third of banking assets, with subsidiaries of Austrian and Italian banks accounting for another third. Clearly, the depth of the recession in Bulgaria had an effect on banking stability in these eurozone countries, especially if one took into account that the same eurozone banks operated in Hungary and Romania. At this stage at least, this interdependence was not considered important by the ECB. I stress this because three years later, during discussions on the shape of the banking union, the position of the ECB under Mario Draghi was very different. Draghi and his ECB colleague Jörg Asmussen often expressed the view that the banking system of the European Union was so interrelated that single banking supervision could not proceed in the eurozone without having the same rules and practices for noneurozone countries. I wish that view had prevailed in 2009.

Meanwhile, the United Kingdom was gearing up for elections amidst worsening public financing. "Britain is at risk of following Greece with rising interest rates and soaring debt repayments," shadow chancellor George Osborne said on December 20, 2009.[3] The pre-budget report, prepared by Alistair Darling, the chancellor of the exchequer, was playing with economic fire by failing to produce a credible plan to tackle the national debt. This may explain why during the various Ecofin meetings in late 2009 and early 2010, Darling was frequently absent and generally kept a low profile. That changed significantly after May 2010 when George Osborne came to his first Ecofin.

2010 Begins on an Up Note

And yet with all these difficulties 2010 got off to an optimistic start. In Davos, the Swiss ski resort where every year the world's famous and powerful meet, Finance Minister George Papaconstantinou said Greece would not need a rescue package. Also in Davos, EU Commissioner Joaquín Almunia announced there was no "Plan B" for Greece. "Greece will not default. In the euro area, default does not exist."[4] But the markets thought otherwise. After these comments, the yield on a Greek 10-year bond reached 6.248 percent, a euro-era high at the time.

---

3. James Kirkup, "George Osborne: Britain Risks Greek Tragedy over Deficit," *Telegraph*, October 20, 2009.

4. Lin Noueihed, "EU's Almunia: No Chance of Greek Default, Eurozone Exit," Reuters, January 29, 2010.

Figure 5.2   Greece: 10-year bond yields, 2010

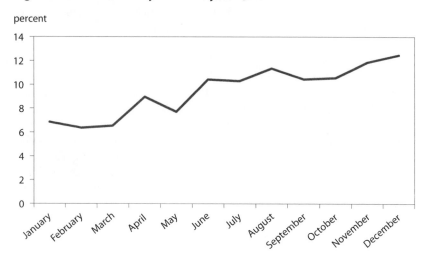

percent

Source: Bloomberg (accessed on April 1, 2014).

Two weeks later, Papaconstantinou changed his tune: "We are basically trying to change the course of the *Titanic*. People think we are in a terrible mess. And we are."[5] After another two weeks, the government lost control of the situation—literally; on March 4, 2010, protesters seized the finance ministry in Athens. And yet denial was still pervasive throughout Europe. Later the same month, in a *Financial Times* interview, former Italian prime minister Romano Prodi said, "Greece's problems are completely over. I don't see any other case now in Europe."[6] The same day, Ireland said its banks needed to raise an additional €31.8 billion ($44.1 billion) in capital.

At the beginning of February 2010, Greek 10-year bond rates spiked to more than 7 percent (figure 5.2) and Portuguese rates reached 4.725 percent. By contrast, the yield on German bonds was 3.03 percent. Contagion from the Greek problems affected Portuguese bonds more than those of the rest of the southern rim countries mainly because figures for 2009 indicated a much higher than foreseen deficit of 9.3 percent of GDP. The informal meeting of the heads of state and government in Solvay Library on February 11, the first chaired by Herman Van Rompuy as president of the European Council, focused on the financial pressure on Greece. The message was that eurozone member states would take coordinated action to safeguard financial stability

---

5. Lin Noueihed, "Greece Tells Eurozone It Needs Time: We're Trying to Change the Course of the *Titanic*," Reuters, February 15, 2010.

6. Gwen Robinson, "Prodi-ing Along in Greece: 'It's All Wonderful,'" *Financial Times*, March 20, 2010.

in the eurozone as a whole. The emphasis was on Greece, but its government denied having requested any financial support.[7] Bulgaria's prime minister, Boyko Borisov, attended the meeting and spoke several times about the need for fiscal discipline in every European country. At this stage, Bulgaria was viewed rather condescendingly as a country without much to offer to the eurozone debate. But later this attitude changed significantly, and by 2011 other countries would ask both Prime Minister Borisov and me for advice on fiscal measures.

The next day, February 12, data from the Bank for International Settlements revealed that France and Switzerland had more exposure to Greek debt than any other country: €57 billion ($79 billion) each. Germany's exposure was €31 billion ($43 billion). The French bank Crédit Agricole was singled out as being particularly exposed. "It owns Emporiki Bank in Greece, which has been floundering away, and has about €23 billion in loans there," the analysis said.[8] This was a watershed moment for Bulgaria and some other countries in the Balkans. Prior to that, it was widely assumed that the trouble in the Greek banking system was mostly affecting the countries in which Greek banks had subsidiaries such as Bulgaria, Romania, and Serbia. Suddenly, the focus shifted elsewhere.

On March 3, 2010, Jean-Claude Trichet commended the Greek government's additional fiscal consolidation measures and advised on swift implementation.[9] There was still hope that the Papandreou government could avoid default. But by the time the European Council met on March 25 it was obvious that Greece would need financial assistance. Despite Dutch and German resistance to any form of a sovereign bailout, most eurozone governments announced their readiness to contribute to coordinated bilateral loans as part of a package involving substantial IMF financing.

On April 8, 2010, Eurostat revised Greece's 2009 budget deficit to 13.6 percent of GDP, higher than the government's previous forecast of 12.9 percent. In two weeks, the Greek government requested a loan from the European Union and IMF to cover its financial needs for the remainder of 2010. Papandreou called the bailout "a new Odyssey for Greece." "But we know the road to Ithaca and have charted the waters," he added, referring to the return of the mythological hero Ulysses to his island home.[10]

---

7. See Statement by the Heads of State or Government of the European Union, Brussels, February 11, 2010.

8. Jill Treanor, "France and Switzerland Most Exposed to Greece's Debt Crisis, Say Analysts," *Guardian*, February 11, 2010.

9. Jeremy Warner, "Greece Is a Harbinger of Austerity for All," *Telegraph*, March 5, 2010.

10. Maria Petrakis and Jonathan Stearns, "Papandreou's Greek 'Odyssey' Challenged by Parliament's Vote on Confidence," Bloomberg, June 7, 2011.

Volcano Builds Camaraderie at Ecofin

On April 14 during the informal Ecofin meeting in Madrid, Eyjafjallajökull, a volcano in Iceland, erupted. All European air travel was cancelled, and we finance ministers spent four days together. The first day was devoted to discussing a Greek rescue. As time went by, however, informality really kicked in—for the first and only time in my tenure at Ecofin. There was even singing—it turned out that Fernando Teixeira dos Santos, the Portuguese finance minister, was quite a virtuoso. So was Christine Lagarde. Other informal Ecofins were in fact quite formal. Each time the presidency of the European Union rotated—twice a year—an "informal" meeting would be held in the country holding the presidency. "Informal" meant that one did not have to wear a tie. Otherwise, the program was the same as in a formal meeting. That was a pity because more informal meetings would have advanced the euro agenda a lot further. As it was, informal Ecofin meetings served simply to keep the media at arm's length.

Work continued the following week, after we had traveled home and again to Brussels. The eurozone reached an agreement on April 24 on a €45 billion ($62 billion) package for Greece—one-third from the IMF and the rest in the form of bilateral loans from eurozone member states. The same weekend, Greek finance minister George Papaconstantinou visited IMF headquarters in Washington for a meeting with Managing Director Strauss-Kahn. Following their discussion, Strauss-Kahn issued a statement saying that talks on further restructuring of the Greek economy had accelerated. The statement also expressed confidence in Athens's determination to get the Greek economy back on track.[11] In Paris, French finance minister Christine Lagarde clarified that the amount of the Greek bailout package was just for the first year of a three-year program. Indeed, it would rise to €110 billion ($152 billion) on May 2, after Greece asked for the first tranche to be released.

Meanwhile, anger had built up against Greece for the way its public officials had handled information on the true condition of the country's public finances. It was most visible in the comments of Jyrki Katainen, the Finnish finance minister, and Ján Počiatek, the Slovak minister. The Germans seemed peeved as well. On April 28, 2010, at a conference at the headquarters of the Organization for Economic Cooperation and Development in Paris, German chancellor Angela Merkel said it was a mistake for Greece to have been allowed to join the single currency. "In 2000 we had a situation when we were confronted with the question of whether Greece should be able to join the Eurozone," she said. "It turned out that the decision [in favor] may not have been scrutinized closely enough."[12]

Approval of the Greek bailout package depended on national parliamentary confirmations in most of the participating member states. Many states

---

11. Tim Webb, "Greek Bailout Not Limited to €45bn, Ministers Warn," *Guardian*, April 25, 2010.

12. Larry Elliott and Ian Traynor, "Greek Debt Crisis: Europe Feels Shockwaves as Bailout Falters," *Guardian*, April 28, 2010.

were skeptical about the bailout of Greece, and the Slovak government decided not to participate at all. The skepticism was warranted; the package lacked structural reforms. In effect, the painful but necessary restructuring that was forced on the Baltics and Romania by denying them access to the ECB's instruments was not imposed on Greece. Quite the contrary, the Greek banking sector's access to the extra liquidity ensured that the Papandreou government did not feel pressured to take reforms seriously. That only made the costs of subsequent bailouts and related reforms higher. I think that if IMF managing director Dominique Strauss-Kahn and ECB president Jean-Claude Trichet had taken the view that tough reforms at the onset would be rewarded, Greece would have exited the recession by early 2012. However, they chose to take a wait-and-see approach and magnified the costs severalfold.

Both the financial markets and the Greek public understood this reality quickly. Because of the mounting public anger in Greece at the scale of the cutbacks, throughout April the market pressures on Greece increased, with 10-year bond interest rates spiking above 12 percent on May 7, 2010. The contagion affected all of the most vulnerable eurozone economies—Ireland, Portugal, and Spain, in particular. Portuguese bonds reached 6.285 percent.

New Financial Facility Unveiled

On May 7, the EU heads of state came together in an emergency meeting in Brussels and agreed to create the European Financial Stability Facility (EFSF). The facility was intended to provide eurozone member states with financial assistance using funding of €750 billion ($1.04 trillion), one-third of which would be supplied by the IMF. Members of Ecofin were asked to hammer out the details, which we did in a long, tense meeting on Sunday, May 9, that finished just before the opening of the Asian markets on Monday. Significant concerns were raised by Germany, Luxembourg, Sweden, and the United Kingdom about the legality of the facility under the EU treaty. It was clear to many others that the EFSF was only barely in line with the treaty, but the heads of state would not tolerate any more delay and so the decision was made.

Market reactions to Ecofin decisions became a bigger part of our considerations from this moment on. There was an explicit discussion in Ecofin of how much information would be sufficient to placate markets on any one issue. Some of the ministers, such as Swedish minister Anders Borg, had prior experience in the financial markets and a good sense of their reactions. For the rest of us, it was more of a guessing game. Generally, I think market pressure played a positive role in the pace of decisions. Without it, little would have been decided at all. In fact, the inertia continued until well into 2011, and the European Commission did not feel sufficiently empowered to make bold proposals. This changed in 2011 after the second Greek bailout.

As for the EFSF, the decision to create this temporary entity was aptly communicated by the head of the eurozone, Jean-Claude Juncker. The immediate effect was positive, with interest rates falling considerably in all the southern rim economies. But that happy effect lasted only 10 days, and then the pressure quickly escalated again. As a next step, the ECB said it would buy government and private debt in the largest attempt yet to soften the crisis. Bundesbank president Axel Weber immediately criticized the idea of ECB bond purchases. His main reason was that the bond purchases would reduce governments' incentives to adopt strict fiscal policies. This sentiment was shared by the German finance ministry as well. I, too, shared it, and on multiple occasions in Ecofin or in bilateral meetings with other finance ministers I expressed this view. If a country's bonds were purchased, its government would renege on previously announced reforms and privatization targets. Greece was the classic example.

The EFSF came into play almost immediately. By June 2010, it was obvious to markets and international institutions that the first Greek rescue package was a failure. The deepening recession meant fewer tax revenues, while rising unemployment increased social security payments. The Greek government was facing bankruptcy. A new rescue was therefore needed. The Troika (European Commission, ECB, and IMF) began to work on a second Greek package. This time, the conditions would be stringently followed.

France: "Increase Taxes"

At the June 2010 Ecofin meeting, the main topic of discussion was the financial transaction tax proposed by the European Commission. The tax would be collected on behalf of the European Union in all eurozone countries and those noneurozone countries that wished to join voluntarily. Commission experts had calculated that the tax could raise as much as €35 billion ($49 billion). It would be levied on transactions between financial institutions: 0.1 percent on the sale of shares and bonds and 0.01 percent on derivative contracts. The tax would be applied even if just one of the financial institutions resided in a country signatory to it.

When this idea was presented, four countries were against it: Bulgaria, the Czech Republic, Malta, and the United Kingdom. Cyprus, Denmark, and Sweden announced they would not participate—they saw it as a potentially extraterritorial issue. Finland was originally strongly in favor of the tax, but over time it joined the undecided group. France and the European Commission were the biggest proponents. The position of Commissioner Algirdas Šemeta at the time was understandable: Brussels was under pressure to provide more money for social programs in the member states, and a common tax was the easiest way to increase funding without asking the net donor countries such as Germany and the Netherlands to contribute more.

My view of the financial transaction tax was simple. Even though Bulgaria would not be affected by the introduction of such a tax because its financial system was still evolving, I opposed the idea. The reason was that once the European Commission managed to introduce one common tax, it would not be long before other taxes were introduced and tax harmonization would gradually creep in through the back door. There was also the question of whether this tax avoided the democratic budgetary process that consisted of a debate and then a vote in national parliaments. This view was shared by the Czech Republic, and especially by its president, Vaclav Klaus.

The United Kingdom had different issues with the financial transaction tax. It feared that if such a tax were introduced, London would lose its place as a preeminent financial center and businesses would run to New York and Hong Kong. George Osborne made this point over and over in the many meetings held on the tax. Eventually, the idea was applied in part of the eurozone, but not in the whole European Union. I consider this one of my successes in Ecofin: arguing forcefully that the tax was not in the interest of the European Union. It was later challenged on treaty grounds by the UK treasury, and its challenge succeeded.

On July 23, 2010, the Committee of European Banking Supervisors reported the results of bank stress tests. Of the 91 institutions tested, five failed in Spain and one each in Germany and Greece. These banks needed only to raise €3.5 billion ($5 billion) in fresh capital to make themselves secure, much lower than the €30 billion ($42 billion) regarded as the minimum by the market before the tests were completed. The markets then calmed down temporarily. Meanwhile, many questions were raised about the stress test methodology—whether it had been purposefully too benign. The answer was yes, it was far too benign, and stress testing lost much of its credibility. Fortunately, it was already summer, and market analysts soon went on holiday and forgot the issue.

Romanian Finance Minister Sacked

By August 2010, concerns about the Irish banking sector were turning the pressure on again. The decision by the Irish government at the end of September to bail out the Anglo Irish Bank gave rise to a new spike in interest rates in Ireland and, by contagion, also in Hungary, Portugal, Romania, and Spain. In Romania, Prime Minister Emil Bok was under severe pressure after following the advice of the IMF and raising the value-added tax from 19 to 24 percent a few weeks earlier. With the increase in interest rates, he took a desperate gamble by firing all five of his ministers responsible for the economy, including Finance Minister Sebastian Vladescu. Vladescu had been in this position in a previous government, between 2005 and 2007, and was widely respected for his long-term career at the finance ministry. He was also one of the few outspoken finance ministers from Eastern Europe at Ecofin.

The week after his departure from the government I met Vladescu in Bucharest at a conference organized by the leading Romanian business association. I asked him whether the move was a surprise to him. "Not at all," he replied. "Once people start averting their eyes when you are in the grocery store, you know the time has come. And the problems at home are made all the more difficult from constant bad news from Greece."

Theory of a Euro Holiday

With the contagion rapidly spreading through the southern rim, Martin Feldstein, erstwhile chief economic advisor to President Ronald Reagan and longtime president of the National Bureau of Economic Research (NBER), suggested that countries like Greece, and perhaps Portugal and Spain, should take a euro holiday.[13] The basic idea was simple: A country would commit to rejoin at a depreciated exchange rate in the future (say, in three years), and in the meantime it would undertake the reforms necessary to maintain its competitiveness in the long run. Bank balances would remain in euros, so there would be no run on the banks.

How would this work in Greece? It would go off the euro and let the drachma depreciate to the point that 1 euro equals 1.30 drachmas. Argentina had effectively done the same thing in 2001, ending the dollar peg. In one year, the peso fell to a quarter of its previous value, imports declined by half, and inflation rose to 44 percent. Iceland was another example, although it did not detach itself from a peg. In 2008 its currency fell by half against the euro and the dollar. Inflation rose from 2 to 12 percent.

The idea immediately attracted opponents. Chief among them was US economist Barry Eichengreen. In his critique, he cited the significant technical difficulties associated with euro holidays.[14] All contracts would have to be rewritten in the new currency, and vending machines and meters would have to be rewired. At best, preparation for a euro holiday would take a year. (Just ask Estonia, the latest country to enter the eurozone. It needed about a year to prepare for entry.) A systemwide bank run would then follow. And the financial sector would collapse.

And that comparison was even friendly to Feldstein's idea. The difference between the transition to the euro and the transition back to national currencies is that in the first instance there is no reason to expect subsequent changes in exchange rates and thus little incentive for currency speculation in the international markets. In the second case, such changes would be viewed as virtually inevitable, and speculators would swarm.

When the ruble zone broke up in the 1990s and new national currencies were introduced, the successor states of the former Soviet Union were unable to limit the destabilizing financial consequences, and hyperinflation ensued. They could to a certain extent limit the substitution of foreign assets for domestic assets by imposing exchange controls, but that option is not available to EU members.

The same issues were evident in the breakup of the Czechoslovak monetary union in 1993. The Czechs and Slovaks agreed to political separation as of January 1, 1993, but initially kept their monetary union in place in order to minimize disruptions to economic activity. Although the Czech and Slovak

---

13. Martin Feldstein, "Let Greece Take a Eurozone 'Holiday,'" *Financial Times*, February 16, 2010.

14. For a summary of Eichengreen's arguments, see Eichengreen (2010).

Republics agreed to maintain a common currency for a minimum of six months, the markets did not find this agreement credible. They expected the Slovak authorities to push for a much looser monetary policy and their Czech counterparts to reject the consequent high inflation.

The result was a flight of currency and deposits from Slovakia to the Czech Republic. The authorities then quickly reversed course and decided in favor of monetary separation. The demise of the monetary union was announced on February 2, 1993, just five weeks after it had commenced operation, and separate national currencies were quickly introduced. Czechoslovak banknotes were stamped and then replaced with new national banknotes. During this period, currency could be transferred or exported abroad. Again, the relatively underdeveloped financial system accommodated such transitional arrangements. Moreover, the fact that the old Czechoslovak currency disappeared at the end of the six-month transition eased the process of dissolving the currency union. By contrast, if an individual member exited the eurozone, the euro would continue to circulate in the rest of the zone. Thus nothing would prevent a Greek or a Cypriot from holding onto euro banknotes and moving them to northern Europe sometime after the restrictions are lifted.

A euro holiday would have serious political costs as well. The Treaty on European Union makes no provision for exit. Everything would have to be resolved by political negotiations, which brings uncertainty about conditions and timing.

Meanwhile, exit by one member would raise doubts about the future of the monetary union and would likely precipitate a further shift out of euro-denominated assets, which would upset the remaining members. It might damage the balance sheets of banks in other countries with investments in the country abandoning the euro—for example, French banks that hold Greek assets. The defector would be relegated to second-tier status in intra-European discussions of nonmonetary issues. And, insofar as they attach value to their participation in this larger process of European integration, countries would be reluctant to leave. This is what the Germans have effectively been saying over the last few years: whoever leaves the euro leaves the European Union.

And no one, even the harshest critics of the euro, really wants to leave the European Union. The transfers from Brussels are welcome contributions to national well-being. When the radical left Syriza party in Greece wanted all kinds of concessions from Brussels, it did not for a moment think of leaving the European Union. Neither has Viktor Orbán, Hungary's prime minister, despite his almost daily criticism of Brussels.

Cyprus Almost Goes on Holiday

Cyprus came the closest to leaving the European Union. Its governing party considered dropping out of the eurozone at the peak of its financial crisis in early March 2013 as it faced a standoff over the terms of an international bailout.[15] But the exit idea was shelved after it was estimated that reinstating the Cypriot pound would have caused an immediate 40 percent drop in the value of the new currency, ruining a small island that relies heavily on imports.

At the time, the notion of a euro exit for Cyprus had a wide following. US economist Paul Krugman wrote on his blog: "So here it is: yes, Cyprus should leave the euro. Now. The reason is straightforward: staying in the euro means an incredibly severe depression, which will last for many years while Cyprus tries to build a new export sector. Leaving the euro, and letting the new currency fall sharply, would greatly accelerate that rebuilding."[16]

So possible was the Cypriot exit that Moody's put out a research note highlighting the likely costs as it lowered Cyprus's sovereign rating to Caa2: "An exit would result in large losses to investors due to the redenomination of government debt and private debt securities issued under Cypriot law. It would also lead to further severe disruption to the country's banking system and additional acute dislocations in the real economy. Such disruption would generally imply additional losses for holders of debt securities issued by Cypriot entities, irrespective of their governing law."[17]

Notwithstanding the costs, an early April 2013 poll found that 67.3 percent of Cypriots favored their country exiting the eurozone and strengthening relations with Russia. But an exit implies the willingness of the ECB and eurozone officials to assist Cyprus in the transition. Such assistance was not forthcoming, and with this episode the likelihood of an assisted exit for Cyprus or any other eurozone country is effectively nil. Feldstein's original idea was therefore put to rest. In truth, this idea was never discussed at Ecofin, either formally or informally.

The Euro without Germany?

In 2012 a new version of the euro holiday idea appeared: Germany should leave the eurozone. Germany is one country that could exit the eurozone without precipitating a run on its banks. Because the "new deutsche mark" would likely strengthen against the euro, money would flow into the German banking system, and so banks would not have to close for an initial period. And Germans are so technically efficient that vending machines and ATMs would be adjusted to the new currency almost overnight.[18]

Proponents of this view, mostly German academics, cited four reasons for a German eurozone exit. First, the legal framework of the euro had been repeatedly violated since its creation. The Maastricht Treaty criteria—limited

---

15. Interview with Cyprus foreign minister Ioannis Kasoulides, "Cyprus Considered Exiting the Euro Zone in March," *Washington Post*, May 9, 2013.

16. Paul Krugman, "Cyprus, Seriously," The Conscience of a Liberal blog, March 29, 2013.

17. Moody's, "Cyprus Country Ceiling Lowered to Caa2," March 18, 2013.

18. For a while, Finland was also rumored to be ready for exit. But the source of this rumor was likely a purposeful leak by the government in the run-up to the Finnish parliamentary elections.

Figure 5.3 Eurozone current account balances and real effective exchange rates, 2012

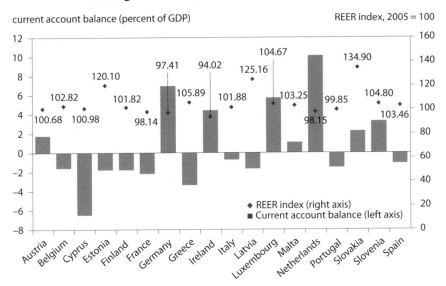

Sources: IMF, *World Economic Outlook*, October 2014, www.imf.org/external/pubs/ft/weo/2013/02/weodata/index.aspx (accessed on February 26, 2014); Eurostat, http://epp.eurostat.ec.europa.eu/portal/page/portal/statistics/search_database (accessed on February 26, 2014).

budget deficits, prohibition of bailouts, and a ban on state financing via monetary policy—had all been breached. The result was mistrust of the law. Second, Germany had already spent billions to support insolvent member states such as Greece.[19] Third, German consumers could benefit from the lower import costs that a rising currency would bring to improve their purchasing power. And, fourth, adherence to the euro was poisoning Europe's political environment. The euro had been introduced primarily as a political project intended to build up European identity. It turned out to be counterproductive, however, because Chancellor Merkel was seen as Europe's budget cop, and German citizens were increasingly suspicious of the ability of the southern rim governments to make tough decisions.

All that said, German industry depended significantly on exports, which would be hurt when the deutsche mark appreciated against the currency of the country's European neighbors. For that reason, German businesses remained firmly in favor of the euro throughout the euro crisis. The country's export competitiveness was greatly enhanced by a euro exchange rate that had remained at reasonable levels because Germany shared the currency with weaker European economies (figure 5.3). German businesses also understood

---

19. This argument was made by Stefan Homburg, economics professor at Leibniz University in Hannover, in an editorial for the *New York Times*, "Germany Should Leave," March 18, 2013.

that a move to reintroduce the deutsche mark would create massive financial crises in other European countries, as individuals there shifted their bank deposits to Frankfurt. More financial crises in other European countries were not in Germany's economic interest.

Most important, I think Germany needed to stay in the eurozone so it could remain the leader of reforms in the European Union. Otherwise, its position would be shaky, and its commitment to European integration would have been questioned. And this is what Germany did. The resounding victory of Chancellor Merkel's party in the September 2013 parliamentary elections showed that she had made the right calculation on the future of the eurozone and Germany's place in it.

6

Deauville Blunder and Perils of 2011

On October 18, 2010, in the run-up to the October meeting of the European Council, German chancellor Angela Merkel and French president Nicolas Sarkozy met in the French resort town of Deauville. There, they issued a fateful declaration attaching conditions to the establishment of a permanent crisis management mechanism to replace the temporary European Financial Stability Facility (EFSF) in 2013. The main condition called for losses to be imposed on private creditors in any future rescue of a country or a financial institution. The same declaration was repeated by Merkel and Sarkozy 10 days later at the October 28–29 meeting of the European Council. There, it was affirmed that a role for the private sector would be included in the features of the future mechanism. The term *private sector participation* was a polite way of saying that the private sector would bear a substantial share of the losses. This development was certain to bring on anxiety in the financial markets.

Deauville ushered in a new round of ideas on dealing with the euro crisis, most of them well intentioned. The main idea was to force creditors to pay for their mistakes. I supported this idea: There was no reason why taxpayer money should be used to cover the mistakes of private investment bankers. But the idea was introduced without a full assessment of how the financial markets would react. Deauville also spurred other intellectually interesting ideas such as setting up a two-tier eurozone, one for northern Europe and one for southern Europe, or allowing a temporary exit from the euro, as described in chapter 5. However, these ideas were impractical. They merely wasted people's time and raised fears of bank runs. None of them was truly the subject of discussion in Ecofin. Unlike in the United States, where academic researchers were active participants in the debates on crisis resolution, in the European Union they remained silent. As a result, there was a big disconnect between what was discussed publicly in the media and what was taking place in Ecofin and in the Eurogroup, which was made up of the finance ministers of the 18 states that had adopted the euro.

Second Tipping Point

Introducing publicly the notion of private sector participation in the middle of a volatile market without detailing how it would work was a mistake. And, indeed, this was the second tipping point in the euro crisis (see the chronology). Ecofin was blindsided—we had not discussed this matter in September. And there was no formal analysis to back up the declaration. At the October meeting of Ecofin after Deauville, French finance minister Christine Lagarde was defensive and provided no further details. Without additional clarity on what was meant by private sector participation, borrowing costs soared for both Ireland and Portugal after the Deauville declaration and continued to do so after the meeting of the European Council. Jean-Claude Juncker, the head of the eurozone, who usually tried to be restrained in his comments on Franco-German proposals, this time was openly critical.

In fact, several times during the crisis France and Germany met and announced decisions without providing any details on their rationale and implementation. On later occasions, they provided no clarity either. Simply put, their decisions were neither specific nor backed by serious analysis. As a result, often those decisions were disregarded and quickly sank into oblivion. The financial markets would be left wondering what precipitated this change in policy direction. The truth was that there was no coherent policy to begin with. In perhaps a holdover from an earlier period in the evolution of the European Union, the Franco-German duo attempted to direct the work of Ecofin. That was problematic for a number of reasons, but chief among them was the fact that neither France nor Germany had recently dealt with a crisis of this nature. They needed to rely on the experience of others, but they were unwilling to do so. Finland and Sweden had gone through major banking crises in the early 1990s, and their policymakers knew what had and had not worked. The East European and Baltic countries had gone through dramatic crises a decade earlier and also had experiences to share. But, to the detriment of crisis management throughout the eurozone, that experience was not used.

After Deauville, the crisis in Ireland spread outside the banking sector. On November 14, 2010, Irish enterprise minister Batt O'Keefe said Ireland did not need a bailout. That announcement did not help—Standard and Poor's (S&P) cut Ireland's credit rating by two steps, to A from AA−. One could not fault the minister. In crises, circumstances change quickly and so do decisions, especially if the minister has to react to an out-of-the-blue Franco-German declaration. Such declarations were a constant irritant for finance ministers during the Merkel-Sarkozy years. With the election of François Hollande to the French presidency in 2012, the duo never regained their previous importance, and we were spared such nasty surprises.

Irish Worries Redux

In Ireland, the situation was worsening—the pressure from the markets and the size of the Irish public debt incurred by assuming the enormous liabilities from bad banks were growing larger. On November 22, 2010, Ireland reversed its stance and requested access to the EFSF. At their November 28 meeting in Brussels, Ecofin and eurozone ministers agreed on an €85 billion ($118 billion) package. The goal was to immediately strengthen and entirely overhaul the Irish banking system. The initial proposals included large losses to bondholders, as stated at Deauville. The Irish treasury was against such losses and succeeded, after tough negotiations, to uphold its views at the expense of Irish taxpayers.

Half a year later in one of his last interviews, Brian Lenihan, the Irish finance minister, described his experience: "I've a very vivid memory of going to Brussels on the final Monday to sign the agreement and being on my own at the airport and looking at the snow gradually thawing and thinking to myself, this is terrible. No Irish minister has ever had to do this before."[1] And yet a Portuguese minister had to do the same about a year later, and a Cypriot minister two years after that.

At the Ecofin meeting, the Eurogroup also issued a statement meant to allay market fears on the issue of private sector participation in the upcoming European Stability Mechanism (ESM). The ESM would provide for the case-by-case participation of private sector creditors, consistent with International Monetary Fund (IMF) policies. In this context, the ministers made a clear distinction between solvent countries whose private sector creditors would be encouraged to maintain their exposure according to international rules and insolvent countries that would have to negotiate a comprehensive restructuring plan with their private sector creditors with a view toward restoring debt sustainability. It was decided that the standard collective action clauses would be included in all new eurozone government bonds. Furthermore, any private sector involvement, including the use of collective action clauses, would not become effective before mid-2013. This action seemed to be after the fact and defensive, and it did not have much of an effect, especially because the governments of Finland and the Netherlands kept insisting publicly on private participation. Jyrki Katainen and Jan Kees de Jager made this point during many of our discussions.

By the end of 2010, Ecofin and the Eurogroup had agreed on the main changes to the economic governance and had achieved what a year before would have been thought unlikely. Stricter sanctions would be linked to budget discipline and macroeconomic supervision. A new framework for economic coordination in the context of the European semester[2] would take

---

1. Dan O'Brien, "Ireland 'Forced' to Take Bailout," *Irish Times*, April 23, 2011.

2. An annual economic policy coordination cycle set up by the European Commission (EC), in which member states undergo a detailed analysis of their economic and structural reforms. On that basis, the EC gives its assessment and recommendations for the next 12–18 months.

effect in early 2011. Financial assistance facilities were up and running, helping euro members in difficulty. These temporary facilities would be replaced by a permanent mechanism in 2013.

Nevertheless, the feeling at the last Ecofin was that the European Union had been running behind events associated with the crisis and sometimes even provoking them, such as the dispute over private sector involvement. In reality, political agreement had been extremely difficult to achieve. Perceptions about the crisis, as well as economic situations, differed considerably between the countries on the periphery and those in central and northern European. The political interests within some countries also differed. Clearly, two views dominated Ecofin: the German view, supported by Austria, Bulgaria, Estonia, Finland, the Netherlands, and Slovakia, and the French view, supported by Greece, Italy, and Portugal. The United Kingdom had a distinct view on most issues related to the crisis, but when George Osborne became its finance minister it mostly aligned with the German camp. Olli Rehn, representing the European Commission, did not have a consistent view and gravitated toward whoever made up the majority. That made it difficult for Ecofin to stay ahead of crisis events.

Meanwhile, a significant part of the electorates in northern European countries believed the culprit behind the crisis was the fiscal mismanagement in the southern eurozone. And some eurozone countries were faring quite well out of the recession (figure 6.1). The central and northern eurozone countries all posted growth figures above 2 percent in the second half of 2010 (Austria, 2.4 percent; Belgium, 2.8 percent; Finland, 5 percent; Germany, 4.4 percent; the Netherlands, 2.1 percent; Slovakia, 4.7 percent). These outcomes made European solidarity even harder to achieve and charged the saving-the-euro debate.

The year 2011 then arrived, bringing many perils. And many more politicians turned toward Frankfurt to provide the answers, pointing to the two rounds of quantitative easing in the United States. There was significant pressure on Jean-Claude Trichet to follow the example of US Federal Reserve chairman Ben Bernanke and flood European markets with additional liquidity. Although the European Central Bank (ECB) had aggressively lowered interest rates and provided liquidity through covered bond purchases, unlike Bernanke, Trichet was not willing to use other instruments. I fault Trichet for not assisting the noneurozone countries during the early stages of the crisis. But on the bigger question of using outright monetary purchases, I think he was right to be cautious.

Portugal: Headed for Trouble

In January 2011, a series of news stories on Portugal, usually based on anonymous senior eurozone sources, reported repeatedly either that core EU member states were pressuring for financial assistance for Portugal and that Portugal would not hold out for long, or that somewhere a plan was being prepared to respond to an imminent request from Portugal for financial assistance. For example, in early January Der Spiegel reported that Germany and France

Figure 6.1   GDP growth per quarter in northern, eastern, and southern rim eurozone countries, 2007–12

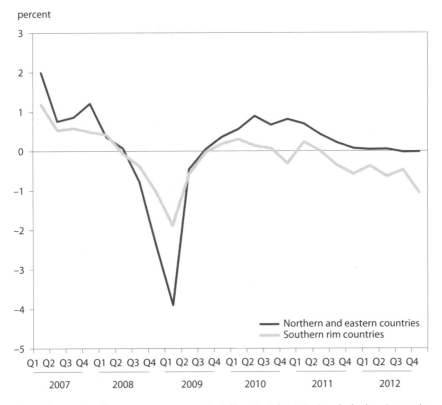

percent

Northern and eastern countries
Southern rim countries

Q1 Q2 Q3 Q4 Q1 Q2 Q3 Q4 Q1 Q2 Q3 Q4 Q1 Q2 Q3 Q4 Q1 Q2 Q3 Q4 Q1 Q2 Q3 Q4

2007   2008   2009   2010   2011   2012

Source: Eurostat, http://epp.eurostat.ec.europa.eu/portal/page/portal/statistics/search_database (accessed on February 28, 2014).

were trying to persuade Portugal not to postpone the inevitable bailout.[3] This report was denied by the three governments mentioned, but four days later, when Portugal held its first government bond auction of the year, the three-year bonds were offered at the relatively high price of 5.4 percent.

The European Council met again on February 4, 2011, in a summit intended to focus on energy and innovation. Instead, the center of attention was a new Franco-German idea to create what was called at the time a "Competitiveness Pact." Details of the pact were left for later negotiations between experts, and yet eurozone leaders endorsed the idea of achieving a new quality of economic policy coordination in the eurozone to improve competitiveness. Strikingly, the Franco-German team provided nothing on paper. As in the Deauville episode, there was a discussion but no prior analysis.

---

3. Brian Rohan, "Germany and France Want Portugal to Accept Aid," *Der Spiegel*, January 8, 2011.

The pact targeted eurozone members, although nonmembers were invited to participate. Presented to journalists by Chancellor Merkel and President Sarkozy in Brussels on the day of the European Council meeting, it was aimed at stronger policy coordination. It also created a blueprint for countries to converge toward the German competitiveness model, targeting four main areas: (1) unit labor costs, notably by abolishing wage indexation schemes; (2) pension systems, by raising retirement ages; (3) a higher degree of tax harmonization, by creating a common base for corporate taxes; and (4) fiscal discipline, by making it a constitutional violation to exceed limits on national debt.[4] I found it too ambitious and too stingy with details. I asked some of the other finance ministers what they made of this—for example, Anders Borg from Sweden, Luc Frieden from Luxembourg, and Jan Vincent-Rostowski from Poland. Each had spoken to the Germans or French and seemed to know some of the rationale. The entire matter reminded me of a children's game in Bulgaria called broken telephone, in which one child whispers a sentence in the ear of the person next to him, she does the same to the next person, and so on. By the time, the sentence has passed to the other side of the room, it has changed completely. Proposals for crisis resolution should not rely on a broken telephone.

The Council's communiqué after the summit included an assessment by the European Commission of how much progress eurozone members were making in implementing measures to strengthen fiscal positions and growth prospects. It was also a message to Portugal to quickly put forward contingency measures that would take into account the lower growth prospects for the eurozone.

After the February 4 summit, market pressure increased with the news that the Germans were resistant to the idea of strengthening and extending the flexibility of the EFSF. The ECB then began to once again buy Portuguese debt in an attempt to contain yields that went above 7 percent for 10-year bonds. Simultaneously, Portuguese government officials met with European Commission and ECB officials to discuss the 2011 fiscal gap. The longer-term measures needed to meet the 2012 and 2013 deficit targets of 3 percent and 2 percent of GDP, respectively, were also on the agenda.

On February 11, 2011, Axel Weber resigned from the Bundesbank after opposing the ECB's crisis policy. He was a staunch and vocal opponent of the ECB's bond-buying program. He also doubted that the significant reduction in interest rates by the ECB would do anything to change market sentiment. Most important, he argued that the actions of the ECB were undermining sound fiscal policies in the crisis-affected countries. In three separate informal Ecofin meetings also attended by heads of central banks, I had agreed with Weber's views: The extra liquidity extended to the banking sectors of the southern rim countries reduced the impetus for reforms. Because the European Commission had been slow in responding to the crisis, the ECB had truly become the savior

---

4. See Statement by the Heads of State or Government of the Euro Area and the EU Institutions, Brussels, February 4, 2011.

of last resort. This was classic economics: Once the first-choice policy was not available in time, the second-choice policy, albeit distortionary, was in order.

On March 3, 2011, the ECB warned of a rate increase in April that could send Portugal and Ireland closer to bankruptcy. ECB president Trichet said it was possible that the base rates on the continent could be raised to calm inflation. He maintained that the ECB was prepared to act "in a firm and timely manner" to prevent inflation from racing out of control. "Strong vigilance is warranted with a view to containing upside risks to price stability."[5] My guess is that this message was in part a response to Axel Weber's resignation. Trichet was showing toughness to appease the Germans.

On March 9, 2011, the new Irish government was sworn in, and Michael Noonan became the finance minister. Two weeks later, I visited Dublin to give a talk at the invitation of the Irish Tax Institute. The topic was corporate taxation in Europe. My views were well known by then through various statements at Ecofin and in the media. In short, I held that tax issues were in the hands of national parliaments and that the European Commission could not weigh in, even in bailout discussions. This view was especially salient in Ireland, whose low corporate tax, 12.5 percent, was under scrutiny by the European Commission and the IMF. I met Michael Noonan and Enda Kenny, the prime minister, both of whom expressed resolve to support my view. They said that, as in Bulgaria, the low corporate tax had become one of the recognized comparative advantages of Ireland, and they intended to keep it that way.

Northern Euro: Another Good Idea in Theory

During my talk in Dublin, someone asked about another idea on how to save the euro: create its northern version. The idea of having a strong northern euro had been around since the creation of the euro itself. And the euro crisis had only increased its attractiveness. No self-respecting politicians would admit to considering it, and yet leaked reports from meetings suggested it was on their minds. A December 2010 *Wall Street Journal* article had described a meeting between Czech prime minister Petr Necas and German chancellor Angela Merkel in which the two leaders began to talk about ways to save the euro from its problems.[6] During the informal part of their meeting, Merkel asked Necas to bring his country into the eurozone. Fiscally sound Czechs would help Germany increase the weight of prudent eurozone members in contrast to the profligates such as Greece, Italy, Portugal, and Spain. "The reply by Prime Minister Necas was that if a northern European euro area existed, the Czechs would join the next day," an inside source reported.

The leaked discussion at the Czech-German meeting on a dual-speed eurozone actually mirrored the idea of a "core Europe" offered as early as

5. Reuters, "ECB's Trichet Says 'Strong Vigilance' Warranted," March 3, 2011.

6. Leos Rousek, "Czech, German Leaders Daydream about Northern Euro," *Wall Street Journal*, December 13, 2010.

1994 by Wolfgang Schäuble, a German parliamentarian at the time. The idea centered on creating an economically and strategically stable core of the continent, composed of Austria, Belgium, France, Germany, Luxembourg, and the Netherlands, that would adopt its own separate currency, thereby shielding itself from the fiscally loose southern rim governments. Over the years, Schäuble, now German finance minister, had changed his views. In 2011, he no longer thought a separate currency was either smart or practical.

But other people did, and they saw the adoption of another currency proceeding as follows. First, smaller countries such as Austria, Finland, or the Netherlands would exit the euro and then build up the northern euro, possibly joined by Denmark and Sweden. Second, Germany would join them, as well as the Baltics, Bulgaria, the Czech Republic, and Slovakia. The southern rim countries would remain with the existing euro. After initial inflation, they would benefit from a strong devaluation. Their manufacturing exports would become competitive, and the competitiveness of their tourism sector would increase. They could also pursue their own monetary policy.

The German economy would remain competitive even with a strong northern euro, if that euro did not appreciate too quickly. The competitiveness of the southern economies would increase as well. But their productivity loss would be twofold: first, from euro entry, and, second, from the loss of labor-intensive manufacturing such as textiles because of globalization. Thus the southern rim businesses would be caught in a trap between cheap labor in the former communist countries and the technologically advanced German exports. Italian labor costs would be close to Germany's, but they would be four times higher than those in Slovakia or Estonia.

Accepting a monetary partition was simply agreeing that Germany and other northern countries would have their own currency, a "northern euro." It would be about 30 percent more expensive than the euro used in the countries in the south. At first, for a brief period, only credit card payments would be possible, and then some newly printed northern euros would replace the southern euros in the northern countries. The purchase of southern euros under the supervision of a northern European central bank would reassure markets and maintain the 1.30 exchange rate between the two currencies. Cross-border capital controls would be in place for a short period—something used not long ago in the Cyprus bailout. Until recently, the IMF was against imposing capital controls, and they are explicitly prohibited by the EU treaty. However, they seemed to have worked well in Cyprus, thereby setting a precedent.

There would, however, be a downside for the northern banks and rich depositors. They would realize some losses from their holdings in southern euros, but less than the many transfers from Germany to the periphery. Currency purchases of the northern European central bank would replace Bundesbank losses on Target2 and on ESM and EFSF by the northern states.[7] German industry

---

7. Target2 is the real-time gross settlement system owned and operated by the Eurosystem. Target stands for Trans-European Automated Real-time Gross Settlement Express Transfer system.

and exporters would also complain about the strong northern euro. And so its introduction would have to be accompanied by a compensatory mechanism.

Meanwhile, the central banks of the northern euro and the southern euro would need to work together to prevent a sudden appreciation of the northern euro. A rise of more than 10 percent per year against the southern euro would have to be prohibited. If the limit were reached, the northern European central bank would be obliged to purchase southern euros to limit the appreciation of its northern currency.

All this seemed unlikely. As economist David Schawel vividly described the scenario:

> If the Greek Government were to devalue the new Drachma (to perhaps a third the value of the Euro) then the banks (which are loaded with Greek Sovereign paper) would default. Even Hellenic Telecom would default because they would be forced to repay their billions of Euro borrowings whilst collecting only Drachma phone bills.

> If you were Greece you would take this option without hesitation. However this option has explosive implications for Europe. You see a bank deposit in Athens is going to turn your Euros into Drachma. Overnight it will lose 70 percent of its valuation.

> One weekend we will just find that the Greeks have done it. But now suppose Greece does pull this trick. The day after we have a Drachma—deposits are in Drachma. We might print a single 10 drachma note and allow it to settle against the Euro—then over time print more. This should work for Greece.

> Now if you are Irish or Italian or Portuguese (or even Spanish) you know the rules. You get to get your Euro out of the PIGS [Portugal, Italy, Greece, and Spain] and into the core (Germany) as fast as possible. So max all your credit cards (for cash), draw all your bank deposits and load them in the boot of your car and make the drive to Switzerland or Germany. Somewhere safe. Otherwise you are going to lose half the value the day that the rest of the PIGS do a Greece.

> And this bank run—a run including tens of thousands of Italians driving their Fiats—will surely blow apart every Italian bank.[8]

This scenario seemed to bring the integration of Europe to an end. However, some economists, a clear minority, argued just the opposite—that a split euro would help to unite Europe. One of them was Bernd Lucke, a University of Hamburg economist who in 2012 founded the Alternative für Deutschland Party to further this cause. Here was his rationale:

> We think that the euro currently splits the European Union into two parts—a segment of an economically unsuccessful southern part, and a more northern,

8. David Schawel, "What History Tells Us about a Potential Greek Exit," Economic Musings blog, May 13, 2012.

or more central, European part, which currently seems to benefit from the misery of the southern European countries, because all of the capital flows back from southern Europe to Germany, and the Netherlands, and other stable countries, where it helps us to do cheap investment, but which is at the expense of those southern European countries, and which certainly is the cause for envious sentiment and angry sentiment in the southern European countries, so that the political tensions within the European Union actually rise.[9]

The majority of economists, myself included, did not agree. The idea of the northern euro came with two major problems. First, the northern countries would likely see a significant deterioration of their exports to the southern countries. If Italy is included, these exports account for 2 percent of Finnish GDP, 4 to 5 percent of German and Austrian GDP, and 7 percent of Dutch GDP.

Second, it was unlikely that the Greeks, Spaniards, Portuguese, and Italians would be able to agree on the policy coordination and solidarity needed to keep the smaller euro club together. Europe might be left with a strong northern euro and a group of weak southern currencies.

Still, the proponents of the northern euro would not give up. Allan Meltzer, a professor at Carnegie Mellon University in Pittsburgh, provided a solution. Once devaluation restored competitive prices in the southern euro countries, they could be admitted to the new currency arrangement if they committed to the tighter fiscal arrangement. If all countries rejoined, the euro+ system could restart with a more appropriate, binding fiscal policy rule.[10]

But like the euro holiday, the northern euro was never considered seriously at Ecofin. As a response to the crisis, it went against the grain of a more integrated Europe. During my first two years as Bulgaria's finance minister, I had underestimated the importance of integration and often argued with other finance ministers that some sort of temporary southern exit would be beneficial for the eurozone. This happened several times during the informal European People's Party breakfasts before Ecofin. Wolfgang Schäuble would listen politely and then ask, "Do you have other ideas that are workable?" Luc Frieden, who chaired the breakfasts, together with Jan Kees de Jager, the Dutch finance minister, were also skeptical. Gradually, they changed my views. By late 2011, I no longer thought a solution to the euro crisis would entail an exit of a country or a group of countries. What was needed was more patience in finding long-term solutions.

---

9. Matthew Boesler, "Meet the Influential German Professor Who Wants to Get Rid of the Euro in Order to Save Europe," *Business Insider*, May 30, 2013.

10. Allan Meltzer, "Leave the Euro to the PIGS," *Wall Street Journal*, September 14, 2011.

7

Portuguese Bailout and ESM-Eurobond Debate

By March 2011, Portugal had entered a full-blown crisis. Its difficulties were different from those of Ireland, where banks became overleveraged during a real estate boom that went bust. They were also different from those of Greece, where hidden financial commitments came to light and overwhelmed it with debt. Although the crises in Ireland and Greece had consumed much of Ecofin's time in 2010, the crisis in Portugal did not receive much attention until it was too late. (The same would happen to the crisis in Cyprus in 2012.)

The Portuguese turmoil raised again the question of how extensive the European backstop mechanism should be and whether it should be provided in the form of a European Stability Mechanism (ESM) or eurobonds. It initiated an intense period of debate, in which Finland, Germany, the Netherlands, and their allies in Eastern Europe supported the ESM, whereas France and the other southern rim countries supported the issuance of eurobonds. The International Monetary Fund (IMF) wavered between the two options, while the European Commission favored eurobonds. As with previous decisions, Ecofin did not have enough analysis of the legal aspects of each option and had to rely on the opinions of member countries. Several of them, including Luxembourg and the United Kingdom, which had taken a neutral position on the issue, argued that eurobonds would not be legal under the EU treaty.

By 2011 the Portuguese finance minister, Fernando Teixeira dos Santos, was the longest-serving minister in Ecofin. He had left his academic career at the University of Porto to join the government in 2005. A very polished politician, he skillfully diverted attention from Portugal during the early stages of the crisis, and, as a result, it rarely entered our discussions. By late 2010, however, the trouble in other southern rim countries was taking a toll on Portugal, combined with its poor growth record.

Portugal's own troubles stemmed from a decade of measly growth, averaging 0.7 percent a year before the crisis, during which it had amassed huge debts. The two large Portuguese banks—Banco Português de Negócios and Banco Privado Português—were effectively bankrupt. They had been accumulating losses for years because of bad investments, and, as it turned out, because of accounting fraud as well. The case of Banco Português de Negócios was particularly serious because of its size, its market share, and the political implications. Portugal's president, Cavaco Silva, and some of his political allies had maintained personal relationships with the bank and its president, who was eventually arrested for fraud. On the grounds of avoiding a potentially serious financial crisis in the Portuguese economy, the Portuguese government decided to bail out the banks, Irish style, at the expense of taxpayers.

And yet resistance to an IMF-EU bailout was supported by a majority of the population. They still remembered the two earlier IMF interventions in Portugal, in 1978 and 1983, following balance of payment crises. Both led to lower salaries and prolonged recessions.

I visited finance minister Teixeira dos Santos in Lisbon on March 15–16. He had expressed an interest in the flat tax regime that Bulgaria had adopted in 2007, and I had volunteered to bring some analysis on how it was implemented and on the fiscal results in the years after the reform. The timing of my visit could not have been worse. Teixeira dos Santos had just come back from a session of parliament focusing on tax increases. Midway through our conversation, he was called to parliament again. The discussion continued with his secretary of state and eventually Teixeira dos Santos returned, this time looking very concerned. That evening, we learned the opposition had called a no-confidence vote for the following week.

On March 23, 2011, Prime Minister José Sócrates resigned following the no-confidence vote over spending cuts. In little more than a week, between March 24 and April 4, Fitch cut Portugal's credit rating from A+ to BBB–, and Standard and Poor's (S&P) cut it from A– to BBB–. The agencies based their cuts on the conclusion of the March meeting of the European Council that "sovereign debt restructuring is a potential pre-condition to borrowing from the European Stability Mechanism." The bigger problem now became political instability. Yields on 10-year government Portuguese bonds climbed considerably (see figure 7.1).

National Elections: Getting in the Way

Bailouts had become an issue in the Finnish electoral campaign, which was in its final stages in March 2011. The National Coalition Party, led by Finance Minister Jyrki Katainen, was ahead in the polls, but the nationalistic True Finns Party was benefitting from its radically negative stance on assistance to Greece and Portugal. The True Finns were running ahead of the Social Democrats and rapidly closing in on Katainen's party.

Figure 7.1   Portugal: 10-year bond prices, 2011

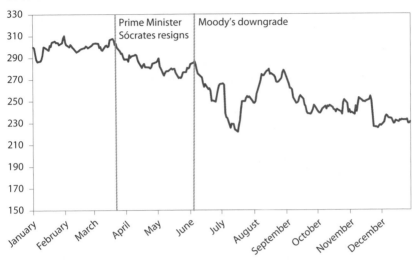

Source: JPMorgan, Datastream (accessed on February 27, 2014).

On the day the Portuguese government resigned, the regular Ecofin meeting agreed on mechanisms that would allow the eurozone's permanent bailout vehicle, the ESM, to lend €500 billion ($693 billion) beginning in 2013. The mechanism would draw on €80 billion ($111 billion) of paid-in capital. France initially insisted on increasing the fund to €1 trillion ($1.386 trillion), but Germany and Finland strongly opposed such a move, and the Finnish finance minister even hinted that Finland might leave the eurozone. This was three weeks before the Finnish parliamentary elections, and clearly the rhetoric was directed at the Finnish electorate. However, because this viewpoint was that of the pro-euro party, the ministers thought it best to wait until after the Finnish elections to have another discussion. This was one of many instances in which the upcoming elections in one country or another influenced the flow of decisions at Ecofin. The same situation would play out later with French, Greek, Italian, and Dutch elections.

While waiting for the results of the Finnish elections so it could continue its discussions of the ESM, Ecofin turned to the Euro Plus Pact. Joined by Bulgaria, Denmark, Latvia, Lithuania, Poland, and Romania, the pact laid out guidelines for convergence between its members in competitiveness, employment, public finances, and financial stability. A coalition of Nordic and East European countries managed to remove most of the tax harmonization language from the pact, even though France vociferously objected. I was quite active in the discussions, as were Anders Borg, Swedish finance minister, and

Jürgen Ligi, the Estonian minister. Germany initially took the French side, but fell quiet as the discussion progressed.

There was also an agreement on reinforcing the effective financing capacity of both the ESM, to €500 billion ($693 billion), and the European Financial Stability Facility (EFSF), to €440 billion ($610 billion). A first step was taken toward lowering the price on loans from the ESM and EFSF; Greece received a lower interest rate (100 basis points less) and longer maturity (7.5 years). But the enhanced flexibility of these instruments did not meet the expectations of analysts, who were looking for a bigger solution for the eurozone. Some pushed for ESM interventions in the debt primary market, but only exceptionally and in the context of a full assistance program with strict conditionality. Germany strongly objected to such an idea, followed by even stronger objections from Finland and the Netherlands.

No reference was made to secondary market interventions. The decision on flexibility fell short of what the markets felt was needed to give the eurozone an instrument to fight market disruptions. It remained up to the European Central Bank (ECB) alone to try to do that job. But, politically, that was all that was possible. The coming Finnish elections were on everyone's radar screen.

Two weeks later, on April 6, 2011, Portugal requested financial assistance from the IMF and the EFSF. A longer wait would have led to further deterioration in the sovereign bond market. The announcement fueled the final days of the True Finns campaign, and now they were running neck and neck with the National Coalition Party. For a few days, we all followed the Finnish news on our Blackberries.

On April 17, Katainen's party won the Finnish election with 20.4 percent of the vote. The Social Democrats came in second, with 19.2 percent of the vote. The True Finns, who took 19.1 percent of the vote, were third. As in the Greek parliamentary elections a year later, had the True Finns won the elections—and they came very close—the eurozone might have been very different today. As it was, the two largest parties established the new government, and the leader of the Social Democrats, Jutta Urpilainen, became finance minister.

Faulty Portuguese Statistics?

On April 24, 2011, following a Eurostat report on financial irregularities, Portugal was forced to revise upward its budget deficit and public debt figures for recent years (figure 7.2). The corrections implied budget deficit figures of 10.1 percent of GDP for 2009 and 9.1 percent for 2010, instead of 9.3 and 6.8 percent of GDP, respectively. The numbers for public debt were also raised, to 83 percent for 2009 and 93 percent for 2010 (Lourtie 2011, 13–14). This was reminiscent of the revisions made in the first days of the Papandreou government in Greece, although at smaller magnitudes. Still, it not only raised the issue of what the national statistical office had missed, but also questioned the credibility of Eurostat.

Figure 7.2 Portugal's public debt and budget deficit, 2006–13

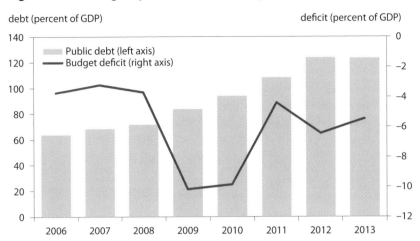

Source: Eurostat, http://epp.eurostat.ec.europa.eu/portal/page/portal/statistics/search_database (accessed on February 27, 2014).

The new figures were the result of several previous omissions in the budget accounts: (1) the state's financial assistance to banks (Banco Português de Negócios and Banco Privado Português); (2) three public transportation companies (REFER, Metropolitano de Lisboa, and Metro do Porto); and (3) the full comprisal of three public-private partnerships for toll-free motorways that, after the introduction of tolls, had to be considered public assets and registered as an investment expenditure. It was difficult to imagine how Eurostat had missed these corrections. I was familiar with its work in Bulgaria and knew how detailed their questionnaires were and how meticulous Eurostat experts were at checking such details. Clearly, the Eurostat experts dealing with Portugal were laxer. But shouldn't EU institutions have a role in catching such irregularities earlier? In both Greece and Portugal, Eurostat and the Commission's directorate dealing with economic and financial affairs had missed obvious signs of the problems to come.

May 2011 was one of the worst months of the euro crisis. On May 13, Eurostat published new debt and deficit forecasts and predicted that in Greece, Ireland, and Portugal the public debt would exceed the total GDP. In other words, even if their governments managed to deal with the budget deficits, the issue of the large debt overhang would remain. During the meetings of finance ministers, this issue was raised repeatedly, and the common—and reasonable in my view—point made was that it was better to deal first with the short-term deficit issue and then worry about how to resolve the debt issue. This was why the first Greek package and the Irish package did not foresee any solutions to the debt issue and concentrated on deficit-cutting measures.

The same week, Dominique Strauss-Kahn resigned from the IMF. I had never been one of his fans because of the design under his tutelage of the first Greek bailout package. It was short on structural reforms and long on liquidity—an odd outcome from the person who implemented the largest privatization program in French history during the socialist government of Lionel Jospin. In my view, the first rescue package for Greece extended the country's recession for another two years because insufficient steps were taken early on to address the causes of the crisis. It quickly overwhelmed the government, and so the later steps had to be much larger (more expensive).

On May 17, 2011, the eurozone heads of state approved a €78 billion ($108 billion) bailout package for Portugal. Three months of work went into the package, and some of the lessons learned from the failure of the Greek package were taken into account. For that reason, it did not raise the same concerns.

A Nervous Summer

On May 22, 2011, Spain's ruling Socialists suffered the worst local electoral defeat in 30 years. The opposition center-right People's Party won 38 percent of the vote, thereby gaining control of all of Spain's largest cities, including Barcelona, which had been controlled by the Socialists since 1979. Mariano Rajoy, leader of the People's Party since 2003, had called for parliamentary elections after Spain's statistical office announced that the country's public debt would double in just four years, between 2009 and 2013, from 40.2 percent to 85 percent of GDP.

Greece, where the daily strikes continued, was constantly in the news. On June 17, Papandreou appointed Defense Minister Evangelos Venizelos to replace Papaconstantinou as finance minister. The idea was to reduce the pressure on the government and get tougher with the European Union. By then, a second bailout loan of €130 billion ($180 billion) was being prepared for Greece, but activation was made conditional on further austerity measures and restructuring of the sovereign debt. Just a few weeks earlier, Papaconstantinou had visited me in Bulgaria and had described the enormous daily pressures of putting together a reform program. He also said something that every newly elected politician should remember: "Many times I wanted to blame my predecessors for the situation. But the sign in front of me says 'Greece,' not 'current Greek government' so I refrain from criticism."

In his new position, Evangelos Venizelos did not engender trust. In previous Greek governments, he had held nearly every ministerial position, including minister of the media, culture, justice, transport, defense, and development. He was an accomplished politician like few others in Europe, but in successive Ecofins he stubbornly held to written statements and would not engage in open discussion about progress on reforms. During his tenure as finance minister, there was little confidence in the transparency of the Greek position.

Perhaps this why in early July the new Finnish finance minister, Jutta

Urpilainen, stated publicly that "Finland would consider leaving the Eurozone rather than paying the debts of other countries in the currency bloc. Collective responsibility for other countries' debt, economics and risks; this is not what we should be prepared for. We are constructive and want to solve the crisis, but not on any terms."[1] Patience was running thin.

The credit rating agencies, which repeatedly had been caught unprepared for crisis events, decided to act preemptively. On June 5, 2011, Moody's cut Portugal's rating to junk, the lowest rating possible. A week later, Moody's cut Ireland's rating to junk. On August 5, 2011, the ECB sent Italy a letter asking for more austerity measures and a plan to balance its budget in 2013 rather than 2014. Italian president Silvio Berlusconi announced he would seek a balanced budget amendment and pledged more austerity. But Italian yields rose above Spanish yields for first time since May 2010. Later that day, the United States lost its AAA credit rating. The decision by Standard and Poor's to cut the US debt rating could increase the cost of borrowing for the United States.

The only response of EU officials to this barrage of bad news was to increase the ECB's bond purchase program. Jean-Claude Trichet obliged, but unwillingly. Then on September 9, Jürgen Stark, the ECB's chief economist, resigned from his post after long opposing the bank's bond purchases. "It's generally known that I'm not a glowing advocate of these purchases," Stark said in a Bloomberg interview. "I see the rationale. Our accommodative monetary policy isn't being transmitted in certain regions. So it's justifiable from a policy point of view. But there's an important point—we are also reducing interest rates for the sovereign. That's where the problem is."[2]

After this nervous summer, the council of finance ministers was to meet informally in Poland, which had the rotating EU presidency. But there was a surprise. On September 17, US Treasury Secretary Timothy Geithner joined Ecofin in Wroclaw and urged EU officials to deal with the crisis and avoid "catastrophic risks."[3] But, if anything, his comments backfired. "I remember sitting at the meeting and wondering who is he to tell Ecofin what to do? The US fiscal situation is in as much of a mess," said one of the most respected finance ministers after the meeting. Apparently, this feeling was shared by many because Geithner got a cold reception. He attended Ecofin meetings two more times without impressing anyone with either his knowledge of the euro crisis or his vision of how to improve the US fiscal condition. It also did not help that he had with him a retinue of a dozen or so aides, whereas the rest of us were limited to having two in the room. Moreover, his aides often giggled and were generally obnoxious. They fulfilled to a tee the American stereotype.

1. Andrew Walker, "Finland Mulls over Its Eurozone Future," BBC World Service, August 14, 2012.

2. Matthew Brockett and Jeff Black, "ECB Dealt Blow as Executive Board Member Stark Resigns before End of Term," Bloomberg, September 9, 2011.

3. Dominic Rushe, "Eurozone Debt Crisis: Tim Geithner Rebuffed over Cash Injection—as It Happened," The Guardian blog, September 17, 2011.

Calls for Higher Taxes, Again

On September 28, 2011, the president of the European Commission, José Barroso, unveiled a plan to create a financial transaction tax "to make the financial sector pay its fair share."[4] Two weeks later, we discussed the proposal at Ecofin, where the same views and coalitions emerged that had been formed during the June 2010 discussions of the financial transaction tax. The United Kingdom was against it, citing evidence from the introduction of a similar tax in Sweden that led to a 90 percent reduction in derivatives transactions. More important, the tax would lead to an increase in capital costs and from there to a long-run drop in GDP in the European Union by up to 2 percent. The European Commission responded that this scenario could be avoided by imposing the tax on secondary markets only and that it would curtail high-frequency trading. Such trading was frequently blamed for the woes of the European economy, especially in the run-up to the presidential elections in France.

Bulgaria and the Czech Republic had a different worry, which we expressed at Ecofin. Once the financial transaction tax was introduced, it would set a precedent for the European Commission to propose and implement common taxes. It would not be long before that would lead to demands for tax harmonization.

Denmark and Sweden had another issue. The design of the tax proposal would unfairly hurt countries outside the tax zone because it would be levied on transactions there as well if one of the parties in the transaction was located in the European Union. In other words, the tax would cover all transactions that involved firms or individuals of signatory countries, no matter whether the transactions took place within those countries or elsewhere, such as in Sweden.

After 15 hours of debate on the issue, it became clear that a consensus could not be reached. This was not the outcome the European Commission wanted because then the financial transaction tax could be claimed as a source of revenue for the EU budget. First France and then Germany and Austria threatened to go ahead and implement the tax through the use of "enhanced cooperation"—that is, the tax would be implemented only in the states that wished to participate. Under the EU treaty, such cooperation is permitted. Nine states, a majority in the eurozone, were needed for enhanced cooperation. Because the early count easily reached that number, the process went ahead, with the expected date of approval in the spring of 2012 and a start date in January 2013. These dates would soon fall by the wayside, however, just like most of the dates agreed on for other issues.

---

4. José Barroso, "Financial Transaction Tax: Making the Financial Sector Pay Its Fair Share," European Commission, September 28, 2011.

Third Tipping Point

On October 13, 2011, Slovakia became the 17th and final country to approve the expansion of the eurozone's rescue fund, two days after rejecting the plan. The parliament in Bratislava ratified the extension of the EFSF to €440 billion ($610 billion). But approval came at a high cost—the conservative government of Iveta Radičová fell as a result, less than a year into its term. This was the third tipping point in the crisis—this time in a positive direction (see the chronology). The Slovak finance minister, Ivan Miklos, was an acquaintance of mine from his previous stint as finance minister from 1998 to 2006. He had managed to turn Slovakia into the fastest-growing economy in Europe by slashing taxes and attracting foreign investment. He took the "Doing Business" reforms I had championed to heart, and Slovakia shot up to be among the 30 best-regulated countries in the world. It was disappointing to see him go.

On October 26 and 27, 2011, EU leaders held a crisis summit. After 10 hours of talks, the leaders agreed on the following: to leverage the European Union's temporary bailout fund to €1 trillion ($1.386 trillion), to force private investors to accept a 50 percent "haircut" on Greek bonds, to push European banks to raise €106 billion ($147 billion) in new capital, and to extend a new aid package worth €130 billion ($180 billion) to Greece. The measures were aimed at calming markets. And so they did, albeit for a much shorter time than we all expected.

Eurobonds: A Possible Solution?

After the collapse of Portugal, the heads of states of the southern rim countries pushed hard for another rescue option—eurobonds. The idea of eurobonds had been around for some time among global currency portfolio professionals. A eurobond would be attractive to central bankers and other portfolio investors around the world, both to achieve higher expected returns than on US Treasury bills and to diversify risk.

But Germany opposed eurobonds on the grounds that if national governments were allowed to issue them freely, the knowledge that somebody else was paying the bill would make the incentive to spend beyond their means even higher. "We must, and this is the lesson, move away from a debt union and toward a sustainable stability union. This won't be easy but it is right," said Chancellor Merkel in a speech at the Frankfurt auto show in September 2011. "This can't happen overnight, with some sort of one-off big-bang solution. It can only happen in a controlled, step by step process. Eurobonds are absolutely wrong. In order to bring about common interest rates, you need similar competitiveness levels, similar budget situations. You don't get them by collectivizing debts." Rainer Brüderle, the leader of Chancellor Merkel's coalition partner, the Free Democratic Party (FDP), described eurobonds as "interest socialism."

The distaste of Germans for eurobonds increased significantly over time: from 57 percent opposed to them in November 2011 to 79 percent in May 2012. Germans feared that the creation of eurobonds would lead to a "transfer union"—a permanent bailout mechanism. During a speech before the German Parliament on June 27, 2012, Merkel argued: "Growth on credit would just push us right back to the beginning of the crisis and that is why we should not and will not do it." A similar view was held by the governments of Austria, Finland, and the Netherlands.

This was the view of not only German politicians such as Chancellor Merkel, Rainer Brüderle, and Wolfgang Schäuble, but German bankers as well. When it appeared that the German government would yield to pressure from France, Axel Weber, the head of the Bundesbank, resigned over the issue in 2011.

The staunch German view was influenced by Germany's experience with financing German reunification. The result of Germany's first full-blown bailout to pay for the integration of East Germany (home to only 17 million people) was a tripling of German debt over a decade—from €430 billion ($595 billion) in 1989 to €1.2 trillion ($1.7 trillion) in 1999. Germany had greatly underestimated the integration costs. The country then saw a long phase of slow growth until just before the financial crisis hit.

Jens Weidmann, the current head of the Bundesbank, had many times explained his opposition to debt sharing prior to the establishment of a fiscal union. "The attempt to communitize debt prior to a deepened integration threatens to endanger the currency union," he wrote in *Suddeutsche Zeitung* in May 2012. "The creation of a debt union in which decisions are not anchored in responsibility, and in which liability for others takes place without controls, would only increase the current political and economic instabilities."

This was, however, what the opponents of fiscal responsibility wanted. For example, French president François Hollande made it a central part of his presidential campaign in 2012. Hollande had supporters among the southern rim heads of state, as well as some investors who had bet on the wrong side of the euro crisis and wanted their money back. Some well-known economic thinkers were also on his side such as billionaire and philanthropist George Soros. In early April 2013, Soros even went to Frankfurt to give the Germans some advice: Drop your opposition to eurobonds. Soros said that German fears that countries from the southern rim would abuse eurobonds by breaking budget rules were ill founded. The European Union's Fiscal Compact would ensure that the participating countries could not use eurobonds to cover additional debts. Soros also pointed out:

> If countries that abide by the Fiscal Compact were allowed to convert their entire existing stock of government debt into Eurobonds, the positive impact would be little short of the miraculous. The danger of default would disappear and so would the risk premiums. The balance sheets of banks would receive an immediate boost and so would the budgets of the heavily indebted countries because it would cost them less to service their existing stock of government debt.

Italy, for instance, would save up to four percent of its GDP. Its budget would move into surplus and instead of austerity, there would be room for some fiscal stimulus. The economy would grow and the debt ratio would fall. Most of the seemingly intractable problems would vanish into thin air. Only the divergences in competitiveness would remain unresolved. Individual countries would still need structural reforms, but the main structural defect of the euro would be cured. It would be truly like waking from a nightmare.[5]

The miracle would be reduced yields. Researchers had calculated that the yield of eurobonds would be 0.5 to 0.6 of a percentage point above German bonds (Assmann and Boysen-Hogrefe 2011) because fiscal variables were the main determinants of bond spreads (Ang and Longstaff 2011). In fiscal terms, the eurozone aggregate was comparable to France's. Therefore, the yield on eurobonds would be roughly equal to that on French bonds.

Other researchers claimed that US yields, adjusted for the exchange rate premium, were a good benchmark for yields on eurobonds because with such bonds the eurozone bond markets would be similar to the US market in terms of credit risk and liquidity (Favero and Missale 2011, 27–28). They found that in the years before the financial crisis the yield disadvantage of German over US government bonds had been around 40 basis points, which would represent the liquidity gains from issuing common bonds under the same conditions as US bonds.

The same studies found that the AAA-rated countries did not benefit from reduced yields. It was no wonder, then, that this solution was not embraced in Berlin or Vienna. There had, however, been progress on alternative solutions. For example, a variation of the eurobond proposal was proposed in Germany: In 2010 the German Council of Economic Experts proposed a European Redemption Fund. The plan would convert into eurobonds the existing debt of (approved) member nations in excess of 60 percent of GDP, the threshold specified in the Maastricht criteria. The European Redemption Fund bonds would then be paid off over 25 years. Steps toward this proposed solution to the short-term debt problem were predicated on approval of the Fiscal Compact, Chancellor Merkel's proposed solution to the long-term problem.

Red and Blue Eurobonds

The notion of eurobonds created a bigger problem than it solved because all debt above the legal criterion would become eligible for eurobond financing. Thus the incentive for countries to go deeper into debt increased. Another proposal had a better chance: the "blue/red bonds" proposed by Jacques Delpla and Jakob von Weizsäcker (2011) at the Brussels think tank Bruegel. Under

---

5. Nils Pratley, "George Soros: Germany Must Choose between Eurobonds or Euro Exit," *Guardian*, April 9, 2013.

their proposal, which had attracted support in northern Europe, only debt issued by national authorities below the 60 percent criteria would receive eurozone backing, would be declared senior notes, and would effectively become eurobonds. Investors would then find these "blue bonds" safe. When a country issued debt above the 60 percent threshold, the resulting junior "red bonds" would lose eurozone backing, and the individual member state would be liable for them. These bonds would command higher interest rates, in effect penalizing the issuer for breaching the Maastricht limit.

The enticing feature of this proposal was that the red bond mechanism was automatic, save for any incorrect accounting by the ECB of the debt-to-GDP ratio. In the meantime, however, private investors could determine for themselves the merits of each bond issuance. The resulting market interest rates would provide discipline. Compliance would not rely on the discretion of the national governments or Brussels. Nor would it require unenforceable debt ceilings legislated at the national level.

The euro countries could not, however, jump to a blue/red bond regime without first solving the problems of debt overhang and troubled banks. Otherwise, the plan by itself would be destabilizing—just like the introduction of the euro itself—because it would put almost all eurozone countries immediately into the red. Even Germany, with its 82 percent debt-to-GDP ratio, would suffer. In fact, only four eurozone members—Estonia, Finland, Luxembourg, and Slovakia—met the debt criterion in the Maastricht Treaty and the Fiscal Compact. Perhaps this is why Mario Draghi said that regardless of their color "eurobonds make sense only if you have a fiscal union"—and if there was progress toward reducing debt levels.

The Green Paper

All these options were theoretical because it was not clear whether eurobonds were legal under the EU treaty. Bond purchases were forbidden under Article 123 if they constituted monetary financing of government deficits (which was very much what eurobonds would be used for). For this reason, the European Council asked the European Commission for a legal opinion. The resulting document was more than a legal treatise; it laid out some options about eurobond issuance and coined a more acceptable term, *stability bonds*.[6]

The Green Paper raised many questions in my mind. It said, for example, that Article 125 of the EU treaty prohibited one member state from assuming the liabilities of another member state. Eurobonds under joint and several guarantees would lead to a situation in which the prohibition on bailing out would be breached. In such a situation, a member state would be held liable irrespective of its regular contribution should another member state be unable to honor its financial commitments. In other words, it seemed to me that the

---

6. The European Commission issued its "Green Paper on Stability Bonds" on November 23, 2011.

treaty had to be amended. That would most likely require a unanimous vote of the European Council and the consent of the European Parliament. The issuance of eurobonds would also require significant changes to the laws of a number of member states.

The Green Paper also raised another hurdle to be crossed before euro-bonds could be issued: Who would issue them? Issuance could be centralized in a single agency, or it could remain at the national level with coordination among the eurozone members. The distribution of revenue flows and debt servicing costs linked to the eurobonds would reflect the issuance shares held by individual members. Member states could accept joint and several liability for all or part of the associated debt servicing costs, implying a corresponding pooling of credit risk. Overall, all this sounded complicated, and nothing like it had ever been done before.

If a central debt agency were established, an important issue would be how it would on-lend the funds raised to the member states. There were two options: (1) on-lending in the form of direct loans in which a member state would receive its funding through a loan agreement or (2) the direct purchase from the member states of all government bonds, or the amount agreed on, by the debt agency in the primary market. The second option would allow the agency to buy outstanding government debt in the secondary market if needed.

The repayment of eurobonds would also have to be considered. The easiest way would be through transfers by the national authorities to the issuing agent, which would then organize the repayment to the bondholders. To assure market participants that the servicing of debt would always be guaranteed and that delays of payments would not occur, the debt agency would have to be endowed with a stable revenue stream. National debt management offices were part of the national fiscal institutions, and they were backed by the governments' authority to raise taxes. But a debt management office at the eurozone level would have no such direct link to tax revenues. The lack of such a direct link would reduce the market's acceptance of the bonds to be issued.

Putting these legal and organizational hurdles aside, the European Commission described three scenarios for possible eurobond issuance: (1) full substitution of eurobonds for national issuance, with joint and several guarantees; (2) partial substitution of eurobond issuance for national issuance, with joint and several guarantees; and (3) partial substitution of eurobond issuance for national issuance, with several guarantees only.

In the first option, eurozone government financing would be fully covered by eurobonds through the creation of a single eurozone debt agency. This agency would issue bonds in the market and distribute the proceeds to member states based on their financing needs. On the same basis, the agency would service the eurobonds by gathering interest and principal payments from the member states. The bonds would be issued under joint and several guarantees provided by all eurozone members, thereby pooling all credit risk.

The full substitution of eurobonds for national issuance would assure member states that they would receive full refinancing no matter the condition of their national public finances. This approach would also create a large market, with important advantages in terms of liquidity and reduced liquidity risk. Finally, the eurobond would provide the global financial system with a second safe haven that in size and liquidity would be comparable to that of the US treasury market.

At the same time, this option would involve significant risks. Member states could effectively free ride on the discipline of others, without any implications for their financing costs. Accordingly, this approach would have to be accompanied by an enhanced Fiscal Compact for delivering budgetary discipline, economic competitiveness, and fewer macroeconomic imbalances at the national level. And because of the joint and several guarantees and the upgrade needed in the Fiscal Compact, the treaty itself would have to be changed.

The second option was Bruegel's blue/red bond approach. The eurozone bond market would have two distinct parts. The first part would be eurobonds (blue bonds), whose issuance would occur only up to some predefined limits and thus might not cover the full refinancing needs of each country. These bonds would benefit from a joint and several guarantee and a uniform refinancing rate for all member states. The second part would be national government bonds (red bonds), which would be issued under national guarantees. National bonds would therefore be junior to eurobonds. The scale of national issuance would depend on the agreed-on scale of common issuance of eurobonds and its overall refinancing needs.

The credibility of the ceiling for the eurobond issuance was the main problem with this proposal. Once the blue bond allocation was exhausted, the financing costs for a member state would automatically increase. This increase could result in turn in political pressure to increase the ceiling. Unless there were strong safeguards against such pressure, anticipation of a "soft" ceiling would largely eliminate the disciplining effects of the blue/red bond approach. Anyone who has had to defend a budget in parliament knows that the pressure from politicians to incur more debt is constant. Therefore, the fiscal ceiling would have to be tied to the Fiscal Compact and written into law.

In the third option, eurobonds again would substitute only partially for national issuance, but this time they would be supported by the pro rata guarantees of the eurozone member states. This approach was also called the Juncker-Tremonti approach, after its main champions, Jean-Claude Juncker and Giulio Tremonti, the Italian finance minister.[7] This approach differed from the previous option in that countries would retain liability for their respective shares of eurobond issuance. This option would require that fewer preconditions be met and could be pursued without treaty changes. Because of the several but not joint guarantees, member states subject to high market risk would benefit considerably less from the creditworthiness of low-yield member states than in the previous two options.

---

7. Jean-Claude Juncker and Giulio Tremonti, "Stability Bonds Would End the Crisis," *Financial Times*, December 5, 2010.

Eurozone Ministry of Finance

Other paths to financial rescue were proposed as well. Stijn Claessens, an economist at the IMF and my mentor at the World Bank, and his coauthors designed two paths forward (Claessens, Mody, and Vallée 2012). The first path would be eurobills and project bonds and would take five years to complete. The second path would be the creation of a redemption fund, and it would take 25 years. In both cases, the authors provided solutions to the nagging technical questions surrounding eurobonds—who would issue and who would repay. The answer was the new Eurozone Ministry of Finance.

How likely was it that any of this would happen? That Angela Merkel was not a fan of eurobonds was quite clear. But on June 25, 2012, she was clearer than usual. During a meeting with parliamentarians from the Free Democratic Party, her junior coalition partner, she said there would be no full debt sharing through eurobonds "as long as I live." Several Free Democrats allegedly responded, "We wish you a long life."[8] For this reason, eurobonds were not even discussed in 2013, the year of Germany's parliamentary elections. A further discussion of eurobonds is likely to proceed only in the context of a broader discussion of a fiscal union.

---

8. From the Editor, "The Coming EU Summit Clash: Merkel Vows 'No Euro Bonds as Long as I Live,'" *Der Spiegel*, June 27, 2012.

8

Ongoing Turmoil, Sprouting Theories of Euro Devaluation

On October 31, 2011, in a move that caught everyone by surprise, Greek prime minister Georgios Papandreou announced plans for a referendum on the new bailout plan. Even his finance minister, Evangelos Venizelos, was unaware of the referendum idea. Meanwhile, the eurozone leaders were seething. All the work of the past months to show European resolve in dealing with the Greek crisis was being put in jeopardy. Public opinion in Greece was clearly against the proposed conditions of the bailout, and the referendum would probably result in a rejection of these terms. But where would Greece and the European Union go from there? A suspension of aid to Greece and a subsequent default and exit from the eurozone seemed the most likely route.

Papandreou's move indicated that he was uncomfortable about meeting the demands imposed on the rescue by Berlin, Brussels, and the Eurogroup. He was not alone: Similar misgivings had been voiced by the prime minister of Italy, Silvio Berlusconi; Spain, José Luis Rodríguez Zapatero; and Hungary, Viktor Orbán. This could have turned into a power struggle within the European Union had the European powers shown the kind of hesitation typical of their decision making during the eurozone crisis. But there was no hesitation here.

Fourth Tipping Point

This was the fourth tipping point in the eurozone crisis: Greece's decision to test the resolve of eurozone leaders (see the chronology). Events then began to unfold quickly. On November 2, 2011, European leaders cut off aid payments to Greece and said it must decide whether it wanted to stay in the eurozone. The ultimatum was at odds with the text of the Maastricht Treaty stating that monetary union is "irrevocable." But Papandreou's gamble on the referendum had tested what little patience remained in Berlin and Brussels. By the end of the week, Papandreou had resigned, and, with the agreement of the other parties, former central bank governor Lucas Papademos was appointed prime minister of a caretaker government. The markets found Papademos, also a former vice president of the European Central Bank (ECB), to be a trustworthy figure. And it was clear that his service as prime minister was a stop-gap measure to avoid default. New elections were needed.

On November 8, 2011, the European Council adopted a package of six legislative proposals, the so-called six pack, aimed at strengthening economic governance in the European Union. The package contained a regulation amending previous texts on the surveillance of member states' budgetary and economic policies; a regulation on the European Union's excessive deficit procedure; a regulation on the enforcement of budgetary surveillance in the eurozone; a regulation on the prevention and correction of macroeconomic imbalances; a regulation on enforcement measures to correct excessive macroeconomic imbalances in the eurozone; and a directive on requirements for the member states' budgetary frameworks.

This was one of two major decisions adopted by Ecofin during my time as finance minister (the other was adoption of the single banking supervisor in December 2012). These measures strengthened substantially the Stability and Growth Pact, and provided both the tools to foresee problems (the imbalances procedure) and a mechanism to penalize countries that had strayed from fiscal prudence (the excess deficit procedure). This was also an initiative that European Commissioner Olli Rehn handled well. Although most of the discussions in Ecofin meetings focused on bailouts, Commissioner Rehn managed to push through these legal changes with lots of determination. Together, they would strengthen the eurozone and the European Union's fiscal position.

Berlusconi Resigns

A few days later, on November 12, 2011, Italian prime minister Silvio Berlusconi resigned. After losing his parliamentary majority the previous week amid an ongoing sex scandal, Berlusconi had promised to resign when the austerity measures demanded by the ECB won approval in parliament. The package included an increase in the value-added tax from 20 percent to 21 percent; a freeze on public sector salaries until 2014; measures to fight tax evasion, including a limit of €2,500 ($3,465) on cash transactions; and a special tax on the energy sector.

Berlusconi's exit paved the way for a new government of technocrats led by Mario Monti, a former member of the European Commission under Jacques Santer, Romano Prodi, and Manuel Barroso. He, too, was a highly regarded European technocrat like Lucas Papademos. His mandate was to push through measures to reduce Italy's €2 trillion ($2.772 trillion) public debt. His immediate proposals included selling state assets and raising the retirement age from 65 to 67 by 2026. He would also attempt to reduce the power of professional guilds, privatize municipal services, and offer tax breaks to companies that would hire young workers.

Monti's government came with high expectations, and somehow it managed to receive high marks from the international community and the media. It may have been because Silvio Berlusconi's reputation had sunk so low prior to his resignation. A closer look at the government's efforts would, however, reveal two things. First, the Monti government was not technocratic. Most ministers had previously sat on the boards of state-owned companies, and as such they were part of the old political elite. Second, the government did not achieve much in terms of reforms: A lot was said and little was done. None of the stated reforms were completely carried out, and many did not go beyond the initial intention. Mostly likely, what saved Monti's reputation was the work of another Italian, Mario Draghi, the former governor of the Bank of Italy who became president of the ECB in November. Had the ECB not intervened so extensively in the financial markets the following year, Monti's legacy would be quite poor.

At first, Monti combined the jobs of prime minister and minister of finance, and so he attended Ecofin meetings. At these, I had an opportunity to listen to his comments and to discuss his views on the eurozone crisis. In my view, Monti knew well what had to be done, but he was unsure of how much time he would have to carry out the needed reforms. Over time, he also grew afraid of trying and relinquished the finance ministry. In July 2012, Vittorio Grilli was appointed minister of finance. A former academic at Bocconi University, Grilli served as vice president of the Economic and Financial Committee of the European Union from March 2009 to March 2011, and then was chosen to chair the Economic and Financial Committee until January 2012, when Thomas Wieser replaced him. He had originally joined the Italian government as a deputy minister of economy and finance.

Approving the Fiscal Compact

Early December was especially busy at Ecofin, probably because Europeans seemed to work only when the prospect of ruined holidays was upon them. Two consecutive meetings were held to agree on the Fiscal Compact. On December 9, eurozone leaders agreed on its text after heated discussions that were leaked to the press.[1] Jean-Claude Juncker went so far as to reprimand Austrian finance minister Maria Fekter for worrying more about her image in the international media than the future of the eurozone. This would happen again and again in later eurozone meetings.[2] Fekter, who sat next to me at Ecofin meetings, was

---

1. For the confusion that EU summit meetings usually cause in markets, see Nicolas Véron, "Why Do Markets Disdain Euro Summit Accords?" Peterson Perspectives Interviews on Current Issues, Peterson Institute for International Economics, December 15, 2011.

2. Jeff Black and Josiane Kremer, "Euro Spat Erupts as Fekter Upstages Juncker at Crisis Talks," Bloomberg, March 30, 2012.

Figure 8.1 Euro-dollar foreign exchange spot rate, March 2012

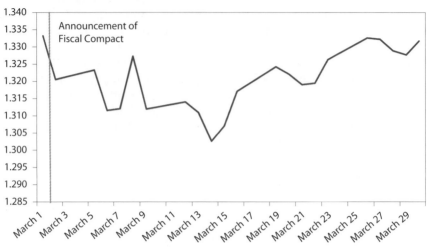

US dollars per euro

Announcement of
Fiscal Compact

Source: WM/Reuters, Datastream (accessed on February 27, 2014).

simply the type of person who gave a straight answer if asked. Normally, such behavior is welcome, but these were not normal times.

The Fiscal Compact was a step toward a European fiscal union. It called for government budgets to be balanced or in surplus—requirements that would have to be inserted either in a member country's constitution or in an organic budget law. In other words, it provided for a national legal limit on deficit spending (it had become obvious that the Maastricht criteria did not provide a legal limit because they were based on international law). With the Fiscal Compact in place, opposition politicians in every European country could demand that the government fulfill the Maastricht criteria or resign. Constitutional courts could also weigh in on possible infringements of the law. In short, political and judiciary control was moved from Brussels to the national capitals.

In the same December 9 meeting, the heads of state also agreed to move forward to July 2012 the entry into force of the European Stability Mechanism and to reassess the adequacy of the €500 billion ($693 billion) ceiling on bailout funds in March 2012.

Adoption of the Fiscal Compact had a positive effect on the financial markets—the euro went up nearly 2 percent against the US dollar on the Monday after the signing of the Fiscal Compact on Friday, March 2, 2012 (figure 8.1). And European leaders had another positive announcement in store. On December 22, the last working day before Christmas, the ECB allotted €489 billion ($678 billion) to 523 banks in the first step of a 36-month longer-term refinancing operation, similar to the quantitative easing operations of the US Federal Reserve. Mario Draghi had hinted at this move a few months earlier, on August 2. Announcing it just before the markets closed for the holidays was an effort to end the year 2011, the most difficult one in the euro crisis, on a high note.

Draghi's gesture was well timed. During a financial crisis, journalists and analysts hang on every word said after EU meetings—and for good reason. All decisions were made either in informal breakfast or lunch sessions of Ecofin, or at the informal eurozone dinner the previous night. Thus anyone looking at the transcript of a formal Ecofin meeting would learn little about what was going on. The communiqués, however, might reveal details on the main points of tension. It is true that some ministers always spoke their mind. In addition to Fekter, the straight talkers were Anders Borg, the Swedish finance minister; the two Finnish ministers, Jyrki Katainen and then Jutta Urpilainen; the two Dutch ministers, Jan Kees de Jager and then Jeroen Dijsselbloem; Luc Frieden, the Luxembourg finance minister; and all the Germans present at Ecofin— Wolfgang Schäuble; Jörg Asmussen, first as a deputy finance minister who stood in for Schäuble when he was sick and then as a representative of the ECB; and Klaus Regling, the managing director of the European Stability Mechanism. When a draft communiqué was distributed for comments before the end of Ecofin and the press conference, these were the people who would demand clear language. Thus when little progress was made on particular issues, the communiqué should say so. When partial progress was made, it should state what was achieved and what remained unresolved. This approach avoided a lot of confusion, such as that characterizing the Franco-German summit meetings. It also laid the foundation for giving the markets positive signals. When the Fiscal Compact was adopted, that truly was a positive decision.

Even though 2011 ended with positive momentum, 2012 still started badly. On January 13, Standard and Poor's (S&P) downgraded the credit ratings of France and eight other eurozone countries, blaming it on the failure of eurozone leaders to deal with the debt crisis. One of the reasons cited: France had not achieved a balanced budget since entering the eurozone. Three days later, S&P downgraded the temporary bailout fund, the European Financial Stability Facility.

France's response was quick: The government would sue S&P. At the next Ecofin meeting, the French finance minister, François Baroin, suggested that the European Commission create its own credit rating agency. That idea surfaced repeatedly whenever some country felt treated unfairly by the credit rating agencies. It was first tabled by Christine Lagarde in 2010, after the Greek downgrades. And it was picked up by Italian finance minister Giulio Tremonti on several occasions. Fortunately, it never materialized. One can only imagine the political pressure it would come under.

When the Fiscal Compact was signed by the heads of state on March 2, 2012, the United Kingdom abstained, as did the Czech Republic. However, the other 26 members signed on to the new rules that made it harder to incur large budget deficits. Bulgaria joined the Fiscal Compact but took exception to the section on tax harmonization. I recognized that the Fiscal Compact would help future finance ministers resist the demands from policymakers for more spending. They could simply say, "This is unconstitutional." That would be a good insurance against populist policies, which were widespread in Bulgaria. At the same time, I voted against the section on tax harmonization because it simply meant that everyone should adopt the kinds of high taxes found in France and Italy. I went so far as to submit a bill in parliament that would forbid this and future governments from participating in tax harmonization treaties at the EU level.

Papademos Takes Over in Greece

After the Papademos government was in place, weeks of negotiations ensued between Greece, private lenders, and the Troika—the European Commission, the ECB, and the International Monetary Fund (IMF)—as Greece sought a debt write-off and even more spending cuts in order to receive a second bailout. On February 10, the Papademos government agreed to the package proposed by the Troika. It required Athens to implement a further €325 million ($450 million) in budget cuts to receive the bailout. On February 12, 2012, the unpopular austerity bill passed the Greek Parliament. The mass demonstrations that followed were in the hundreds of thousands.

On February 21, 2012, the eurozone finance ministers agreed on the basic principles of the second bailout package, including stronger on-site monitoring by the European Commission, creation of an escrow account for the bailout installments, private sector debt restructuring, and additional retroactive lowering of the interest rates of the Greek Loan Facility. The European governments whose central banks held Greek government bonds in their investment portfolios agreed to pass on to Greece until 2020 an amount equal to any future income accruing to their national central bank stemming from this portfolio. During this stretch of the arduous negotiations, conference calls among the finance ministers were organized nearly daily to communicate progress.

March began with the news that the eurozone jobless rate had hit a new high. At the same time, in its spring forecast the European Commission predicted that the eurozone economy would contract by 0.3 percent in 2012. More support for the foundering European economy was needed, and it came from the only possible source, the ECB, which promptly announced an allotment of €530 billion ($735 billion) to 800 banks in the second 36-month longer-term refinancing operation. On March 8, the ECB also reactivated the buyback scheme for Greece and decided that marketable debt instruments issued or fully guaranteed by Greece would again be accepted as collateral in Eurosystem credit operations without applying the minimum credit rating threshold for collateral eligibility. This action somewhat calmed the markets about the Greek banking sector. On March 13, the eurozone backed a second Greek bailout of €130 billion ($180 billion). Of the member states, France was the most active in pushing the bailout along—perhaps out of solidarity, but the more likely reason was that French banks held the majority of bad Greek debt.

Just as the immediate concerns about Greece waned, other concerns sprang up elsewhere. On April 12, Italian borrowing costs increased in a sign of new worries among investors about Italy's ability to reduce its high levels of debt. In an auction of three-year bonds, Italy paid an interest rate of 3.89 percent, up from 2.76 percent in a sale of similar bonds the previous month. Attention shifted to Spain the next day, with the stock market hit by worries over the country's economy. The Spanish government's 10-year cost of borrowing returned to above 6 percent. On April 18, the Italian government cut its growth forecast for the economy in 2012. It was previously predicting that the economy would shrink by 0.4 percent, but was now forecasting a 1.2 percent contraction.

On May 6, 2012, the majority of Greeks voted in a general election for parties that rejected the country's bailout agreement with the Troika. New Democracy, the conservative party of Antonis Samaras, came in first in a field of six parties that entered parliament. But no clear winner emerged because Samaras had no plausible coalition partners. Syriza, the coalition of radical left parties led by Alexis Tsipras, came in a close second but could not organize a government either. New elections were then announced after attempts to form a coalition government failed. This time, the opinion polls gave Syriza a significant lead. Tsipras declared he would annul the Troika agreement on his first day in power.

In the month leading to the repeat elections, the ECB flooded Greek banks with additional liquidity. This was Europe's indirect effort to stave off a resurgence by nationalist parties in the coming election. And it worked. On June 17, 2012, Greeks went to the polls again, and the pro-austerity party, New Democracy, received a higher percentage of the votes, nearly 30 percent, thereby allaying fears the country was about to leave the eurozone. Syriza came in second, with 27 percent, thereby gaining more seats in the parliament. The remaining parties all lost seats. New Democracy received support from PASOK (Panhellenic Socialist Movement), led by the former finance minister Evangelos Venizelos, and ANEL (Independent Greeks), another conservative party led by former New Democracy politician Panos Kammenos, to form a cabinet.[3] Together, the three parties held 182 seats in the 300-seat parliament.

Meanwhile, the rest of the southern rim countries continued to slide into trouble. On May 25, Spain's fourth largest bank, Bankia, asked the government for a bailout of €19 billion ($26 billion). Next door, woes in the Portuguese banking sector were deepening. On June 7, 2012, Portugal's largest bank in assets, Millennium, was rescued by the Portuguese government, now headed by conservative Passos Coelho, using €3 billion ($4.16 billion) from the bailout

---

3. Jacob Kirkegaard, "Europe after the Greek Election," Peterson Perspectives Interviews on Current Issues, Peterson Institute for International Economics, June 21, 2012.

package. On June 7, 2012, after emergency talks with eurozone leaders, Spain's finance minister, Luis de Guindos, said that the country would shortly make a formal request for up to €100 billion ($136 billion) in loans from the eurozone bailout fund to shore up its banks. In an odd twist, de Guindos had been an advisor for Lehman Brothers in Europe and director of its subsidiaries in Spain and Portugal, where he served from 2006 until the firm collapsed in 2008. Prior to that; he had held several appointments in the Spanish administration. His background was useful when he had to describe to the eurozone group and Ecofin the kind of bailout package Spain needed.

Theories of Euro Devaluation

By the spring of 2012, the US Treasury was becoming increasingly agitated about the prolonged uncertainty in the eurozone and was beginning to make public comments about individual countries' bailout packages and the overall coordination of support in the eurozone. Usually off-target, the comments from Washington, following the academic tradition in the United States, were generally snide about the euro. Two years earlier, European economists Lars Jonung and Eoin Drea (2010) had summarized the differences in opinion about the euro between US and European economists. The title of their journal article reflected the pessimism being expressed by US scholars: "The Euro: It Can't Happen, It's a Bad Idea, It Won't Last. U.S. Economists on the EMU, 1989–2002."

One of the papers singled out by Jonung and Drea was by Charles Calomiris at Columbia University. As early as 1999 in a paper entitled "The Impending Collapse of the European Monetary Union," Calomiris had predicted that roughly a decade after its creation either some members of the eurozone would be forced to leave or the currency would depreciate dramatically as a means of keeping those countries in the eurozone. The reason he cited was the lack of competitiveness within Europe. Indeed, from 2000 to 2007, after the introduction of the euro and before the financial crisis, Portugal grew by only 1.2 percent a year and Italy by 1.3 percent a year, close to stagnation. Yet this was a time of loose fiscal and monetary policy. In fact, both Portugal and Italy deployed a great deal of fiscal stimulus during that period. Portugal had an average budget deficit of 4.3 percent of GDP, and it never complied with the Maastricht budget ceiling of 3 percent of GDP. Italy's average budget deficit was 3.2 percent of GDP, and it complied with the Maastricht budget ceiling only in 2007.

So even in good times the southern rim countries could compete within the eurozone. Calomiris did, however, point to a solution. If the euro were devalued against other global currencies, then the eurozone would survive. This idea attracted many followers because in this way the struggling southern rim economies could regain their competitiveness. Economic reforms alone would not do the trick for countries such as Italy and Spain.

Problems with Euro Devaluation

Devaluing the euro, however, would be fraught with problems. The first problem with a euro-area-wide devaluation would be the internal differences between euro members in competitiveness. Devaluation would only affect the eurozone's trade links with the rest of the world, while leaving the cost differentials, say, between Germany and Greece and between Slovakia and Spain unchanged. But the eurozone's aggregate trade relationship with the rest of the world was part of the issue: Greece and Portugal were not able to compete against China.

The second problem with a euro devaluation was that it would not help the eurozone as a whole. To understand why, one has only to consider the structure of eurozone imports. In 2012 fuels accounted for 29 percent of EU imports—the eurozone is energy-poor and heavily dependent on oil and gas imports. The higher energy costs from devaluation would offset some of the competitiveness gains, particularly for the manufacturing sector. They would also make the average household poorer.

The third problem was that a euro devaluation would boost just German exports. In 2012 only 38 percent of German exports were going to other eurozone countries. The devaluation would not affect this intra-euro-area trade, but it would extend Germany's trade surplus with the rest of the world, spurring concerns in the United States and China. Thus in April 2013, Jens Weidmann, head of the Bundesbank, said that "politically brought about devaluations" do not lead to improved economic competitiveness. He also pointed out that indicators suggested the euro was not overvalued.

A fourth problem was that a weaker euro could start a sell-off of bonds in the southern rim countries. Holders of bonds from southern European countries would sell them to avoid a net loss because of the new exchange rate.

For these reasons, an overall devaluation of the euro was an unlikely scenario. An alternative was a devaluation within the eurozone. Southern Europe traditionally had low productivity growth, particularly in tradable goods. This relative productivity growth gap with the north was likely to persist as a result of the human capital differences, rigid labor laws in the south, and low labor mobility in Europe. According to the Balassa-Samuelson model of real exchange rates, if two countries with persistent productivity growth differences in their tradable goods sectors adopt a common currency, eventually the country with slow productivity growth will experience recessionary pressure. After a period, that country will have to either suffer from continuing price deflation or devalue its currency.

And what about labor costs? The average hourly labor cost in Spain in 2012 was €32 ($45) an hour, whereas in Slovakia it was only a third of that cost, €12 ($17) an hour. In Germany and Italy, it was about €80 ($111) an hour. To avoid a permanent crisis, the southern rim countries had to see their labor cost fall, until it reached approximately €25 ($35) an hour. For the Slovaks for the same period, the labor cost would have to go up. In the meantime, it was clear that foreign investors would prefer to invest in Slovakia rather than in

Spain. Indeed, since 2004, when Slovakia entered the European Union, large segments of the Spanish car industry have shifted to Bratislava. Italian wages would also have to fall, while German wages, which had been stable since adoption of the euro, would rise even higher. Both Italy and Spain would then focus on their export-oriented manufacturing sectors.

The southern countries with export traditions could gain the most. Others would find new markets and expand production, mostly focused on the domestic market—for example, agricultural produce in Greece and Portugal. The favorable exchange rate prior to euro entry made it possible for the relatively inefficient, often family-owned firms in Italy to sell their products abroad. Their experience and upgraded technology would keep them competitive internationally. Italy also has some competitive industries—well-to-do families around the world were wearing Armani, Cavalli, and Prada, buying Italian furniture, and even driving the occasional Fiat or Lamborghini. Spain was also known for fashion—Desigual, Zara, and Mango—and was a traditional exporter of food products.

Entering the eurozone improved credit conditions, but at the cost of manufacturing competitiveness. Devaluation might give eurozone countries an export boost, relieving some of the rising unemployment affecting their industries, but it was still unlikely that at any exchange rate France would ship Citroëns to Stuttgart. At the right exchange rate, however, Citroëns could appear in Asia or Latin America.

Over the short term, overvaluation implied that the southern euro countries would have to cut wages and deficits, and northern euro countries would have to increase wages and public spending. If Europe were to keep the euro, the southern rim would have to deflate prices and wages 2 or 3 percent a year for several years. Germany would have to go in the opposite direction. Does this sound reasonable? Not in the least. No government could endure several more years of deflation on top of what had already been five difficult years in Europe.

In Bulgaria, I oversaw austerity measures in a much more benign environment, and it was hard—very hard. When people see more of the same belt-tightening year after year, praise from Brussels and credit rating agencies falls on deaf ears. It becomes even more difficult at election time. How can one promise his constituents fiscal stability and falling prices? They want their standard of living to rise—higher pensions and wages and more money for health care and education. But by then, all (or most) of the inefficient expenditures have been squeezed out, and there is simply nothing left to cut.

During this crisis, an additional growth stopper in Europe was the large intratrade linkages. When the entire eurozone was experiencing zero growth, exports also slowed down. So this dependence, which was to some extent a result of the euro adoption, became a burden. To export more, either the northern countries needed to spend more (i.e., reduce austerity) or the southern economies needed to become more competitive against imports from China and other countries outside Europe. The latter was possible either through a rapid rise in productivity or through devaluation.

There were straightforward calculations on how much devaluation was needed for the southern euro members to increase (and then retain) competitiveness. The answer was somewhere near 30 to 40 percent. For example, estimates by IMF chief economist Olivier Blanchard suggested that Portugal would require a 25 percent real depreciation to restore its competitiveness (Blanchard and Portugal 2006, 108–207). But this analysis was carried out before the crisis and did not account for the additional rise in unemployment and the increase in the current account deficit.

Krugman's Idea on Devaluation

US economist Paul Krugman argued that gradual devaluation in the south could happen only through a higher inflation target in the north. A downward nominal wage adjustment was next to impossible. It would lead to protests in the streets, something the world had grown accustomed to seeing in Greece and Spain over the last three years. This meant that "internal devaluation" through deflation, which is basically equivalent to reducing labor costs, would be avoided by governments. And so the burden of adjustment would fall on the north through increases in public sector wages, increases in the minimum wage, and larger social schemes for the unemployed and those otherwise underprivileged. If the overall eurozone inflation rate were higher, Cyprus, Greece, Spain, and other peripheral eurozone members would be able to restore competitiveness simply by lagging inflation in the northern countries.

Other economists doubted that this gradual approach would succeed. Since 1990, there had been only two examples of a gradual devaluation. The first was in Hong Kong in 2001–03, when a drop in demand for its goods and services following the merger with China led to a fall in prices while the nominal exchange rate was pegged to the US dollar. The second was in Japan in 1998–2004.

By contrast, depreciations associated with changes in the nominal exchange rate are common. Over the last 50 years, there have been over 250 episodes of a real depreciation. It may be that a nominal depreciation is simply easier compared with measures aimed at reducing labor costs. And internal devaluations are still quite feasible—that is, in many cases in which a nominal depreciation generated a real depreciation, perhaps a real depreciation would have occurred even if the exchange rate had been fixed. One could turn to price evidence from within a currency union to see whether there were substantial relative price adjustments. Again, the evidence was discouraging for countries hoping to pursue this strategy.

Jay Shambaugh (2012), a Georgetown University economist, turned to price data for 27 US metro areas from 1961 to 2010 to determine whether metro areas could have falling prices relative to the rest of the United States. He used the same standards for an internal devaluation as used in international studies, but he compared each metro area with the median inflation rate for the nation. The evidence showed that in the United States measures aimed

Figure 8.2 Consumer price inflation rates for Greece, Germany, and Spain, 2007–12 (as measured by the Harmonized Index of Consumer Prices)

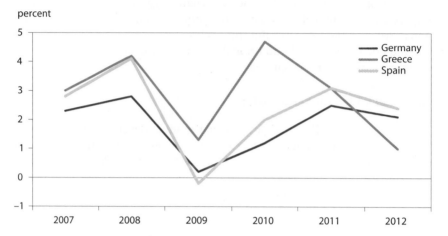

Source: Eurostat, http://epp.eurostat.ec.europa.eu/portal/page/portal/statistics/search_database (accessed on February 27, 2014).

at reducing labor costs did take place, but rarely. And they did not happen after the United States entered a lower inflation period after 1990. US inflation averaged over 5 percent from 1968 to 1990 but averaged 2.5 percent from 1991 to 2010. There were also no internal devaluations during the period 1961–68 when inflation averaged just 1.7 percent. Just as nominal devaluations may be the path of least resistance, labor mobility in the United States may take place before a reduction in labor costs is needed.

These results suggest that in the eurozone a rapid and substantial shift in relative prices through wage or price compression was unlikely (figure 8.2). Some southern rim countries had lost considerable cost competitiveness over the last decade. In Greece, prices had risen roughly 30 percent since 1999 relative to those in Germany and 20 percent compared with the eurozone outside Germany. In Spain, prices rose by 20 and 10 percent, respectively. To regain competitiveness at a rate of 5 percent over three years would require a decade of reducing labor costs in Greece.

An internal devaluation comes with another challenge as well. If wages and prices fall, nominal GDP could fall even if there were real GDP growth—that is, the denominator in the debt-to-GDP ratio did not grow. Thus even if the southern rim countries were able to restart real growth by reducing labor costs, only when they restarted nominal growth would real growth help their debt sustainability.

Yet another challenge during the euro crisis was resolving the large outstanding sovereign and company debt in countries such as Cyprus and Greece.

Holding the nominal exchange rate fixed and relying on lowering labor costs did not make debt more manageable. The real value of the debt rose over time, increasing the need for cost adjustments.

A Fiscal Devaluation

Another course of action was devaluation through changing the tax structure, a so-called fiscal devaluation. Raising the value-added tax and cutting payroll taxes would produce some of the effects of currency devaluation. The higher value-added tax would make imported goods more expensive because foreign companies exporting to the country would have to pay duties on their products. Simultaneously lowering payroll taxes would allow domestic companies to offset the higher value-added tax while not raising prices. Because domestic company exports are not subjected to the value-added tax, they can sell their products abroad at a lower price, exactly as though the euro had been devalued.

France did just that in late 2012 when President François Hollande took office. The IMF recommended the same to the Monti government in Italy. There, a shift of 2 percent of GDP from social security contributions to the value-added tax could lift the level of GDP and employment by about 1 percent over the long run. In addition, the cut in social security contributions would target the lower wage levels to reduce the cost of the measure, but also to benefit low-wage earners, women, and young workers.

There are a number of reasons why fiscal devaluation might work well in France and Italy: its high labor tax wedge, wage rigidity, and the fact that the fixed exchange rate covers a large proportion of trade. Fiscal devaluation would facilitate the wage and price adjustments needed to restore France's and Italy's external competitiveness in the absence of an exchange rate adjustment.

Slovenia also took this approach, announcing an increase in the value-added tax from 20 to 22 percent in July 2013. If privatization targets were met later in the year, the government was going to reduce social security payments. The effect, however, was small relative to the gap in competitiveness to be filled. And the costs accrued disproportionately to the poor because the value-added tax and other indirect taxes were on consumption, not income. Consumers took another hit from more expensive imports. Thus a change in the tax structure should be coupled with increases in the social payments to some underprivileged groups. Examples would be increases in unemployment benefits and the lower pensions as well as the minimum wage.

Recently, Portugal tried this combination of reforms, in part out of the need to increase budget savings after the constitutional court struck down some of its earlier expenditure-cutting measures. On April 5, 2013, the court ruled that four government austerity measures, including the planned cuts in public sector pay and state pensions, violated the constitution. A €1.3 billion ($1.8 billion) hole in the 2013 budget, 0.8 percent of GDP, was therefore opened. A week later, the government announced plans to cut the corporate income tax from the current 24 percent. The value-added tax had been increased to 23 percent the previous year.

Overall, the advice on devaluation from the US Treasury and various US economists seemed ill-timed and likely to fail. Fortunately, after the onset of the crisis finance ministers from southern rim countries became increasingly knowledgeable as they weighed their countries' options. Finance Ministers Luis de Guindos from Spain, Vítor Gaspar from Portugal, and Yannis Stournaras from Greece were all first-class economists. They understood that the US plan would not work and that they needed other ideas on how to revive their sagging economies. The devaluation idea was chimerical.

9

Progress toward Fiscal Union

Until the spring of 2012, the discussions on bailout packages and euro-zone issues in Ecofin meetings had generally been peaceful—that is, if one did not count the occasional raised voice and finger-pointing by Austrian finance minister Maria Fekter (dubbed "The Witch of the South" by the German media) and the forceful comments by Finnish finance minister Jutta Urpilainen, when the subject of Greece's lack of progress with reforms was broached. These discussions took a decidedly different turn when the new Spanish finance minister, Luis de Guindos, joined Ecofin. He would lash out at any finance minister who dared to suggest that the new Spanish government was taking too much time to decide on the size of its bailout package. German finance minister Wolfgang Schäuble was especially insistent on quick action in Spain, pointing out that further delay would endanger the whole eurozone because the size of a delayed package could be larger than what the eurozone countries could afford. Tempers flared quickly anytime Spain was discussed.

And for good reason. The experience with the bailout packages had been disappointing. The packages had always been smaller than the markets needed, and each bailout announcement had helped only temporarily. It was also clear that the European Stability Mechanism (ESM) had insufficient funds to cover all of Spain's banking problems, let alone deal with those of Italy or France. Moreover, nothing we did in Ecofin seemed to calm investors long enough that we could focus on broader solutions such as the fiscal union or the single banking supervisor. We had to take a bigger step.

Fifth Tipping Point

And that step was taken on July 26, 2012, when European Central Bank (ECB) president Mario Draghi announced that the bank would do whatever was necessary to save the euro. That did the trick—it saved the eurozone. Whether it was Draghi's decision, or whether—as I suspect—he did it at the urging of Germany, the bank's move enabled European leaders to turn to broader solutions to the euro crisis such as a fiscal union. This, then, was the fifth tipping point in the euro crisis (see chronology of events at the back of the book).

On June 27, 2012, the new Spanish government led by Mariano Rajoy finally requested financial assistance from the eurozone. The request was a long time coming. Since January, we had devoted time at every Ecofin meeting to discussing what assistance Spain would need and when it would be appropriate to request this assistance. Jean-Claude Juncker and Schäuble thought it should be done immediately, whereas Luis de Guindos argued that his government needed to wait until the summer so that it had a better idea of the financing needs of the banking sector. However, the social situation in Spain was deteriorating—action was needed now.

On July 11, thousands of coal miners converged on Madrid to protest the reduction in mining subsidies. Dozens were injured as demonstrators clashed with police. Later that day, Prime Minister Rajoy announced an austerity budget that included €65 billion ($90 billion) in additional spending cuts and tax increases. Spain's value-added tax was raised 3 points, to 21 percent, and unemployment insurance payments and government wages were slashed. By the end of the second quarter of 2012, the unemployment rate had reached 26 percent (figure 9.1).

On July 20, 2012, the eurozone finance ministers agreed to give Spain the financial assistance it needed for the recapitalization of the country's financial institutions. The discussion then moved to Ecofin. We agreed that the funds would be channeled to the financial institutions in the Spanish Fund for Orderly Bank Restructuring. That decision seemed to have a calming effect on the markets for a day or two, and then they began to slide again because of doubt that the Spanish bailout was large enough to cover the bad assets in the banking sector.

This kind of doubt arose regularly during the euro crisis. The agreed-on packages would always be smaller than the markets wanted, and each bailout announcement would calm the waters only a few days before another panic started. The other reason for this uncertainty was the lack of a fund large enough to cover possible future bailouts. For example, it was clear to Ecofin ministers that the money in the ESM would barely cover an earnest bailout of the Spanish banking sector, not to mention the Italian or French banking sector. And with no solution in sight for possible calamities in the near future, no single decision, no matter how well designed, could calm investors. They needed to hear that the eurozone would be saved as a whole.

Figure 9.1 Quarterly unemployment rate in the eurozone, 2011–13

percent

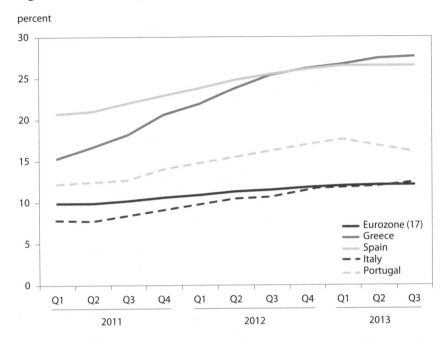

Source: Eurostat, http://epp.eurostat.ec.europa.eu/portal/page/portal/statistics/search_database (accessed on February 27, 2014).

By July 26, 2012, the crisis was getting out of control. That was when Mario Draghi, in the fifth tipping point in the crisis, announced that the ECB would do "whatever it takes" to keep the eurozone together. The markets gave a sigh of relief, and yields in the troubled European countries fell sharply. With Draghi's statement, investors became more comfortable buying bonds issued by the region's southern rim governments. Draghi's announcement was the single key act that saved the eurozone and changed the course of the crisis. Had he been more reticent, as Jean-Claude Trichet was before him, some eurozone members might have exited by the end of 2012. Draghi's determination made everyone more confident that the remaining issues could be resolved over time.

How much of this was Draghi's own doing and how much of it was a German decision (it was clear that Jörg Asmussen had a major role in it) I do not know. What I do know is that the ECB gained a lot of credibility and overnight became Europe's most trusted institution. This enhanced credibility would be useful later in the discussion of the banking union. And in my view, it explains why Ecofin shifted toward work on the banking union, thereby abandoning two years of effort on the fiscal union. For the banking union, it was clear who would play the major role—the ECB. That was another main turning point in the euro crisis.

Outright Monetary Transactions

On September 6, 2012, a month after Draghi's announcement, the ECB issued a description of the technical features of the Outright Monetary Transactions (OMT) program, which allowed unlimited bond purchases in secondary sovereign bond markets. Participation in the program was conditional on countries taking part in either a full European Financial Stability Facility (EFSF) program, a full ESM program, or a precautionary program. The OMT program applied to bonds with a maturity of one to three years.

The OMT program was similar to the quantitative easing programs of the US Federal Reserve. The Fed had implemented quantitative easing by buying financial assets from commercial banks and other private institutions, thereby increasing the monetary base. Brussels and Frankfurt had carefully watched the Fed programs since the launch of the first program in November 2008. Because that program was judged a success, the heads of state of the southern rim countries demanded a similar program in Europe. Apparently, however, the Fed's first program proved to be insufficient, and so it launched another round two years later, in November 2010. The second program began to raise doubts about diminished efficiency. Quantitative easing was presented as an unconventional tool for Fed policy. If it was continually needed, then it would become a standard monetary policy. But such a tool distorts market signals— for example, the interest rate becomes less meaningful. The launch of the Fed's third program of quantitative easing in September 2012, soon after Draghi's announcement, was not met with enthusiasm.

Sensing that the momentum had shifted, the European Commission decided to move quickly on other issues as well. At the next Ecofin meeting, in October, the financial transaction tax was put up for discussion again. An enhanced cooperation agreement, supported by 11 eurozone states representing more than 90 percent of eurozone GDP, was tabled. Austria, Belgium, France, Germany, Greece, Italy, Portugal, Slovakia, Slovenia, and Spain signed the agreement, but Finland, an early supporter, did not. Domestic politics had shifted since the first debates in the summer of 2010, and the True Finns Party had managed to change public opinion. The tax was now seen as one on disciplined countries and transactions in their markets—that is, a handout of sorts to undisciplined countries. This view was most strongly and consistently voiced by Czech president Vaclav Klaus, who also pointed to the Swedish experience in 1983–91 as a deterrent. Still, the agreement was approved by the European Parliament in December 2012, with a new expected start date of January 2014. It would soon run into difficulties, however.

The ECB's decisive actions changed the markets' sentiment, but left the issue of the already bankrupt Spanish banks to Spain's government. Simply buying its bonds would not help because the share of nonperforming loans was too high. The government would have to step in and manage the assets. For this reason, on November 28, 2012, Spain agreed to the terms of a bailout.

According to the European Commission, the bailout would allow three lenders—BFA-Bankia, NCG Banco, and Catalunya Banc—to become viable in the long term without continued state support. Their balance sheets would be reduced by 60 percent by 2017. The fourth, Banco de Valencia, would be sold to CaixaBank and would cease to operate independently.

Steps toward a Banking Union

With the immediate danger of a meltdown in Spanish banks past, Jean-Claude Juncker and Mario Draghi turned to the issues remaining around the earlier proposals on a single banking supervisor. On December 17, 2012, at the last Ecofin meeting of the year, we struck a deal with member states on the structure of the new banking supervisory agency. The aim in setting up a supervisor was to tighten oversight of the eurozone's 6,000 banks and to prevent a repeat of the financial crises that had hit Cyprus, Greece, Ireland, and Spain. Non-euro-area members could also sign up. Under a deal reached by eurozone leaders in June 2011, once the supervisor was fully set up by mid-2014, the ESM could start directly recapitalizing regional banks. That could break the link between the sovereign and bank crises that some countries were facing.

Michel Barnier, the EU internal markets commissioner who pushed the proposal through Ecofin, declared that the deal was the first fundamental step toward a real banking union that would restore confidence in eurozone banks and ensure the solidity and reliability of the banking sector. In reality, though, it was a first small step. The two accompanying reforms—the creation of a restructuring fund and a deposit guarantee fund—were too contentious. But without these, the banking union could not function. Supervision could be guided by officials in Frankfurt, but who would follow up on their recommendations? A single supervisor without a common restructuring mechanism would mean that the burden of dealing with banking troubles would once again fall on the national authorities.

And yet even German finance minister Wolfgang Schäuble acknowledged that this was an important beginning. Just as the adoption of the Fiscal Compact was the foundation for a future fiscal union, the agreement on the single banking supervisor laid the foundation for a future banking union. Together with the existing, albeit imperfect, monetary union, Europe now had the parts it needed for a true economic union—something that had not been achieved in the previous decades of European integration.

There were some reasons for optimism. The year 2012 was better than the preceding one, something that had not seemed possible at the midyear mark. Still, Chancellor Merkel's New Year's address was the soberest yet. "I know that many are also heading into the new 2013 with trepidation. And indeed, the economic environment next year will not be easier, but more difficult. That should not discourage us, but—on the contrary—serve as an incentive." She went on to say that "the European sovereign debt crisis shows us how important this balance is. The reforms we have agreed to are beginning to take effect. But we still need a lot of patience. The crisis is far from over."[1]

After a brief pause in January 2013, bad news started coming in from Portugal. Portugal's woes had been discussed many times at Ecofin in previous months, so the bad news was no surprise. Still, many of us—including me—thought that the actions of the ECB would stave off a crisis in Portugal. But perhaps these actions came a bit too late for Portuguese banks. In early February, the Portuguese government bailed out Banco Internacional do Funchal SA (Banif), its third largest bank, to the tune of €1.1 billion ($1.5 billion). Unemployment in Portugal had reached 18 percent by the end of 2012, and 240,000 people had left the country over the previous two years in search of work and a better life—mostly young, highly educated people fleeing to Switzerland, Brazil, or the oil-rich former Portuguese colony of Angola.

With little new on offer from the ECB, Germany decided to push forward with the idea of a fiscal union. I say Germany because by the time François Hollande's government began to work on eurozone issues, the Franco-German duo had ceased to strive for all-eurozone solutions. Perhaps French and German policymakers were simply too tired to do it on their own, or perhaps they got the message that the rest of the eurozone and of Ecofin did not think highly of their two-step approach: France and Germany would make a decision, and then the rest of us would rubberstamp it. By late 2012, Germany was the only leader in the eurozone.

> The main problem which we politicians are facing is that the public debt crisis in the Eurozone makes people and investors lose confidence in Europe. They do not understand why decisions in Europe take so long. But this is a constitutional element of Europe: Europe is complicated, and if decisions are taken with democratic legitimation, they simply take time. And the longer the crisis in the Eurozone lasts, the more people question whether the euro is worth all the rescue efforts—in terms of painful reform programs conducted by countries in trouble and in terms of credits guaranteed by taxpayers' money of "solid" countries.

These were the words of Wolfgang Schäuble, Germany's finance minister, in his speech to the European Parliament in September 2012. By February 2013, the southern rim countries were much more sympathetic to the idea of a fiscal union for two reasons. First, Greece, Italy, Portugal, and Spain had new political leaders, and they saw a benefit in further integration. Second, the new finance ministers from these countries were better qualified to negotiate within Ecofin the text of a future fiscal union.

---

1. Graeme Wearden, "Eurozone Live: Angela Merkel Warns Crisis Is 'Far from Over,'" *Guardian*, December 31, 2012.

Toward a Fiscal Union

The solution Schäuble proposed was pragmatic: build the fiscal union along-side the existing monetary union block by block. Three such blocks were built during my time as finance minister: the European semester, the Fiscal Compact, and the ESM.

European Semester

The European semester was a new procedure for coordinating national budgets within the European Union. It spanned the first six months of each year when, according to a timetable, member states would receive expert advice and then submit their national reform programs and stability or convergence programs for assessment in Brussels.

Member states also would receive individual recommendations on when to prepare their next year's budget, and, if necessary, recommendations on correcting macroeconomic imbalances. Countries that received financial assistance would not be required to submit stabilization programs or reviews on macroeconomic imbalances. They would only follow the prescribed measures in their adjustment programs.

The European semester focused on three types of policies: (1) structural reforms that brought about growth and employment; (2) fiscal reforms that were consistent with the goals of the Stability and Growth Pact; and (3) macro-economic reforms that prevented a country from entering the macroeconomic imbalance procedure. The European semester had its roots in 2011, when an attempt was first made to coordinate the different policies using one procedure. Prior to 2011, countries had submitted their lists of reforms only after their national budgets were approved, and so the European Commission was unable to recommend any changes.

The recommendations arising from the European semester were published in the *Annual Growth Survey* (European Commission 2013b). In the March 2013 survey, for example, the European Council advised countries to focus on five goals: (1) pursuing growth-friendly fiscal consolidation; (2) restoring normal lending to the economy; (3) promoting competitiveness; (4) tackling unemployment and the social consequences of the crisis; and (5) modernizing public administration.

For the second goal, restoring normal lending to the economy, possible steps included promoting new sources of capital such as issuing corporate bonds and facilitating access to venture capital funds. Another measure was to reduce payment delays by the public administration. In June 2012, the European Union introduced a directive on late payments that limited them to 30 days. In the banking sector, suggestions included protecting vulnerable households from individual changes in mortgage conditions, thereby avoiding a foreclosure and using project bonds as instruments to fund large infra-structure and transport facilities. For municipal projects and transnational infrastructure projects, countries could use the instruments available at the European Investment Bank.

The measures the European Commission proposed for achieving the third goal—promoting competitiveness—were limiting the tax burden on low-skilled labor and introducing subsidies for hiring new workers, especially the long-term unemployed or low-skilled. The Commission also recommended simplifying labor legislation and developing flexible working hours. In linking education to market needs, proposals included reducing the number of early school leavers and facilitating transition from school to work through the development of traineeships (Germany's vocational training in high schools was cited as worthy of study). Yet another proposal introduced a "youth guarantee" that would ensure work or the continuation of education for all those under 25 years of age. It was pointed out that some of these initiatives could be financed by the European Social Fund.

Countries could choose the ways in which to achieve these goals; the Commission would track implementation. In 2011 the Netherlands proposed establishing the position of European commissioner for budgetary discipline who would control the budgets of the member states. Germany supported the idea, but France and the United Kingdom did not, and it was shelved.

In January 2013, the idea resurfaced when the new head of the Eurogroup, Dutch finance minister Jeroen Dijsselbloem, announced that the European Commission would install a so-called European semester officer. The semester officer was intended to act as a watchdog over the national governments, without the status of commissioner.

Fiscal Compact

The second block was the Fiscal Compact. It is widely considered a symbol of German chancellor Angela Merkel's European austerity drive, but in fact it was not responsible for shaping fiscal policy in the eurozone. The Fiscal Compact treaty (formally, the Treaty on Stability, Coordination and Governance in the Economic and Monetary Union) was approved on March 2, 2012, by 25 EU states and entered into force in January 2013. It included many aspects of EU legislation already in place. Ratification by at least 12 eurozone members was required for it to take effect. Finland was the last one to do so, in December 2012.

The Fiscal Compact drew on the "golden rule" that Germany had enacted in its constitution in July 2009. New Article 109 of the German Constitution, besides reaffirming the budgetary autonomy of the Federation and the Länder, stated the general rule: "The budgets of the Federation and the Länder shall in principle be balanced without revenue from credits. The Federation and Länder may introduce rules intended to take into account, symmetrically in times of upswing and downswing, the effects of market developments that deviate from normal conditions, as well as exceptions for natural disasters or unusual emergency situations beyond governmental control and substantially

Figure 9.2 Total government spending in the eurozone, 1999–2012

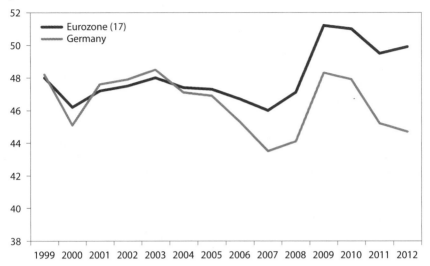

percent of GDP

Source: Eurostat, http://epp.eurostat.ec.europa.eu/portal/page/portal/statistics/search_database (accessed on February 27, 2014).

harmful to the state's financial capacity. For such exceptional regimes, a corresponding amortization plan must be adopted."

Such limits were useful at all times, but especially during crises when public spending in European countries typically increases. A longer-term trend of increasing expenditure was evident as well: Since introduction of the euro, 17 countries in the eurozone had seen government spending rise from €3.3 trillion ($4.6 trillion) to €4.7 trillion ($6.5 trillion) in current euros, or by nearly 40 percent. As a percentage of eurozone GDP, spending increased from 47 to 51 percent of GDP between 1999 and 2009 (figure 9.2).

And yet if one looked at Germany or Finland, the pattern was different. Between 2001 and 2010, government spending in Germany went up by 18.5 percent, from just over €1 trillion ($1.4 trillion) to €1.2 trillion ($1.7 trillion). As a result, the share of public expenditure to GDP remained roughly constant in Germany, despite the crisis and bank bailouts, aid to automakers, and wage increases for public employees. Government spending remained fairly high (48 percent of GDP), but in size it was the same share of GDP as it was in 2001. In Finland, spending actually decreased substantially as a share of GDP during the same period—by about 3 percentage points of GDP.

The data on Germany imply that in the rest of the eurozone without Germany public spending went up at a much faster pace, by 41.5 percent, between 2001 and 2010. This was an increase of 23 percentage points more than that in Germany. For that reason, Chancellor Merkel and Finance Minister

> **Box 9.1   New rules in the Fiscal Compact**
>
> First, eurozone member states had to commit to a budgetary position in "bal-
> ance or in surplus." They further had to pass a national law or an amendment
> of the national constitution that would limit the structural budget deficit to 0.5
> percent of GDP—a deviation was allowed only in "exceptional circumstances."
> This was similar to Article 115(2) of the German Constitution, which states that
> "[r]evenues and expenditures shall in principle be balanced without revenue
> from credits," and clarifies that "[t]his principle shall be satisfied when revenue
> obtained by the borrowing of funds does not exceed 0.35 percent in relation
> to the nominal [GDP]."
>
> The treaty allowed for a transition period, but its length was not specified.
> For countries with a debt-to-GDP ratio "significantly below 60 percent of GDP,"
> the structural budget deficit could be as high as 1 percent of GDP.
>
> Second, a member state could bring another member state before the Eu-
> ropean Court of Justice if it believed that the other state had not fulfilled the
> treaty provisions calling for passing a national "debt brake" into national law.
> For states found guilty, the court could impose a fine of up to 0.1 percent of
> GDP.
>
> Third, a new 1/20 rule allowed the opening of an excessive deficit procedure
> if countries with a debt-to-GDP ratio of more than 60 percent did not bring that
> ratio down quickly enough. The requirement was defined as an annual reduc-
> tion of the debt ratio by 1/20th of the difference between the actual debt-to-
> GDP ratio and the 60 percent threshold. In addition, countries were given a
> three-year grace period after the correction of their current deficit below the 3
> percent target before the 1/20 rule went into effect.

Schäuble insisted that the eurozone adopt the Fiscal Compact and its new
rules (see box 9.1).

The new Fiscal Compact among the euro countries was supposed to make
budget rules more binding by inserting them into laws and constitutions at
the national level. But biased forecasts could defeat budget rules, as had been
demonstrated repeatedly since the creation of the euro (Frankel and Schreger
2013). Penalties for inaccurate forecasts were considered during the discussions on the Fiscal Compact. In the end, however, this idea was dropped for two
reasons. First, the forecasts were typically done by independent agencies and
thus governments could not—at least directly—shoulder the blame. Second,
the errors were typically found several years after the forecast was made, so
fines could not be given on the spot.

Several governments quickly adopted the Fiscal Compact. The Spanish
government rushed a constitutional amendment through its parliament that
established a balanced budget requirement. New Article 135 of the Spanish
Constitution, which was approved in less than two weeks and entered into
force on September 27, 2011, affirms in its first two paragraphs that "all public
administrations will conform their actions to the principle of budgetary sta-

bility. The State and the Autonomous Communities shall not incur a structural deficit that exceeds the standard established by the European Union."

Spain did, however, make the "golden rule" of a balanced budget subject to an exception clause. Article 135(4) states: "The limits of the structural deficit and of the volume of public debt can only be exceeded in cases of natural catastrophes, economic recession or situations of extraordinary emergency beyond the control of the State which considerably endanger the financial situation or the economic and social sustainability of the State, to be assessed by the absolute majority of the members of the Chamber of Deputies."

Italy quickly adopted the prescriptions of the Fiscal Compact as well. The Constitutional Revision Act was signed into law on April 20, 2012. New Article 81 states: "The State ensures the balance between revenue and expenditures in its budget, considering the upswings and the downswings of the economic cycle. The State can resort to the emission of debt only with the purpose to consider the effects of the economic cycle and, upon authorization of the two chambers of Parliament adopted at the absolute majority of its members, in cases of exceptional events."

France was not as eager to adopt the Fiscal Compact. During his election campaign in 2011, François Hollande vowed to renegotiate the compact. A year later, in September 2012, Hollande, now president, explained his long-standing opposition to a constitutional amendment: "I do not consider that a commitment that is obligatory for a few years should be written in stone in our texts." These words notwithstanding, France amended its organic budget law and submitted it to parliament for approval, together with the Fiscal Compact, the EU stimulus package, and the ESM. All were approved in November 2012.

The Fiscal Compact was considered to be a building block of a future fiscal union. "The fiscal compact . . . can create and can be a necessary pre-condition but it will not be sufficient in itself to save the euro," Chancellor Merkel said in a televised interview on June 7, 2012. It could be viewed as an expansion of the Stability and Growth Pact, but primarily focused on debt sustainability. By contrast, the Stability and Growth Pact primarily dealt with the deficit.

European Stability Mechanism

The third building block was the ESM, Europe's permanent bailout fund. It has capital reserves of €700 billion ($970 billion), with €80 billion ($111 billion) in paid-in capital and the rest used as needed. Germany, France, Italy, and Spain contribute the majority of the capital because of their large GDPs. These payments are made periodically.

The ESM itself was authorized to approve bailout deals of up to €500 billion ($693 billion) when all of the paid-in capital is received. In situations in which relying on the public sovereign debt markets is prohibitively expensive, eurozone countries can instead obtain funding through this mechanism at a lower and more stable interest rate. Only countries that agreed to the Fiscal Compact may access the funds.

The €500 billion ($693 billion) ESM was declared operational on October 8, 2012, in Luxembourg. The birth of the fund was eased by the ECB's offer in August 2012 to buy bonds of fiscally struggling countries. This drove down interest rates in Spain and Italy and bought European governments time to address the root causes of the crisis.

The ESM has some advantages over the EFSF. The fact that it was established by treaty gives it legal security relative to the EFSF. The fact that the ESM has paid-in capital, rather than relying, like the EFSF, on contingent guarantees to underpin its lending, also adds to its credibility.

European Monetary Fund

In early 2010, when the bailout for Greece was discussed, German politicians first raised the possibility of creating a European Monetary Fund, an expanded version of the ESM serviced by a wider pool of experts. At the time, they thought that more cooperation was preferable to accepting intervention from the IMF, an option not accepted by Greek prime minister Georgios Papandreou. Such a new fund was also endorsed by President Nicolas Sarkozy—his most potent domestic political rival, Dominique Strauss-Kahn, was at the time managing the IMF. Perhaps Sarkozy believed that the creation of the European Monetary Fund would reduce the power of the IMF.

As German leaders saw it, the European Monetary Fund could also serve as a vehicle for imposing tougher sanctions on eurozone countries that defied the limits on debt. "Accepting help from the IMF would be an admission that the euro countries don't have the strength to solve their own problems," Jean-Claude Juncker told *Welt am Sonntag* in September 2010.

The idea was first suggested by Daniel Gros at the Centre for European Policy Studies in Brussels and Thomas Mayer, the chief economist of the Deutsche Bank in London (Gros and Mayer 2010). They proposed creating a fund with the power to, among other things, lend money to ailing eurozone members or guarantee their bonds and impose sanctions such as cutting off other forms of aid. When a government was in imminent danger of default, the fund would have the power to issue replacement debt. But it would impose a so-called haircut on investors, who would receive only a fraction of the face value of government bonds.

"We have agreed to create the beginnings of a European Monetary Fund," Sarkozy boasted. The move to do so did indeed mean that the EFSF would increasingly resemble the Washington-based IMF. It would be allowed to grant preemptive lines of credit to countries under pressure on the financial markets. It would also be allowed to assist in the recapitalization of stricken banks. Even Chancellor Merkel, who had long been opposed to the idea of a European Monetary Fund, admitted that "one could draw such a comparison" to the IMF.

In 2012 France, Germany, Italy, and Spain were among the European countries that jointly prepared a document that proposed establishing a European

Monetary Fund and urged EU member states to give up some of their national sovereignty in order to increase their solidarity in crisis situations. The report, prepared by Austria, Belgium, France, Germany, Italy, Luxembourg, the Netherlands, Poland, Portugal, and Spain, was sent to the European Commission, the ECB, the Eurogroup, and the European Council. The country concessions would include giving EU institutions the power to supervise national financial and budget policies, as well as ceding some autonomy to decide on economic policies related to the sustainability of the eurozone's economic and employment growth.

The ESM appeared to be a step toward a European Monetary Fund. However, it left several questions unanswered. First was its coverage. Jean-Claude Juncker had insisted that it be retroactive in cases of bank recapitalization. "There is a heavy question mark on the legacy from the past. Can the ESM recapitalize banks by retroactively applying the arrangements that it has, or must we limit the European mechanism's intervention to the new problems that arise? I have a personal point of view to express. I think we must ensure certain retroactivity for the mechanism; otherwise it loses a great part of its meaning."[2]

The issue was especially important for Ireland, which wanted the ESM to cover at least some of the huge debt overhang incurred when the government tried to save banks that were collapsing. It was relevant for Cyprus, Slovenia, and Spain as well. And perhaps over time for Italy.

The second question to be answered was the fund's size. From the outset, the Eurogroup and the IMF wanted a larger fund, as large as €750 billion ($1.04 trillion). The reason was the mounting banking problems in Spain, and the possibility, however remote, of having to aid Italy's banking sector. Germany balked at the need for a larger mechanism, but left open that possibility should the need arise. European Parliament president Martin Schulz, a Social Democrat from Germany, summarized the situation: "The euro backstop fund will be enlarged, whether Angela Merkel wants it or not. In the end, Angela Merkel is always prepared to take the necessary steps. But only in the end. It would be better if she were to take the necessary steps in the beginning."[3]

The establishment of the mechanism was met with stiff resistance from Germany, where many politicians believed they had already been asked to pay too much toward solving the debt crisis. A petition calling for creation of the ESM to be delayed until it was certain it would be subject to democratic control had attracted 37,000 signatures, and a German opposition party and conservative lawmaker had also filed complaints stating that the measure could be unconstitutional.

---

2. EPP TV, "Juncker Sees Difficult 2013, Backs More Flexible European Stability Mechanism," January 10, 2013.

3. Spiegel Online, "Juncker Piles on the Pressure: Merkel Stuck in the Euro Firewall Trap," February 29, 2012.

The German Constitutional Court in Karlsruhe overturned the challenges in September 2012 and ruled that the ESM could be signed into law. But it also imposed several restrictions. First, it set a maximum German contribution of €190 billion ($263 billion) that could not be raised without the approval of the government. Second, the ruling stated that there must be no unlimited liability. Chief Justice Andreas Vosskuhle declared, "The review has concluded that the laws that were challenged, with high probability, do not violate the constitution. Hence the motions for a temporary injunction were to be rejected."[4] The court also gave the go-ahead for a European fiscal treaty designed to force eurozone governments to exert budgetary discipline.

I am a supporter of a fiscal union in Europe; it may push the European Union into a true discussion of competitiveness. If member states were limited in their ability to adopt populist policies—that is, to spend money beyond their means—a focus on competitiveness would become necessary by default. Brussels, then, might decide to concern itself with productivity growth, something that has not been on the European agenda at all. So I view fiscal union as a path toward a more productive Europe. Various discussions with Jean-Claude Juncker, Wolfgang Schäuble, and Jörg Asmussen seemed to indicate that they had that idea in mind as well, but they did not disclose it for fear of further alienating the southern rim governments.

---

4. Matthew Sparkes, "German Constitutional Court Ratifies ESM with Conditions," *Telegraph*, September 12, 2012.

10

Banking Union

The personalities of European Central Bank (ECB) presidents Jean-Claude Trichet and Mario Draghi could not have been more different, at least in the ways they conducted themselves in Ecofin meetings. Trichet craved the spotlight. He was very active at the beginning of each meeting when the media were invited in to take pictures. Then he would read prepared statements, and after that he would fade into the role of passive observer. Often, he would leave the meeting within an hour or two of its opening. By contrast, his successor, Draghi, avoided the cameras, scribbled his talking points on bits of paper a few minutes before the meeting began, tossed out comments throughout the discussions, and stayed until the end—which was frequently in the wee hours of the morning.

I was able to observe the participation of both men at close range. In Ecofin meetings, we sat in alphabetical order by member country name. European Union institutions were assigned seats on the two short sides of the table. And so my neighbors were always the same: To my left was Jürgen Ligi, the Estonian finance minister, and to my right was Josef Pröll, and then his successor, Maria Fekter, the Austrian finance minister. To her right sat the president of the ECB, first Trichet and then, as of 2011, Draghi. At coffee breaks, we sometimes exchanged views, especially when Draghi came on board.

The differences in the personalities of Trichet and Draghi may explain their behavior when at the helm of the ECB. Trichet's methodical, cautious approach precluded quick decisions to address market sentiment. Draghi's more instinctive approach allowed decisive actions to tame the animal spirits of the financial markets. Overall, Draghi's approach seemed better suited for the euro crisis, especially in view of the indecisiveness of the president of the European Commission, Manuel Barroso.

Draghi Takes the Helm

Personality differences were likely also the reason the banking union began to take shape under Draghi's leadership. The idea was not new: In 2010 Germany had wanted the ECB to take on the role of single banking supervisor for the eurozone. The logic was that the euro deepened financial interdependence in Europe and so required integrated supervision. In fact, had such integrated supervision been applied earlier, it might have prevented the buildup of large private financial imbalances in some eurozone countries from 1999 to 2009. With Draghi at the helm of the ECB, the key eurozone politicians—in Berlin, Luxembourg, the Hague, and Paris—were confident that a banking union would finally emerge.

"The ECB's evolution to lender of last resort has blunted market pressure and political momentum," observed a eurozone analyst in May 2013.[1] Indeed, the euphoria surrounding the last days of December 2012 when European Commission president Barroso had outlined an ambitious program for centralized fiscal control in Brussels had quickly subsided. By late January 2013, European politicians were relying on the ECB to pull Europe out of the crisis.

Draghi's announcement in mid-2012 of unlimited liquidity reduced borrowing costs across the southern rim, especially in Italy and Spain. This development in turn allowed Spanish prime minister Mariano Rajoy to avoid a comprehensive aid package and instead focus on assistance for the Spanish banking sector. And it saved Italian prime minister Mario Monti's reputation. His government would likely go down in history as the one that brought Italy back from the brink of collapse. But in truth, the ECB deserved the most credit. Most of the Monti government initiatives died out in the Italian Parliament. And some did not even reach it.

By being decisive when everyone else was waffling, the ECB became Europe's most trusted institution. That reputation was quite different from the one the bank had early in the crisis under Trichet. Then, the ECB did not appear to be doing enough. In response to the global financial crisis that erupted in 2008, the ECB introduced liquidity support to banks in November of that year. That was the only measure taken by the ECB before the sovereign debt crisis blanketed Europe. One result of full allotment was that some of the banks addicted to ECB credit emerged (Eijffinger and Hoogduin 2012).

As noted earlier, the new leadership at the bank and the personalities that went with it made a big difference as well. Trichet had a roundabout way of saying things and would take cautious positions. He often looked tired and showed no resolve. Vítor Constâncio, vice president of the ECB since 2010, usually accompanied Trichet to Ecofin meetings, but he was not a straight talker either. When the new president, Mario Draghi, and Jörg Asmussen, a member of the Executive Board, took over, the atmosphere and energy in Ecofin shifted. Both men were sharp, tireless, and confident. Although much

---

1. Peter Spiegel, "Integration Put on Back Burner," *Financial Times,* May 9, 2013.

credit goes to Draghi, in Ecofin the more trusted figure was Asmussen. We had worked together earlier in his capacity as deputy finance minister. He was outspoken then, and he remained so in his new position as a member of the ECB's Governing Council. At Ecofin meetings, he never hesitated to give his opinion on difficult issues. But, more important, he had one quality few central bankers have—he was a genuinely likeable person. He knew everyone by name, and during coffee breaks and informal meetings, he was willing to talk to anyone. By contrast, during the Trichet era, the ECB representatives would stick together, or they would talk to French finance minister Christine Lagarde or German finance minister Wolfgang Schäuble, or to whoever was being followed by journalists' cameras. I doubt Trichet knew more than a quarter of the EU finance ministers by name. All these differences made an impression on incoming finance ministers, not just on me.

ECB Takes Center Stage

In 2010 resolving the euro crisis seemed a matter for the governments of the eurozone. At the outset of the Greek debt crisis, the ECB identified the underlying cause as excessive deficits and debts. But Trichet was also aware that no immediate remedy was available at the government level. The emergency fund, the European Financial Stability Facility, would not begin operations until much later, and it was going to take time to negotiate an EU-IMF program for Greece.

The creators of the eurozone had paid no attention to banking issues, and especially to the importance of national as opposed to EU-wide guarantees in the eurozone. In Europe, bank bailouts had caused sudden jumps in government debt, most notably in Ireland, where the government's assumption of bank debts abruptly added 40 points to the ratio of public debt to GDP. Belgium, Cyprus, the Netherlands, and Slovenia experienced such troubles as well.

The ECB Governing Council found itself in uncharted territory. It had to decide whether and how to intervene in government debt markets. This was no ordinary monetary policy decision. The fact that intervention intended to calm market turbulence could have been an argument for grounding it in financial stability considerations. But this was not in the ECB's mandate, and for that reason Trichet was indecisive.

Peter Praet, a member of the Executive Board of the ECB, explained the quandary in an April 2013 speech: "The standard monetary policy action was judged as insufficient because, during the crisis and especially from 2010 the interest rate channel of the monetary policy transmission mechanism was impaired. . . . In response to this challenge, the ECB engaged in a series of nonstandard measures to restore a proper transmission of the monetary policy impulses, including lending operations through a fixed rate tender procedure with full allotment, the provision of liquidity with longer maturity and an expansion of the set of assets that could serve as collateral for receiving central bank liquidity."[2]

As a further step, the ECB began to intervene directly in securities markets in order to correct the malfunctioning of certain segments. The first action of this type was the Securities Markets Programme launched in May 2010. The ECB argued that the program, which began to buy government debt in the secondary market, was intended to facilitate the homogeneous transmission of monetary policy.

In June 2010, Trichet told Ecofin that the Securities Markets Programme would be temporary. But as the crisis evolved, the program remained open. Governments did not take sufficient measures to end the market turbulence or to make it possible for the ECB to (gradually) exit the program. Early in the spring of 2011, tensions in the markets did lessen, and the size of the Securities Markets Programme stabilized at €70 billion to €75 billion ($97 billion to $104 billion). It began to look as though the program would die quietly, but then the crisis flared up again when Spain, and later Italy, came under pressure. The result was a very rapid increase in the size of the program to well above €200 billion ($277 billion).

The Securities Markets Programme strained relations between the southern rim governments and the ECB. Trichet became increasingly annoyed with those governments for not taking measures that would go to the root of the crisis. In fact, the ECB had to write governments to force them to take consolidation measures and implement structural reforms as a condition for eventually purchasing bonds. Trichet was clearly upset that politicians were turning more and more for solutions to the ECB. He wanted to run the institution as a conservative central bank and not burden it with unnatural responsibilities akin to expansionary fiscal policy.

When problems mounted again toward the end of 2011, there was resistance in the ECB Governing Council to accelerating purchases of government bonds under the Securities Markets Programme. The new president of the Bundesbank, Jens Weidmann, argued that this would not be compatible with the treaty creating the European Union. Draghi made the point to the Governing Council that governments first had to adopt the Fiscal Compact, which would minimize the risk of similar problems in the future. This was Trichet's view as well at the December 2011 Ecofin.[3]

After Ecofin announced the negotiations on the Fiscal Compact, the majority of the ECB Governing Council looked more favorably on taking additional action in the bond markets.[4] However, resistance by some council

---

2. Peter Praet, speech at the colloquium "The Challenges Ahead," Pioneer Investments' Colloquia Series "Redrawing the Map: New Risk, New Reward," Unicredit, Beijing, April 17, 2013.

3. Mario Draghi, "The Euro, Monetary Policy and the Design of a Fiscal Compact," Ludwig Erhard Lecture, Berlin, December 15, 2011.

4. Mario Draghi, "Remarks at the Annual Reception of the Association of German Banks," Berlin, March 26, 2012.

members against further increasing the Securities Markets Programme had not disappeared. In Germany, there was strong, broad opposition outside the Bundesbank to the program.

As uncertainty kept building after a quiet summer, the ECB took action. In October 2011, Trichet announced two long-term refinancing operations with three-year maturity. The ECB also allowed seven national central banks to accept a wider range of collateral against its refinancing operations. These combined measures led to an injection of liquidity in the European banking sector of over €1 trillion ($1.4 trillion).

At first, it was unclear why the ECB announced two long-term refinancing operations. And why it did choose maturity of three years and not of one? Also, why did the ECB not introduce a cap to remain in control of its own balance sheet? The rapidly worsening market situation at the time provided the answers: The ECB wanted to stop once and for all any speculation that it would not defend the European banking sector. Its action had just put a premium on maturities that were longer than the market had become used to. Eventually, market turbulence disappeared, and the risk premia of Spain and Italy came down. More generally, the eurozone entered a period of relative calm.

Because refinancing operations had been undertaken successfully elsewhere, Draghi was able to benefit from that experience when he took office on November 4, 2011. Both the US Federal Reserve and the Bank of England had created large asset purchase programs. The Fed bought assets to increase the overall expansionary stance of monetary policy and to turn around the reduced flow of credit to housing markets. The Bank of England was also buying assets in an attempt to improve the flow of credit to businesses. As Draghi explained, "What we saw is that after the first [longer-term refinancing operation] the senior unsecured bond market reopened. In the last two months we had something like €40 billion of new issuance, which is about as much as it was in the previous six months or more. We also saw €30 billion in new covered bond issuance. But for the interbank markets to function we need a return of full confidence in the counterparty. We can address only the liquidity side of the problem. But then growth prospects have to pick up."[5]

By acting decisively, the ECB reduced pressure on eurozone governments to increase their emergency funds. An alternative would have been a further increase in the Securities Markets Programme. The program was addressing the problem of sovereign debt at its roots without involving the banking system and without causing the related spillover effects. But that approach was judged to be an insufficient signal to markets.

On December 21, 2012, Draghi announced the results of the ECB's intervention: Troubled banks had received €490 billion ($679 billion) as part of the program. In the weeks that followed, the banks used a sizable share of the cash

---

5. Brian Blackstone, Matthew Karnitschnig, and Robert Thomson, "Q&A: ECB President Mario Draghi," *Wall Street Journal*, February 23, 2012.

to buy the European bonds so desperately in need of customers. It was as if the ECB had injected lenders with infinite liquidity and then asked them to flood the markets.

This determination was applauded by Adam Posen, at the time a member of the Bank of England's monetary policy committee. A scholar on what is often called Japan's lost growth, he argued that the US Federal Reserve and the ECB were making the same monetary policy mistakes that left Japan's economy stagnant for two decades starting in 1990. "The Austrians would say you just have to suffer through it," Posen was quoted as saying, referring to a school of economic thought popularized by Friedrich Hayek and Ludwig von Mises. "But suffering is not good for the soul—monetary policy won't solve all your problems, but it can make things easier."[6]

Under its previous president, Trichet, the ECB had long resisted more aggressive action, unwilling to saturate the market with money (the way the Fed did in 2008) until governments committed to reining in spending and deregulating their economies. According to Jacob Kirkegaard, a research fellow at the Peterson Institute for International Economics in Washington, "By refusing to act decisively at an early stage, they in a sense perpetuated the crisis, creating a situation where in the end the euro-area politicians had no other choice than to do the right thing."[7]

In the meantime, market sentiment shifted again after the summer of 2012, and stability evaporated. On September 6, 2012, the ECB announced it would be undertaking an Outright Monetary Transactions (OMT) program in secondary markets for sovereign bonds in the eurozone. This was the "whatever it takes to preserve the euro" that ECB president Mario Draghi had promised on July 26. Back then, at the Global Investment Conference in London, Draghi had remarked: "Within our mandate, the ECB is ready to do whatever it takes to preserve the euro. And believe me, it will be enough."[8] As noted in chapter 9, this was the fifth tipping point in the euro crisis.

The OMT program called for interventions in government bonds whose remaining maturity was up to three years. It required the governments to accept an arrangement involving support by the European Stability Mechanism (ESM), but stiff conditions would be applied. Such conditions were important to preserve monetary policy independence. Interventions would be ex ante unlimited, which was essential to ensure their effectiveness. They also would be sterilized to ensure that these measures would have no effect on the overall monetary policy stance. Finally, there would be transparency because the stock

---

6. Landon Thomas, "From an American in London, Global Warnings," *New York Times*, September 17, 2011.

7. Quoted in Nicholas Kulish, "Central Bank Becomes an Unlikely Hero in Euro Crisis," *New York Times*, January 20, 2012.

8. Mario Draghi, speech at the Global Investment Conference, London, July 26, 2012.

of securities acquired under the OMT program would be published regularly, together with the average duration.

Draghi Calls for Structural Reforms

Draghi's tactics worked for six months, until the Cyprus crisis erupted. On March 14, 2013, during a meeting of the European Council, Draghi made a presentation to the heads of state and government on the economic situation in the eurozone. His intent was to lay out the reasons for the crisis. He presented two graphs that showed that productivity growth in the surplus countries (Austria, Belgium, Germany, Luxembourg, and the Netherlands) was higher than in the deficit countries (France, Greece, Ireland, Italy, Portugal, and Spain). But wage growth was much faster in the latter group. The lesson: Structural reforms and wage moderation are the keys to success.

Instead, the southern rim heads of state asked the ECB for funding for their real economies—that is, the part of their economies actually producing goods and services. In addressing this request, the ECB could have emulated the Bank of England's scheme in which the access of banks to central bank credit was contingent on how much they then lent to the real economy. The Bank of England's program, introduced in June 2012, allowed banks to borrow up to 5 percent of their existing lending stock at funding costs well below market rates for even the strongest institutions.

The bank's scheme was not a total success, however.[9] It had cut about a percentage point off the deposit rates banks were offering. And there was no boom in lending. In fact, UK credit availability probably would have contracted significantly without the Bank of England's scheme. And that was enough of an incentive for the ECB to push credit into Europe's struggling economies.

A broader proposal, following the call for greater involvement by the ECB, was for the ECB to expand its focus from inflation targeting to output targeting. This notion was supported by French president François Hollande and some of the heads of state of the southern rim countries. Among the measures proposed for macroeconomic supervision by the ECB was a system of progressive reserves on bank loans based on the sector and on the supervision of individual banks. A sector-based reserve requirement could channel funds to those sectors considered important for economic development. Adjusting the reserve requirements to individual banks would make them better match each bank's situation (Richter and Wahl 2011).

The German position, however, was that the ECB should retain its narrow mandate. As Jens Weidmann, the head of the Bundesbank, told Reuters in March 2013, "We must be careful not to further blur the borders between monetary and fiscal policy."[10]

---

9. Alen Mattich, "BOE Offers Lending Template to ECB," *Wall Street Journal*, April 8, 2013.

10. Reuters, Eva Kuehnen and Paul Carrel, "Euro Woes Not Over, Says Crisis-Wary Bundesbank," March 12, 2013.

ECB: Eurozone's Banking Supervisor?

One idea that Germany did like was assigning the role of single eurozone banking supervisor to the ECB. Such a move was also consistent with the prevailing model in European countries of entrusting banking supervision to the central bank. For that reason, the EU treaty had included the possibility of giving supervisory powers to the ECB.

This thinking had its roots in the earliest days of the eurozone. In 1999 Tommaso Padoa-Schioppa, a member of the first ECB board responsible for financial stability, wrote: "I am convinced that in the future the needs will change and the multilateral mode will have to deepen substantially. Over time such a mode will have to be structured to the point of providing the banking industry with a true and effective collective euro area supervisor. It will have to be enhanced to the full extent required for banking supervision in the euro area to be as prompt and effective as it is within a single nation."[11]

The eurozone single banking supervisor is one of several components of a functioning banking union. In a speech at Chatham House in March 2013, Vítor Constâncio, vice president of the ECB, listed the components: (1) a single rulebook for banks; (2) a single framework for banking supervision; (3) a single mechanism for dealing with troubled banks funded by levies on the sector itself; (4) a common backstop in case temporary fiscal support is needed; and (5) a common system for deposit protection.[12]

I take the view that a banking union could have prevented the buildup of large private financial imbalances in some eurozone countries from 1999 to 2009 (figure 10.1)—the increase in private borrowing was made possible by declining interest rates as a result of the monetary union. In fact, the largest imbalances were concentrated in lending to private business. Between 1999 and 2008, the ratio of public sector debt to GDP in the eurozone declined on average by about 6 percentage points, while the ratio of private sector debt to GDP increased by 28 percentage points. At the extreme, in Spain the ratio of private sector debt to GDP increased by about 75 percent, while the ratio of public debt to GDP fell by 35 percent (figure 10.2).

A banking union would also eliminate the so-called bank-sovereign loop that endangered the fiscal sustainability of countries, most recently Cyprus and earlier Ireland and Spain. This vicious cycle was driven by the expectation that governments would have to bail out struggling banks. A Single Resolution Mechanism, the third component of a full banking union as described by Constâncio, would avoid these increases by dealing with troubled banks rather than saving them and by having the private sector instead of the taxpayer pick

---

11. Tommaso Padoa-Schioppa, "EMU and Banking Supervision," lecture at the London School of Economics, February 24, 1999.

12. Vítor Constâncio, speech at the conference "Financial Regulation: Towards a Global Regulatory Framework?" Chatham House City Series, London, March 11, 2013.

Figure 10.1   Private debt in Portugal, Italy, Greece, and Spain, 1999–2012

percent of GDP

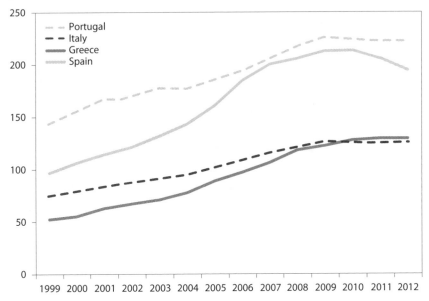

Source: Eurostat, http://epp.eurostat.ec.europa.eu/portal/page/portal/statistics/search_database (accessed on February 29, 2014).

up the bill. Moreover, the residual fiscal burden would be on the eurozone through the ESM.

Finally, a banking union would limit financial fragmentation in the eurozone. A single banking supervisor conducting credible stress tests would erase fears that banks are hiding bad assets in some countries. Depositors' confidence would grow by harmonizing deposit guarantee schemes, thereby discouraging Europeans from moving money from one bank to another based on their beliefs about the soundness of national supervision. This was a point made consistently by Schäuble as a main benefit of a banking union.

By early 2013, some progress had already been made on a banking union. For example, a single rulebook for banks was in place. The creation of a common backstop was already under way as well, with the possibility of direct bank recapitalization by the ESM. This was something on which Eurogroup president Jean-Claude Juncker had insisted. Work on a single mechanism for resolving banks and a common deposit guarantee scheme was still in the early stages, however.

The surprise levy on Cypriot bank deposits as part of the country's bailout in March 2013 gave an additional boost to the belief that Europe should be united in tackling bank problems. "The deeply distressing problems faced by

Figure 10.2　Public versus private sector debt in Spain, 1999–2008

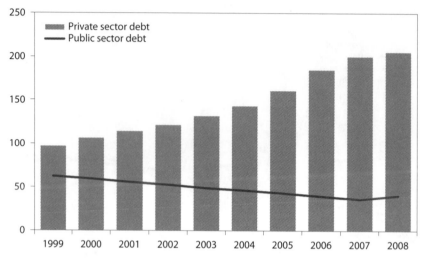

percent of GDP

Source: Eurostat, http://epp.eurostat.ec.europa.eu/portal/page/portal/statistics/search_database (accessed on February 27, 2014).

Cyprus show how insufficient this bailout step is in itself," said Martin Schulz, the German president of the European Parliament, calling for an EU-wide scheme to close failing banks and guarantee deposits.[13]

Sixth Tipping Point

In considering a banking union, Ecofin had made the most progress in putting in place a single banking supervisor. On December 14, 2012, Ecofin approved the appointment of such a supervisor, and the decision was confirmed by the heads of state immediately. This, the sixth tipping point in the eurozone crisis, wiped out any remaining doubts that European politicians were really united in strengthening the euro. The reform required governments to yield control over the supervision of national banks to the ECB in April 2014, or one year after the legislation entered into force after adoption by the European Parliament, whichever came later. And yet Sweden, the United Kingdom, and other non-euro-area countries had safeguards in place to check the power of the ECB and to maintain some influence over the technical standards applied to all EU banks.

---

13. John O'Donnell and Claire Davenport, "ECB Wins Watchdog Role under Cloud over Cyprus Deposit Levy," Reuters, March 19, 2013.

In its new role, the ECB would have direct responsibility for banks with assets of more than €30 billion ($42 billion) or those representing more than a fifth of a state's national output. This definition covered about 150 banks. Another rule called for every eurozone country to have at least three banks directly supervised from Frankfurt, where the ECB had its headquarters. However, the ECB retained the power to intervene in any bank and deliver instructions to national supervisors. Malta's finance minister, Tonio Fenech, objected to the three-bank rule, arguing that virtually the whole banking sector of Malta would be supervised by the ECB. Some other small countries such as Lithuania made the same point. In the end, Malta was exempted from the rule with a special clause.

The much-discussed cutoff of €30 billion made sense. Although the eurozone had over 6,000 banks (much like the United States), the 150 largest banks covered 80 percent of banking system assets. For the rest, delegating them to national authorities was both necessary and useful. Schäuble was particularly animated in all the discussions about the need for a cutoff. Otherwise, the new authority would simply be clogged with work and quickly labeled ineffective. Jürgen Ligi, the Estonian finance minister, supported the same view.

The ECB was also given the task of creating a board of supervisors, made up of one bank supervisor from each supervised country. This board would make decisions on bank supervision that could be vetoed or approved, but not changed, by the ECB Governing Council. The Governing Council, made up of the central bank governors of the eurozone member countries and members of the ECB Executive Board, sets the monetary policy for the eurozone.

A clause inserted into the text creating the single banking supervisor allowed the ECB to take over supervision of a lender at the request of the ESM, the eurozone bailout fund. This paved the way for an emergency injection of capital, but it would require unanimous approval.

Eurozone countries eventually dropped objections to George Osborne's (and thus the United Kingdom's) demands for a "double majority" principle at the European Banking Authority, the EU agency responsible for coordinating the work of national supervisors. Osborne's views were supported in various Ecofins by Maria Fekter, the Austrian minister, and Luc Frieden, the Luxembourg minister. I also chimed in on this issue. This principle ensured that any European Banking Authority decisions were at least approved by a plurality of EU countries outside the banking union—that is, noneurozone countries.

A showdown between big and small countries over the voting arrangements for setting regulations within the banking union emerged as the final outstanding issue. Luxembourg and Austria led objections to scrapping the ECB's one-country, one-vote principle in favor of weighted votes that gave France and Germany greater clout. I was also very active in the discussions, supporting the written views of the Bulgarian National Bank. The final compromise involved combining both voting procedures so that a simple majority and a weighted majority would be required for any decision.

In the negotiations for establishing the single banking supervisor, the ECB insisted that it begin operations by reviewing the participating banks' balance sheets. The objective of this review was to identify past problems and start with a system that avoided reputational risks for the single banking supervisor in the future. Germany supported this proposal, and it was accepted over the objections of several eurozone members such as France and Spain. These countries feared that the review might result in fiscal obligations if impaired assets had to be written down.

The single banking supervisor was open to the participation of all EU countries, including those that had not adopted the euro. At the December 2012 Ecofin, I recounted why a noneurozone country like Bulgaria was interested in participation. The single banking supervisor, and the accompanying single rulebook, would unify supervisory and regulatory practices across Europe, and participation of Bulgarian banks in the system would boost confidence in them as well. Here my views differed from those of the governor of the Bulgarian National Bank. He argued that countries like Bulgaria that had undergone banking crises (for Bulgaria, in 1997–98) had gained significant supervisory expertise and were better off supervising themselves. That point was also made forcefully by former Polish finance minister and central bank governor Leszek Balcerowicz. But what I feared was an imbalance between Bulgarian-owned banks and banks owned by eurozone financial institutions. If Bulgaria opted out of the single banking supervisor, would Bulgarian-owned banks be stigmatized?

Based on my experience with the European semester and analysts in Brussels, I knew Frankfurt-based single banking supervision would take a long time to develop. So it was a reasonable position that for a decade or so national authorities would be in a better position to supervise their own banks. Cooperation would be ongoing between Frankfurt and Sofia, but supervision would be stricter, not more lax, if carried out by Bulgarian experts. By January 2013, I was defending this position.

Putting the Final Touches on the Single Banking Supervisor

In March 2013, the European Parliament approved the European Council's texts on the single banking supervisor with some hotly disputed changes. Most arguments were over the appointment of top officials at the new single supervisor. For example, how would the European Parliament ensure that women were given a fair chance to be board members? The ECB had a dismal record in that area. Martin Schulz, the president of the European Parliament, insisted on having a say in appointments. Draghi was at first incredulous and then indignant. At some point, a humorous counterproposal even emerged: "You appoint our governors, and we would have a say in appointing the leadership of the European Parliament." In the end, a compromise was reached: The European Parliament would have the right to approve the ECB's candidates for chairman and deputy chairman of the supervisory board.

With these final decisions, the single banking supervisor finally took shape. In my view, progress on the details was so brisk because the ECB had won the day in 2012 and now enjoyed a reputation among politicians as the most trusted institution in Europe. Draghi and Asmussen were enjoying their high credibility standings as well. The ECB could handle building a single banking supervision capacity, whereas the European Commission was not viewed so kindly—the majority of Ecofin ministers had misgivings about the capacity of Commission staff to handle a fiscal union.

But just when the preliminary work on the single banking supervisor seemed to be finally done, there was a surprise—this time from Washington. In April 2013, during the World Bank/IMF spring meetings, German finance minister Wolfgang Schäuble and the head of the Bundesbank, Jens Weidmann, caught people off-guard by saying that the European Union should move ahead with the treaty changes they believed were needed to create a banking union for the eurozone. Schäuble argued that although current EU law would allow the ECB to act as a single banking supervisor, setting up a new single resolution authority to restructure or wind up failed banks would require changes to the EU treaties. That process would take years because the revised treaties would have to be ratified by 28 member state parliaments.[14]

I was in Washington at the time and listened to Schäuble's arguments. He had made this point in Ecofin meetings, and he was also among the ministers most actively pursuing an agreement on the single banking supervisor. I thought that, in the end, he had accepted the agreement with its limits on which banks the new authority could supervise. The day of the Schäuble-Weidmann press conference I met Jörg Asmussen in the street and asked whether he was surprised. No, he said. He had worked with both of them and knew their views. Perhaps they were simply being cautious to ensure that unreasonable expectations were not tied to the role of the single banking supervisor.

Asmussen's view was consistent with Schäuble's later explanation. "The German government is willing to change the treaties: the sooner, the better," he pointed out. "Banking union only makes sense . . . if we also have rules for restructuring and resolving banks. But if we want European institutions for that, we will need a treaty change."[15]

To allay Germany's concerns, the ECB offered a gradual plan within days. Asmussen, who was a member of the ECB Executive Board, commented: "In our view this should be dealt with swiftly, since we want to have the bail-in instruments available in 2015, not in 2018."[16]

---

14. For a view of the transitional path toward a full banking union, see Nicolas Véron, "Europe's Banking Union: Possible Next Steps on a Bumpy Path," VoxEU.org, July 12, 2012.

15. Peter Spiegel, "Schäuble Warns EU Bank Rescue Agency Needs Treaty Changes," *Financial Times*, May 12, 2013.

16. Annika Breidthardt, "ECB's Asmussen Wants Single Bank Supervision, Resolution Next Year," Reuters, May 14, 2013.

Treaty changes for a single resolution authority could come later. The policy experts agreed (Véron 2013); the limitations of the treaties did not prevent the establishment of the Single Supervisory Mechanism. Until the treaties could be revised, the ECB would review the banks to come under its supervision and analyze their condition before taking charge of them.

The leaders of southern rim countries argued against such a gradual approach. On May 13, 2013, for example, the prime ministers of Spain and Portugal demanded that the eurozone speed up efforts to create a banking union and complained that credit was frozen in their countries, preventing economic growth and crucial job creation. Many banks were lending at high rates because they were worried about the weak economy. "The money from the banking system isn't getting to the businesses or into the economy," argued Portugal's prime minister, Pedro Passos Coelho.[17]

The German response was swift. "We should not make promises we cannot keep," Schäuble told the *Financial Times* the next day, proposing that Europe first rely on cooperation between national agencies.[18] "Current treaties don't give enough foundation for a European restructuring authority," Schäuble argued. "You can do the same thing very well with a network of national authorities."

Banking Union: A Work in Progress but How Long?

The truth is that no one was prepared for the banking union. Realistically, establishing it would take a decade. For one thing, the ECB does not have enough qualified people; it would have to go on a hiring binge. But because such capacity exists primarily in the national banking authorities, that would mean hiring people away from central banks. For another, just as in a fiscal union, it is not at all obvious that central supervision is superior to national supervision. Bulgaria, for example, has had a strong banking supervisor since the 1997 banking crisis and the creation of the currency board. What guarantees are there that the supervisors in Frankfurt would be as good? And then there is the fact that some countries such as Bulgaria and Poland have fully paid-in guarantee funds in case of bank distress. Other countries have no such funds. Establishing a common fund would mean pooling the assets of existing funds with the nonexistent assets of other countries. Understandably, that would not work.

The first steps toward a banking union will be taken after November 2014, the new date at which the ECB will assume its role as the Single Supervisory Mechanism after examining the balance sheets of the 130 largest eurozone banks. ECB analysis suggests that a period of restructuring in the European banking sector will follow, especially by means of mergers and acquisitions.

---

17. Associated Press, "Spain, Portugal Demand Quick Action on Bank Union," May 13, 2013.

18. Quentin Peel, "Schäuble Calls for Closer EU Integration," *Financial Times*, May 17, 2013.

Such restructuring would make European banks more competitive vis-à-vis their US and Asian competitors.

In the meantime, the discussion about a centralized banking supervisor versus a network of national supervisors continues. In November 2013, ECB president Mario Draghi sent a letter to the heads of EU institutions arguing that "a single mechanism is better placed to guarantee optimal resolution action than a network of national resolution authorities. Co-ordination between national resolution systems has not proved sufficient to achieve the most timely and cost-effective resolution decisions, particularly in a cross-border context."[19] Draghi's letter also suggested there was no need for treaty changes to create a strong, centralized authority.

My view of the actions of the ECB changed over time. In 2009 and 2010, I questioned the refusal of ECB president Jean-Claude Trichet to assist the Baltic banking systems, as well as the Hungarian and Romanian banks, in the same way that the ECB had poured money into southern rim countries. Had Trichet been more decisive, the crisis in these countries would have been less severe. In 2011, when Trichet began to emulate the actions of Federal Reserve chairman Ben Bernanke in the United States, it seemed too late. And it stood in the way of undertaking genuine structural reforms in countries such as Greece and Italy. The chronic hesitation of European politicians to undertake reforms just made the crisis worse and closed many policy options that would have been useful if implemented at the onset of the crisis. Had the ECB not intervened as strongly as it did in late 2011 and then in 2012, the eurozone would have lost some of its members. And so in the end the ECB did the right thing. But it took Mario Draghi and Asmussen to do it. The United States had the right decision makers all along: Ben Bernanke and Obama administration economic advisor Lawrence Summers.

---

19. Peter Spiegel, "ECB on Collision Course with Germany on Banking Union," *Financial Times*, November 8, 2013.

11

Fiascos in Cyprus and Slovenia and the Bumpy Road to Reform

With Cyprus heading toward bankruptcy, Ecofin spent late February 2013 discussing various rescue options. It was obvious, however, that the northern eurozone countries were in no mood for compromises. They wanted to make an example of Cyprus so that France, Italy, and Spain would take note. The previous president of Cyprus had dragged the rescue talks out for over a year, hoping that either the eurozone would soften its stance on needed reforms, or that he would not have to deal with it after the elections. Because President Nicos Anastasiades's opponent had been leading in the polls by nearly 30 percent for much of the election campaign, there was no reason for the government to hurry up. That further angered the eurozone negotiating team, and so when the time came to lay down conditions they let it rip.

Cyprus: A Country in Peril

Cyprus had suffered collateral damage from the Greek crisis because most Cypriot banks held Greek government bonds and were exposed to Greek corporate loans as well. But instead of dealing with the Greek crisis fallout head on, Cyprus's communist government cooled its heels for much of 2011 and 2012, perhaps hoping that the presence of Russian offshore accounts would make it easier to obtain a bailout. When it became apparent that this approach would not work, elections were on the horizon. The outcome of these delays was exacerbation of the initial banking problems, with problems spilling over to the public finances.

The March 2013 Ecofin had a single focus: Cyprus. On March 16, 2013, Cyprus became the fifth eurozone country to receive a bailout. The money, €10 billion ($14 billion), was needed to recapitalize its banking system, but in return Cyprus had to introduce a series of drastic measures that would hit the country's savers. Under the terms of the deal, they would sacrifice up to 10 percent of their deposits to raise €6 billion ($8 billion) in additional revenue for the government. Bank deposits of more than €100,000 ($138,600) would be hit with a 9.9 percent one-off levy. For deposits under that threshold, the levy would drop to 6.75 percent.

Three days later, on March 19, members of Cyprus's Parliament rejected the bailout terms. Cyprus then turned to Russia for help, and Cypriot finance minister Michalis Sarris spent a week in Moscow, meeting with Russian government officials. Sarris had become the finance minister just two weeks earlier, replacing Vassos Shiarly, who had presided over Ecofin for the second half of 2012 as part of the rotating presidency. Sarris came to the finance ministry from the Cyprus Popular Bank, also known as Laiki Bank, where he was chairman. The new government under President Anastasiades was hoping that the large deposits by Russian citizens in Cypriot banks would convince the Russian authorities that they should help find a solution to Cyprus's banking problems. Sarris knew his Russian counterparts from his tenure at Laiki Bank and must have hoped that his contacts would help. But nothing came of it.

Seventh Tipping Point

On March 21, the European Central Bank (ECB) increased the pressure on Cyprus by warning that it would cut off the country's emergency liquidity assistance in a few days unless a European Union–International Monetary Fund (EU-IMF) program was in place. This warning was ironic; in the preceding years the troubled Laiki Bank had received more than €9 billion ($12.5 billion) from the Central Bank of Cyprus, which several times had assured the ECB that Laiki was solvent and that the ECB had no reasons to worry.

The ECB's tough stance could be attributed to German electoral politics. Chancellor Angela Merkel's main opposition, the Social Democratic Party, had identified Cyprus as a wedge issue that it could use to challenge her in the September 2013 elections. The party would simply paint Merkel as too lenient with shady Russian oligarchs and their "black money" held in Cypriot banks. The bluff failed, however, because German finance minister Wolfgang Schäuble held firm on tough conditions against unsecured creditors in Cyprus.

The seventh, final tipping point came on March 25, 2013, when the Eurogroup, European Commission, ECB, and IMF agreed on a €10 billion ($14 billion) bailout for Cyprus. It safeguarded small savers, while inflicting heavy losses on uninsured depositors, including wealthy Russians. And it kept the country in the eurozone. However, Laiki Bank, the nation's second largest bank, would be shut as part of the deal. The cut on uninsured depositors was expected to raise €4.2 billion ($6 billion). Meanwhile, the Bank of Cyprus, the island's largest lender, survived, but investors not protected by the €100,000 ($138,600) deposit guarantee would suffer a major haircut—a loss on the value of their investment on the order of 60 percent.

The European Union was moving toward putting more burdens on bond-holders and fewer on taxpayers. That approach was directed as much at Cyprus as at Slovenia, Spain, and other countries that might fall into further difficulties. The contrast with the approach taken in Ireland was obvious. There, taxpayers footed the whole bill.

Severe capital controls were imposed as well. The restrictions—the first ever imposed in the eurozone—included a daily cash withdrawal limit of €300 ($416) and a cap of €1,000 ($1,386) in cash for people leaving the country. But in an attempt to kick-start spending, the finance ministry eased some of the restrictions, including raising the daily business transaction limit not requiring Central Bank of Cyprus approval from €5,000 ($7,000) to €25,000 ($35,000) and allowing people to make check payments of up to €9,000 ($12,500) a month.

Dijsselbloem Speaks His Mind

Jeroen Dijsselbloem, the Dutch president of the Eurogroup of finance ministers, explained this hard-line approach to bank rescue by suggesting a new doctrine that would put the full burden of future bank restructuring on creditors and depositors rather than taxpayers. "Where you take on the risks you must deal with them, and if you can't deal with them then you shouldn't have taken them on," he warned.[1] He later retracted his comments, but the message was clear: Northern EU members would no longer bail out southern members without private shareholders and investors taking part in the rescue.

The Cyprus bailout involved restructuring the financial sector, with the domestic banking sector reaching the European Union's average indicators by 2018. Pressure mounted and on April 2, Cypriot finance minister Michalis Sarris resigned after less than five weeks on the job. The minister, a former World Bank official who negotiated Cyprus's euro membership in 2008, had come under strong criticism for his handling of the bailout talks. He was thought to have a serious conflict of interest, defending the interests of large Russian bank account holders over those of the Cypriot holders.

Cyprus continued to occupy the headlines for a few weeks, but room eventually had to be made for the bad news coming in from other southern rim countries as well. On April 5, 2013, the Portuguese Constitutional Court struck down a significant part of the government's austerity program. In particular, it ruled against the proposed cuts in holiday bonuses for civil servants and pensioners, as well as against other cuts that would have trimmed the budget by €1.3 billion ($1.8 billion) in order to meet the tough targets set by international lenders. Left with little room to maneuver, Prime Minister Pedro Passos Coelho said the ruling forced him to find further savings. The labor unions immediately called a general strike, saying education and health services were

---

1. Nicolas Véron, "With Cyprus, Europe Risks Being Too Tough on Banking Moral Hazard," *Financial Times*, March 18, 2013.

already in a perilous state after several rounds of cuts since 2008. The same day, Miguel Relvas, the minister for parliamentary affairs and a close advisor to Prime Minister Passos Coelho, resigned amidst allegations that he obtained a political science degree from Lisbon's Universidade Lusófona in only one year, 2007.

On April 14, 2013, Cyprus received the first tranche of the bailout money. It was agreed that Cyprus would have an extra two years, until 2018, to achieve a targeted budget surplus of 4 percent through spending cuts and tax hikes. The extension gave the Cypriot economy more time to recover. Government officials predicted that the country's economic output would shrink by 9 percent in 2013 alone.

In Brussels, Cypriot president Anastasiades asked the European Council for faster progress on the banking and fiscal unions so that Europe could become a truly economic union.[2] Without such a union, countries would be treated according to size of their political muscle. In other words, he was claiming Cyprus was treated harshly because of its small size, while other countries—Spain, in particular—had received more favorable treatment.

On April 30, 2013, the Cypriot Parliament voted 29-27 to accept the terms of the bailout. The new finance minister, Harris Georgiades, had a difficult time convincing politicians that the situation would now improve quickly. "A 'yes' from Cyprus's Parliament is by far the biggest defeat in our 8,000-year history," said member of parliament George Perdikis of the Greens Party. "We know leaving the euro is an equally painful option, but reinstating a national currency could offer prospects for growth in the future," argued Communist Party leader Andros Kyprianou.[3]

It was still unclear exactly how much depositors in the major banks would lose. The Central Bank of Cyprus first published clarifications that financial institutions, government, municipalities, municipal councils and other public entities, insurance companies, charities, schools, and educational institutions would not be subject to depositor haircuts. Insurance companies were later dropped from the list of privileged parties. The ECB's injection of €9 billion ($12.5 billion) in 2012 to keep Laiki Bank temporarily afloat was also exempted from losses.

Several weeks then passed before more accurate numbers emerged. On July 29, 2013, the Cypriot government announced that depositors at the country's largest bank, Bank of Cyprus, would lose 47.5 percent of their savings over the €100,000 ($138,600) insurance limit. Depositors at the second largest bank, Laiki Bank, would lose all of their savings over the €100,000 insurance limit. Many thousands of depositors, however, later filed lawsuits with the European Court of Justice, claiming unequal treatment. As a result, the Cypriot govern-

---

2. Peter Spiegel, "Cyprus President Calls for Bailout Overhaul to Save Economy," *Financial Times*, June 18, 2013.

3. Michele Kambas, "Cyprus Bailout Scrapes through Island's Parliament," Reuters, April 30, 2013.

ment suggested that the losses may be smaller than originally estimated. The precise losses may not be known until the summer of 2014, and that does not instill trust in the Cypriot banking system.

Cyprus was an example of how not to deal with banking problems, and between the Cypriot government and the European Union there was plenty of fault to go around. Cyprus's banking problems were already obvious in 2011, but President Demetris Christofias simply refused to acknowledge them. When he finally did in 2012, his government put such conditions on any rescue package that the European Commission was annoyed and decided to wait to act on the package until after the presidential elections. In normal times, such a delay would probably be inconsequential. In crisis times, it cost Cyprus dearly. The ECB spent a lot of money in 2012 on keeping Laiki Bank afloat, knowing full well that the bank was unsustainable. This was, however, the first true crisis that the ECB had ever encountered, and so it was perhaps normal that its leaders hesitated. It is more difficult to explain why many seasoned politicians in Brussels and in Europe's capitals acted indecisively and made things worse for the Cypriot people.

Slovenia: Latest Troublemaker

Cyprus was not the only small eurozone country to experience severe problems. On April 18, 2013, Slovenia's central bank governor Marko Kranjec said the bad loans held by the country's banks were between €3 billion ($4.2 billion) and €3.5 billion ($4.9 billion), or around 10 percent of GDP.[4] To avoid a bailout, the country would have to adopt swift policy changes, including privatization. A star fiscal performer before 2008 with a debt-to-GDP ratio of only 22 percent, Slovenia's banking sector has been mired in bad loans ever since. Low growth and the slowest privatization of state assets among the East European economies had eaten away at the public finances. The public debt had risen to 54 percent of GDP as a result of large successive deficits during the crisis years. State-owned banks had given money to state-owned companies, thereby bankrupting the banking sector.

In early 2013, I had met twice with Slovenia's finance minister, Janez Šušteršič, on how to reduce the budget deficit. His prime minister, Janez Janša, was the leader of the Slovenian Democratic Party, a member of the European People's Party, and a partner of the ruling GERB party in Bulgaria, engendering immediate trust. Šušteršič was appointed in February 2012, and we spoke frequently during Ecofin meetings. By the time he became finance minister, the situation in Slovenia had gotten out of hand. The previous Social Democratic government, led by Borut Pahor, had adopted the tactic of postponing decisions and hoping the crisis would blow on by. Pahor's finance minister, Franc Križanič, was a very able economist and clearly understood the costs of delay.

---

4. Gabriele Parussini, "Slovenia Central Bank Chief Says Country Can Avoid Bailout," *Wall Street Journal*, April 18, 2013.

He blamed these delays on the politics in parliament—unpopular decisions were simply avoided.

On May 2, 2013, the ECB lowered the interest rate on the main refinancing operations of the Eurosystem to 0.5 percent, the lowest since the introduction of the euro. This was a response to the deepening crisis in Cyprus and the worsening situation in Slovenia. Yields on Slovenian bonds continued to rise, however. On May 2, Moody's cut Slovenia's credit rating to junk status, citing the banking turmoil and a deteriorating national balance sheet. A big sale of government bonds was cancelled because of insufficient demand. Two days later, Slovenia tried again and borrowed $3.5 billion on the international markets at just over 6 percent interest. The government blamed Moody's for intentionally cutting the credit rating ahead of the already announced bond sale and threatened to sue. Yields then increased even more.

In the meantime, Slovenia had entered a political crisis. Prime Minister Janša was implicated in a corruption scandal that revolved around his dealings while mayor of Ljubljana. The scandal quickly engulfed the coalition government, and within a month Janša had lost a confidence vote in parliament. On May 19, the new prime minister, Alenka Bratušek, announced, among other measures, an increase in the value-added tax from 20 to 22 percent, as well as the sale of 15 state-owned firms. Slovenia's second largest bank would also be put up for sale. The government calculated that these measures would raise €900 million ($1.247 trillion). "This program will enable Slovenia to remain a completely sovereign state," Prime Minister Bratušek predicted.[5]

A possible bailout would amount to 20 percent of the country's GDP. Analysts suggested that five of Slovenia's state-run banks had €7 billion ($9.7 billion) in bad loans on their books, twice the amount estimated by the central bank. To avoid collapse of the banking system, the government had to support these banks, yet it did not have enough reserves in the coffers. The economy entered a third year of recession, with unemployment rising to 14 percent. Structural reforms had been twice postponed by the previous governments—in 2010 and again in 2012—after street protests.

On May 24, 2013, Slovenia's Parliament voted 78–8 to change the constitution to require that the government budget be balanced by 2015 and onwards. This move, however, did not pacify the financial markets because a five-year €1.5 billion ($2.1 billion) bond was maturing on April 2, 2014. Time was running short.

Prime Minister Bratušek had to deal with the banking crisis quickly, especially after seeing how the eurozone handled Cyprus. The first order of business was to distance Slovenia as much as possible from any similarities with Cyprus. Slovenia had a relatively small banking industry, with banking assets of 130 percent of GDP, compared with the Cypriot banks' 800 percent of GDP. Still, analysts had bundled the two countries together, and by June 2013 some analysts, worried about the rapidly rising public debt of the two countries,

---

5. Interview with DW, May 2, 2013, www.dw.de.

were comparing them with Greece. In September, the prime minister ordered an independent audit and stress tests of Slovenia's troubled banks to determine how much additional capital they needed. The results implied that recapitalizing the banks would raise the public debt by 11 percent of GDP. In 2008 Slovenia had entered the euro crisis with public debt of just 22 percent of GDP. By 2013 the public debt had risen to 63 percent of GDP. A bank bailout would increase it further, to around 80 percent of GDP.

The lack of reforms weighed down the economy. In 2013 GDP was expected to fall by 2.7 percent, bringing the cumulative decline during the euro crisis to 11 percent, as in Cyprus, and was exceeded in the eurozone only by Greece, at 23 percent. Along with Cyprus, Slovenia is the only eurozone country that the European Commission predicted would remain in recession in 2014, when GDP could fall by another 1 percent.

Slovenia is a good case study for anyone who thinks that fiscal stimulus is the right way to cope with a financial crisis. Once the belt is loosened and the budget falls into a large deficit, there is no political desire to undertake painful structural reforms. The government just bides its time, hoping for a miraculous recovery. But economic miracles rarely happen, so three exits are possible: the fall of the government, an external bailout, or both. In Slovenia, two governments have already fallen in response to the euro crisis. A bailout remains probable.

Balcerowicz's Recipe

In 2012 Polish reformer Leszek Balcerowicz believed he had the answer for Cyprus and Slovenia. He proposed a model for Bulgaria, Estonia, Latvia, and Lithuania (the BELLs), four small European countries that had launched fiscal responsibility measures in response to the crisis and that were the new wave of euro members. Balcerowicz drew on the contrast between the southern rim countries of Cyprus, France, Greece, Italy, Portugal, and Spain, on the one hand, and the BELLs, on the other. The southern rim countries were struggling with stagnant economies, high unemployment, high and increasing debt, and an addiction to too much government spending and high taxes, all of which dampened economic activity. The BELLs, by contrast, had low taxes, lower government debt, and the lowest share of public expenditure to GDP in the European Union. And their economies were the fastest-growing in Europe.

The experience of the BELLs could point the way for the whole eurozone. Balcerowicz argued that they had three initial advantages over the southern rim countries. First, the BELLs lived under communist rule for several decades and knew from experience that a big, overly protective government did not work—thus their mistrust of fiscal stimulus and a drive for austerity. They also recognized that the more money a government spent, the greater was the possibility of corruption. So, fiscal stimulus had a distorting influence on the economy. If one had asked Jürgen Ligi, Estonia's finance minister, or Andris Vilks, Latvia's finance minister, or Ingrida Simonyte, Lithuania's finance minister for much of my term in government, what they thought, they all would have said that budget discipline was the best possible solution both for dealing with the crisis and for reducing corruption.

Second, the BELLs were not protected by the eurozone at the beginning of the crisis, and thus they knew they had to depend only on themselves. This prompted reforms—such as increasing the mandatory retirement age and reforming customs—that were unthinkable in other European countries without external prodding or bailout packages. In Ecofin discussions, both Jürgen Ligi and I often wondered aloud what reforms could be achieved in Greece with so much money pouring in.

Third, the transition from central planning in the BELLs had given them a different perspective on reform horizons. In particular, politicians there did not share the assumption that reforms, although necessary, could bring benefits only in the longer run. This assumption was, however, a mantra in the southern rim countries. For their political classes, the solution to the crisis was a bailout. Every reform was too slow to have an effect. But BELLs finance ministers saw it differently; even if the reform cost the government the next elections, it was worth it. Lithuanian finance minister Simonyte frequently made this point. And her government did implement painful structural reforms. And it did lose elections. Yet in June 2013, Simonyte was appointed deputy governor of the Central Bank of Lithuania in recognition of her good work during the crisis.

The BELLs underwent short-term economic pain so they could eventually recover, which they did. In 2009 Lithuania's economy contracted by 14.8 percent. Growth recovered with a 1.4 percent rise in GDP in 2010, to reach 6 percent in 2011 and 4.5 percent in 2012. Bulgaria saw a 5.5 percent decline in GDP in 2009, but it returned to small growth the next year and reached 1.7 percent growth in 2011. During the crisis, only Poland had better economic performance, although it, too, began to experience problems in 2012.

Latvia Shows the Way

Latvia was the leading example of how to adjust to the crisis by reducing labor costs. After an initial drop of almost 18 percent in 2009, GDP increased by nearly 12 percent from 2010 to 2012, and unemployment fell by almost 7 percentage points from its peak. And Latvia was not alone. If the seven noneurozone countries were grouped together (the BELLs plus the Czech Republic, Hungary, and Poland), they would have had better fiscal and economic indicators than the eurozone. Their average growth rate for 2012 was 1 percent, compared with a contraction of more than 0.5 percent in the eurozone. Earlier, in 2011, it was 3.2 percent, compared with under 1.5 percent in the eurozone (figure 11.1).

The BELLs had two beneficial effects on the eurozone. First, at a time when there was widespread speculation that the eurozone was in for significant difficulties ahead, it was refreshing to have true believers in its long-term

Figure 11.1   GDP growth in the BELL countries, Czech Republic, Poland, and Slovenia, 2006–13

percent change (constant prices)

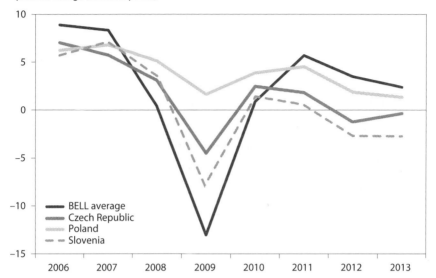

BELL = Bulgaria, Estonia, Latvia, and Lithuania

Source: IMF, *World Economic Outlook,* October 2013, www.imf.org/external/pubs/ft/weo/2013/02/weodata/index.aspx (accessed on February 24, 2014).

future. Second, the entry of these fiscal hawks in the zone would strengthen the German camp, which was numerically in the minority. With the addition of other fiscally disciplined countries, there would be parity in decisions on the future direction. Latvian finance minister Andris Vilks explained how getting his country into the single currency would benefit the rest of the club: "A new, fiscally prudent country with huge experience in the previous crisis, which has learned a lot of lessons, could be a very strong value-added for the eurozone."[6]

Anders Åslund, who together with Latvian prime minister Valdis Dombrovskis wrote the book *How Latvia Came through the Financial Crisis,* has confirmed Balcerowicz's view of the BELLs: "The Balts' rebound (after 2009) stands in stark contrast to the fate of eight mainly southern EU countries—Hungary, Romania, Greece, Ireland, Portugal, Cyprus, Spain, and Slovenia—which either already have or probably will require stabilization programs with external financial support. So what happened? The simple explanation is that the Baltic countries have pursued the opposite policy of the southern Europeans" (Åslund and Dombrovskis 2011, 12).

---

6. Valentina Pop, "Latvia Submits Bid to Join Euro in 2014," *EU Observer,* March 6, 2013.

The BELLs also undertook significant structural reforms, without the need for external prodding. By contrast, the southern rim countries did not reform on their own, and Greece did not reform in earnest even after the first bailout package. At the beginning of his presidency of the ECB in 2012, Mario Draghi was asked to list the regulatory reforms Europe needed to get out of the crisis. He responded: "In Europe first is the product and services markets reform. And the second is the labor market reform which takes different shapes in different countries."[7]

Reforms: Greece, Italy, and Portugal

Why undertake such reforms? Economists agree that European markets are overregulated. IMF chief economist Olivier Blanchard has authored a number of studies on product and labor market deregulation in France (e.g., Blanchard and Giavazzi 2003, 879–907).[8] Harvard University professor Alberto Alesina has conducted similar studies on Italy (Alesina et al. 2010). And the Organization for Economic Cooperation and Development (OECD) has carried out comparative studies for all eurozone countries.

The euro crisis gave finance ministers an opportunity to require reforms from other ministries, which in normal times would have not happened. Most took this opportunity—such as the Polish government. Others talked about it, but did little—such as the Berlusconi and Monti governments in Italy. Much hope was pinned on Mario Monti to start reforms. When coming to power, the Monti government committed itself to introducing several measures to promote competition. They included (1) strengthening the powers of the Competition Authority, including its powers over local public services and the operation of tenders; (2) promoting more competition in public transport, with a new independent regulator; (3) separating network ownership from production and supply in the gas industry; (4) further deregulating some professional services (e.g., abolishing minimum fees, allowing easier access to professions, and reducing compulsory traineeship); and (5) further deregulating the retail sector (e.g., increasing the number of pharmacies and notaries and liberalizing opening hours for retailers)—see Goretti and Landi (2012). In the end, little came of it.

Prior to the euro crisis, some European governments were able to pay generous unemployment benefits. But those benefits were cut rapidly as overall unemployment in the eurozone rose to over 12.5 percent by January 2014. Most eurozone countries initiated labor market reforms, with various degrees of boldness. These reforms most commonly included reductions in severance pay for regular contracts and some simplification of individual or collective

---

7. Brian Blackstone, Matthew Karnitschnig, and Robert Thomson, "Q&A: ECB President Mario Draghi," *Wall Street Journal*, February 23, 2012.

8. Olivier Blanchard, "Reforming the French Job Market," Vox EU, September 30, 2007.

dismissal procedures. By the summer of 2013, such reforms had already been carried out by means of changes in the labor codes in Greece and Portugal.

Greek Reforms

In 2010 Greek lawmakers reduced the overtime pay and the earnings of part-time employees and made averaging of working time possible in an attempt to increase flexibility in the labor market. More labor regulation reforms were forthcoming after the technocratic Papademos government took office because it had become evident that the fiscal consolidation program was derailed. The government introduced a new "mid-term package" in February 2012 that reduced the minimum wage by 22 percent (32 percent for new labor market entrants), decentralized the wage bargaining system (granting seniority to individual contracts over the wage floors agreed on in national and occupational pay agreements), abolished the life tenure rule in large parts of the public sector, and promised to cut public sector employment by 150,000 by 2015 (15,000 each in 2012 and 2013).

During my term in the Bulgarian government, I visited Greece several times and spoke to Greek government officials about their reforms, mostly in the customs and tax administrations. These administrations had roughly three times the number of personnel we had in Bulgaria, even though the countries have about the same population numbers. Despite the reforms, contraband of goods subject to excise duties such as cigarettes and alcohol was rampant, coming through the Greek ports of Piraeus and Thessaloniki. These products were the source of many arguments between Greek and Bulgarian authorities because contraband had increased substantially after the onset of the financial crisis; people had less disposable income across Europe, and so some resorted to buying illegal cigarettes and alcohol. In 2011, for example, Bulgarian customs authorities halted 1.5 billion cigarette sticks at the Greek border, an amount equivalent to 50 percent of the Bulgarian market that year. But the contraband was not intended for Bulgaria—the labels on the cigarette boxes were typically in German because the contraband was simply passing through Bulgaria and Romania on its way to Austria and Germany.

Attempts at Reform in Italy

In Italy, the IMF recommended moving away from using a variety of temporary labor contracts to a single, more flexible contract with phased-in protection that increased with tenure. These kinds of contracts were proposed to boost participation in the labor force. Italian participation rates were low, especially among women—50 percent compared with 65 percent in the rest of the European Union. The Monti government also reduced the incentives to hire workers on fixed-term contracts. The cooling-off period between two fixed-term contracts was extended, and the fiscal incentive for some types of fixed-term contracts was reduced. In particular, employers would have to pay higher social contributions on most fixed-term contracts, which could be reimbursed when the contracts were converted into permanent ones (the so-called stabilization bonus).

"The labor market reform was under expectations," said Tito Boeri, an economist at Bocconi University in Milan. "It didn't do things it could do. It took very long to negotiate, and at the end brought very modest reforms." He added that Monti was "very timid" about liberalizing the guilds that served as entry barriers for most professions.[9]

In April 2012, Monti accused the *Wall Street Journal* of "snap judgments" after the newspaper criticized his "cave-in" over labor reform in an editorial titled "Surrender, Italian Style." The reform Monti's government originally proposed was a modest change that allowed firms with more than 15 employees to fire workers. A final version of the law gave judges greater leeway in determining whether companies were justified in laying off a worker. Because of the judicial bias in favor of workers, the reform was insubstantial.

Portuguese Reforms

Portugal had already begun to reform job creation in 2009, when the socialist government was still in power. The reform substantially eased job protection on regular contracts by simplifying dismissal procedures. This was followed by reductions in severance payments for regular contracts and a narrower definition of unfair dismissal. Further reforms introduced in 2011 and 2012 when Vítor Gaspar was at the helm of the finance ministry provided for easier firing and hiring. Individual dismissals for economic reasons would no longer adhere to a predefined order of seniority. Those based on worker capability became possible in a wider range of circumstances. In both cases, the obligation to transfer the employee to another suitable position was eliminated. Severance pay was reduced from 30 to 20 days per year of tenure (with a 12-month ceiling instead of a 3-month floor), with a further reduction in December 2013.

In May 2011, the Portuguese government froze both the minimum wage and administrative extensions of sector-level collective agreements. The first measure lasted as long as the EU-IMF program, the second until October 2012. The authorities also lowered the threshold above which firm-level bargaining was possible, from 500 to 150 workers. This reduced sector-level bargaining provided additional flexibility. The reform also reduced the disincentives to work by lowering the ceiling on monthly unemployment benefits to €1,048 ($1,450), introducing a 10 percent benefit reduction after six months, and reducing the maximum duration.

---

9. Rachel Donadio, "As a Premier Prepares to Depart, the Talk Is of Lost Opportunities," *New York Times*, December 13, 2012.

Reforms: Pensions and Taxes

Pensions

Greece undertook its most difficult reforms in July 2010. The retirement age was raised from 60 to 65 (from 55 to 60 for special categories) and will be equalized for men and women by 2015. Penalties were introduced for early retirement, and pension payments were suspended for pensioners who were still employed—completely for pensioners below the age of 55 and by up to 70 percent for older pensioners. The number of insurance and pension funds was reduced through mergers and consolidations, all aimed at establishing three unified funds by 2018. The result was a sizable reduction in pension entitlements for a number of professional occupations (lawyers, journalists, doctors, etc.). Finally, limits were imposed on pension transferability (to offspring and widowed spouses).

In 2012 Greece also reduced the generosity of pension benefits, cutting all pensions above €1,500 ($2,079) by 30 percent. Ireland had done the same a year earlier, focusing on civil servants above a pension threshold; it also cut back on early retirements and shortened the list of arduous occupations granted early retirement. Greece introduced a mechanism to index the retirement age to life expectancy.

Italy managed to undertake some pension reforms and for good reason. The public pension expenditure in Italy was 15 percent of GDP in 2010 (figure 11.2), exceeding that of all other OECD countries. Italy therefore increased the mandatory pension age to 66 in stages until 2020. In 2012 it changed the pension system from a defined benefit (based on last salary) to a defined contribution (based on money paid in). The result was a pension reduction of 15 percent. The annual inflation adjustment on pensions was also eliminated for those who collected monthly retirement checks of more than €936 ($1,300). The minimum number of contribution years would rise from 40 to 42 years for men and to 41 years for women from 2012 on. In effect, this change reduced the opportunity for early retirement. And the minimum retirement age for women's seniority pensions was raised from 60 to 62, with financial incentives to try to keep women working until age 70.

Pension system interventions were expected to produce savings, net of fiscal effects on Italy's public finance, that were estimated to reach €7.3 billion ($10.1 billion) by 2014 and almost €22 billion ($30.5 billion) by 2020. As a result of the reform, the average age at retirement (taking into account both the old-age retirement requirements and the early retirement requirements) would increase from 60-61 in 2006–10 to about 64 in 2020, 67 in 2040, and about 68 in 2050.

In Portugal, early retirement was suspended until the end of 2014. By that time, an overhaul of early retirement legislation would be needed. The current rules allow for early retirement at age 55 with 30 years of contributions and a penalty of 0.5 percent for each month not worked. If, for example, a worker

Figure 11.2 Pension expenditures in the eurozone, 2002–11

percent of GDP

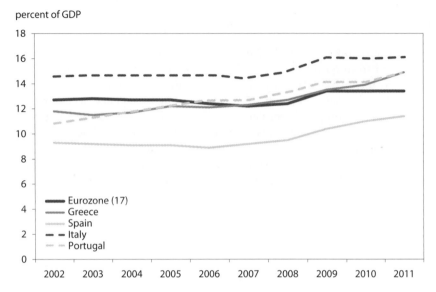

Source: Eurostat, http://epp.eurostat.ec.europa.eu (accessed on February 24, 2014).

retires five years early, he or she would see a 30 percent cut in benefits. There were generous retirement options for workers who became unemployed after age 52. They could retire at age 57, provided they contributed to the pension fund for at least 22 years. But this weighed heavily on the public budget, which subsidized the pension fund.

In Spain, pension spending as a share of GDP was 10 percent in 2010. The pension reforms introduced in 2011 are expected to reduce the projected increase in annual pension spending by half, in part by raising the legal retirement age to 67 for workers who have contribution periods shorter than 38.5 years.

Taxes

Another area of reform during the euro crisis was tax regulation. Tax reforms included (1) broadening the tax base by eliminating some deductions in the personal income tax (Greece, Ireland, and Portugal); (2) broadening the value-added tax base (Cyprus, Greece, Italy, and Portugal) and reforming property taxation, including increasing (Portugal and Greece) or introducing (Ireland) property taxation and introducing a flat stamp duty on all residential property, along with abolishing all existing exemptions (Cyprus, Ireland); and (3) introducing or increasing environmental taxes by increasing the level of carbon taxes and introducing water charges (Ireland) or increasing the car registration tax (Portugal).

In 2011, in the waning days of the Berlusconi government, Italy undertook a number of tax changes driven by fiscal consolidation that have begun to yield results. These were aimed at improving the efficiency of the tax structure, such as cutting labor and corporate taxes, along with raising the value-added tax and local property tax rates. Italy also fought tax evasion and avoidance by strengthening controls and procedures in detecting tax evaders. Other measures included lowering the legal threshold for cash payments to €1,000 ($1,386) and imposing additional obligations on banks and financial intermediaries, such as requirements for disclosure to the Revenue Agency (e.g., of all transactions involving economic agents located in the OECD's "blacklist" countries).

Spain pursued significant tax reforms in an effort to boost public revenues. The most significant measures were the increases in the value-added tax, from 16 percent to 18 percent in 2011 and further to 21 percent in 2012, and the increase in the reduced rate on food and newspapers from 7 percent to 10 percent. Personal and corporate income taxes were also increased; the wealth tax was reintroduced; the deduction for the purchase of one's main residence was abolished; and the tax on income from bank savings was increased in 2012. The government also attempted to collect unpaid taxes through a partial tax forgiveness program.

Although Spain's personal and corporate income taxes had increased substantially, not enough money was raised, mainly because of the deductions that could be applied. For example, if all deductions were eliminated, the expected increase in personal income tax collections in 2012 would have been €9 billion ($12.5 billion), or 0.9 percent of GDP. Spain had high marginal rates for personal income taxes, with a maximum marginal rate of 52 percent, although some regions imposed an even higher marginal rate of up to 56 percent. Corporate income taxes presented the same problem: a high marginal rate (30 percent) but a lower effective rate (below 18 percent). So the reform was clear: eliminate deductions.

As part of the memorandum of understanding with the Troika, Portugal created a new integrated tax and customs authority; a Large Taxpayer Office was set up at the end of 2012. Meanwhile, the tax and customs authority and the social security administration began to share information electronically.

Portugal also expanded the scope of normal value-added tax rates as of January 2012. And it reduced the use of value-added tax exemptions such as the exemption applied to agricultural products. In 2013 the ministry of finance continued to extend the scope of application of the standard value-added tax rate. The logic was that social goals could be met more effectively through job programs than by lower tax rates.

Lack of Reform Leaders

During my tenure in Ecofin, there was not a single official discussion about how regulatory and tax reform in individual EU countries could be supported by the European Commission. This was quite extraordinary because the communiqués associated with bailouts in the eurozone invariably pointed to the need for structural reforms. Why didn't Ecofin take a more forceful rule in prescribing useful reforms? Perhaps because it was too busy with the financial details of bailout packages and with the negotiations on the fiscal and banking unions. My explanation is different: Ecofin was simply not supported by the European Commission in taking on this task. To do so, European Commissioner for Competition Joaquín Almunia and his staff would have had to participate in meetings and prepare analysis. But the Commission's directorates seemed to operate independently and in isolation. I never saw Olli Rehn and Almunia together. The president of the European Council, Herman Van Rompuy, attempted to breach this gap in early 2010, but his initiative fizzled. The EU bureaucracy did not see this as a priority, perhaps because European Commission president Barroso held this view and did not reorganize the Commission to provide this service. Without the Commission, it remained up to individual ministers to show initiative.

This was the main constraint to finding solutions to the euro crisis. The European Commission was not set up as a decision-making body. In the past, it had implemented the decisions of Germany or France and Germany, and in the crisis it continued to operate in this manner. There was no attempt to "graduate" from this patronage.

12

What Now for the Euro?

There are no simple solutions to strengthening the euro. That goal will require a lot of work by politicians in Brussels and the European capitals, by the European Central Bank (ECB), and by academics familiar with the problems. The ideas proposed by scholars during the euro crisis had significant weaknesses. The notion of a euro holiday did not work because there was no credible commitment by those taking a holiday from the eurozone and by the eurozone itself to reentering. The euro holiday also presented significant technical difficulties: All contracts would have to be rewritten in the new currency. At best, the euro holiday would take a year to happen. In the meantime, a systemwide bank run would follow.

For similar reasons, the northern euro was not feasible. Northern industries exporting their products would suffer from a strong northern euro. Meanwhile, the central banks of the northern euro and the southern euro would have to work together to prevent a sudden appreciation of the northern euro. It was also unlikely that the Greeks, Spaniards, Portuguese, and Italians would be able to maintain unity. Europe would be left with a group of weak southern currencies, thereby reversing the tide of integration in Europe.

Eurobonds were not a salvation either. First, it was not clear whether eurobonds were legal under the EU treaty. Second, it was not clear who would issue them and who would repay them. And, third, what level of guarantees would they have? In other words, eurobonds would have to wait until there was a common fiscal policy—up to 10 years, said French president François Hollande.

A big devaluation of the euro was just as unlikely. The problem with a eurowide devaluation was that euro members were still competitive, and a euro devaluation would boost only German exports, creating even greater disparity in the current account balances in Europe. An internal devaluation—through higher inflation in the north and lagging inflation in the south—was problematic as well. If wages and prices fell, even if there was real GDP growth, nominal GDP in the south could fall. Thus the denominator in the debt-to-GDP ratio would not grow, and debt sustainability in the south would suffer. The real value of the debt would then rise over time, increasing the need for austerity.

So what ideas actually did work? After I became finance minister of Bulgaria early in the euro crisis, I was a witness to and participant in the peripatetic progress toward fiscal and banking stability in Europe. This progress featured the tipping points described in this book that defined how European leaders dealt with the crisis. It also featured some notable policy successes and some spectacular failures that are described in the sections that follow.

Some Notable Successes

Indeed, there were some notable successes during my term in Ecofin. The march toward a common fiscal policy yielded some progress—such as the introduction of the Fiscal Compact and the European Stability Mechanism—and that progress should continue. Much work remains to be done, however, before a federal budgetary structure emerges. The European Central Bank played a stabilizing role throughout the euro crisis and came to be seen as the most trusted European institution. For that reason, progress with the banking union outpaced progress with the fiscal union.

Overall progress was helped greatly by the work of several people: Jörg Asmussen, first as the deputy finance minister of Germany, and then as a member of the ECB's Executive Board; Wolfgang Schäuble, the German finance minister; Mario Draghi, president of the ECB; Jean-Claude Juncker, prime minister of Luxembourg, and Luc Frieden, his finance minister; Anders Borg, the Swedish finance minister; Thomas Wieser, president of the Economic and Financial Committee of the European Union; and EU Commissioners Michel Barnier, Algirdas Semeta, and Janusz Lewandowski. Most active during the discussions on how to bring back stability in Europe were Jan Vincent-Rostowski, the Polish finance minister; Maria Fekter, my Austrian colleague; and Jan Kees de Jager while he was the finance minister of the Netherlands. Jyrki Katainen, during his tenure as the finance minister of Finland, was also very helpful in finding solutions to the various crises engulfing Ecofin.

The entry of Estonia and Latvia into the eurozone during these tumultuous times was another success for the eurozone and the Estonian and Latvian governments. It strengthened the implicit principle that the health of the euro was paramount to the health of the political union in Europe. Also, their entry clarified the concept of Europe at a time when it was in doubt—it confirmed that monetary, fiscal, and banking unions are part of the main building blocks of the European Union, not an extension.

Table 12.1 Economic and Monetary Union convergence criteria, 2013
(percent)

Country	Consumer price inflation	Budget deficit to GDP	Debt to GDP	ERM II member	Long-term interest rates
Reference value	2.70	3.00	60.0	2 years	5.50
Bulgaria	0.40	1.80	16.0	No	3.47
Czech Republic	1.40	2.90	47.6	No	2.11
Hungary	1.70	2.70	79.8	No	5.92
Poland	0.80	4.60	57.6	No	4.03
Romania	3.20	2.30	38.1	No	5.41
Croatia	2.30	4.70	57.8	No	4.68

ERM II = Exchange Rate Mechanism II

Sources: Eurostat, http://epp.eurostat.ec.europa.eu (accessed in February 2014); IMF, *World Economic Outlook,* October 2013.

Finally, the entry of Estonia and Latvia provided the euro with long-term security, making it explicit that it was part and parcel of the European Union. It also meant there would be a better balance of power within the eurozone on matters of fiscal discipline. The East Europeans had a tradition of fiscal austerity and structural reforms superior to that in the southern rim countries. Germany would more easily find friends in Eastern Europe when discussing the fiscal union.

Estonia and Latvia charted the way for others to follow, including future EU members. It helped that many of the accession countries either had already adopted the euro on their own (Kosovo and Montenegro), were members of a currency board (Bosnia), or had a fixed exchange rate to the euro (Macedonia). The euro has been the official currency of Montenegro since 2002, when it went into circulation in the rest of the eurozone. Prior to that, Montenegro used the deutsche mark. Macedonia, Kosovo, and Bosnia followed essentially the same route (Dushko, Cikarska, and Koteski 2011).

For those Eastern European Union countries not participating in Exchange Rate Mechanism II (ERM II)—Bulgaria, Croatia, the Czech Republic, Hungary, Poland, and Romania—a rapid path toward ERM II entry should be prescribed (table 12.1). Bulgaria already meets the criteria. Croatia has a narrow managed float against the euro of 6 percent, and has maintained it since 2004. It would not be difficult for the country to fulfill the exchange rate Maastricht criterion: the target zone of ERM II. Other criteria are tougher to meet.

The rest of the countries are close to entry. They could be given a year's time to get their finances in order to enter ERM II. Once in, they would have another two years to adopt the euro. Poland's prime minister, Donald Tusk, has agreed with the opposition that Poland should hold a referendum on euro accession. This could happen in early 2015. By then, Lithuania would already be in the eurozone.[1]

Is such a rapid path to the euro feasible? The ECB and the Eurogroup need to be convinced that, apart from solid fiscal and macroeconomic indicators, East European countries can maintain stability over time. Asmussen has listed the needs: "While the Treaty prescribes the criteria for joining the euro, convergence means more than meeting a set of nominal criteria at a point in time. It has to involve laying the foundations to prosper in EMU over the long-term. There cannot be labor markets that protect insiders; product markets that shield closed professions; education systems that hinder innovation; public administrations that fail to collect tax or pay arrears; or judicial systems that cannot enforce contracts in reasonable time."[2]

Spectacular Failures

While finance minister of Bulgaria, I also witnessed some spectacular failures at Ecofin. The first and most important was the initial rescue package for Greece. That package was insufficient and ill designed to stem the tide of investor worries. A more determined action taken early on would have shortened the Greek crisis and limited the spillover to other southern rim countries. A second failure was the handling of the adoption of the European Stability Mechanism. It was amateurish and led to the fall of the Slovak government. Brussels should have foreseen the dangers in the Slovak Parliament and given Prime Minister Iveta Radičová much more support in the same way it helped Finnish finance minister Jyrki Katainen during his election campaign. Then, Ecofin ministers and heads of state were working hard to find ways to allay concerns in Finland over the Greek and other southern rim bailouts. The third failure was the collapse of Cyprus. It was avoidable. The mishap was partly due to the change at the helm of the eurozone—Jean-Claude Juncker would have handled it more smoothly. Meanwhile, many European politicians were angry at Greece—and they found a victim in Cyprus. Some eurozone members wanted the Cyprus resolution to be noisy and calamitous to appease their audiences at home—an immature tactic, to be sure.

How the Euro Crisis Changed My Mind

When the notion of writing this book came up, I had some ideas about what I wanted to say. Some of these ideas jelled and strengthened as the writing progressed. One was the need for austerity. Austerity simply means that governments spend what they earn, or close to it. In other words, it is fiscal responsibility. People agree with this principle when it is applied to a house-

1. Anders Åslund, "Paul Krugman's Baltic Problem," *Foreign Policy*, September 13, 2012.

2. Jörg Asmussen, "Central and Eastern Europe and the Eurozone," blog on beforeitsnews, April 29, 2013.

hold budget. A July 2013 poll in Bulgaria found that only 17 percent of respondents wanted their families to live in debt during the crisis. Yet when they were asked the same question about their country, 58 percent said they wanted a looser budget.[3] Someone else should pay the government's bills.

Europe must practice fiscal responsibility. Otherwise, inefficiencies in certain countries and sectors will continue. Moreover, large public expenditures open more opportunities for corruption—a main reason for the strikes in the Czech Republic, France, Slovenia, and Spain from 2011 to 2013. Understandably, patience was running thin. Not only was there less money to go around, but public officials misused it to their benefit.

This is also why I agree with the German view that eurobonds would just make the current imbalances worse. It is like writing a blank check to undisciplined governments and saying. "Here, spend more." I had a first-hand experience fighting the logic of taking on cheap loans. In late 2012, when the interest rates on eurobonds fell substantially because of the interventions of the European Central Bank and a successful sovereign issue, members of the majority in Bulgaria's Parliament began agitating for a large loan to finance the consumption expenditure. The idea was to increase pensions and public salaries ahead of the coming elections. "Who would pay for this?" I asked. "The next government" was the answer. Neither Prime Minister Borisov nor I bought into the idea, but the same logic was likely on the minds of many European politicians.

I have been firmly against tax harmonization in the European Union, and I remain so. For me, this is just an excuse to increase the tax burden on business and claim it is part of European solidarity. If Europe has a common monetary and fiscal policy and achieves a banking union, tax policy remains the only tool left in the hands of national parliaments to encourage investors. Countries that can collect their taxes and spend their revenues only on growth-enhancing measures can have lower taxes. This is what Bulgaria by and large does. Countries in which tax loopholes proliferate and where collection is suspect and countries that choose to spend their citizens' money lavishly can keep their tax rates high. This is a national preference that does not endanger the stability of the euro or the political union.

In various Ecofin gatherings, formal and informal, I also supported the idea of a euro holiday for Greece. As finance minister of a neighboring country, I saw the ineffectiveness of the Greek tax and customs administrations and recognized that the ambitious privatization program promised to the European Commission and the International Monetary Fund was unlikely to see the light of day. It was better that Greece have an opportunity to devalue, get its real economy in order, and then rejoin the eurozone at a more appropriate exchange rate.

---

3. Alpha Research, poll, General Views of the Bulgarian Population on Political Developments, Sofia, July 2013.

Now I see things differently. Once one eurozone member left, politicians in other troubled countries would have been subject to enormous pressure to leave as well. And it would have put a heavy burden on the European Central Bank. Because there were no clear exit rules, such an exit would have set back European integration significantly. Anders Åslund made this point by historically comparing a eurozone exit to the collapse of the Habsburg Empire, the Soviet Union, and Yugoslavia—not good examples to follow (Åslund 2012).[4]

Also during my tenure as finance minister of Bulgaria, I witnessed how the euro crisis removed one divide in Europe and created another. Prior to 2008, the divide was east-west. Citizens from the newer members of the European Union would go to the old ones in search of better job prospects. And policy discussions and academic research focused on how quickly Eastern Europe could catch up with Western Europe. Since 2011, the divide had turned north-south, with Eastern Europe closer to the disciplined and responsibility-driven north. The experience of Eastern Europe with structural reforms was also frequently used to urge southern rim governments to take those painful but necessary steps. The euro crisis may yet provide the wake-up call needed to stir Europe out of its complacency. And the integration of Eastern Europe into the eurozone may create the missing momentum.

---

4. Anders Åslund, "Why Greece Must Not Leave the Euro Area," EconoMonitor, March 12, 2012, www.economonitor.com/piie/2012/03/12/why-greece-must-not-leave-the-euro-area.

References

Alesina, Alberto, Yann Algan, Pierre Cahuc, and Paola Giuliano. 2010. *Family Values and the Regulation of Labor.* NBER Working Paper 15747. Cambridge, MA: National Bureau of Economic Research.

Alesina, Alberto, and Francesco Giavazzi. 2006. *The Future of Europe: Reform or Decline.* Cambridge, MA: MIT Press.

Alesina, Alberto, and Francesco Giavazzi, eds. 2010. *Europe and the Euro.* Chicago: University of Chicago Press.

Ang, Andrew, and Francis Longstaff. 2011. *Systemic Sovereign Credit Risk: Lessons from the US and Europe.* NBER Working Paper 16982. Cambridge, MA: National Bureau of Economic Research.

Asdrubali, Pierfederico, Bent Sorensen, and Oved Yosha. 1996. Channels of Interstate Risk Sharing: United States 1963-1990. *Quarterly Journal of Economics* 111, no. 4: 1081-110.

Åslund, Anders. 2010. *The Last Shall Be the First: The East European Financial Crisis.* Washington: Peterson Institute for International Economics.

Åslund, Anders. 2012. *Why a Breakup of the Euro Area Must Be Avoided: Lessons from Previous Breakups.* Policy Brief 12-20. Washington: Peterson Institute for International Economics.

Åslund, Anders, and Valdis Dombrovskis. 2011. *How Latvia Came through the Financial Crisis.* Washington: Peterson Institute for International Economics.

Assmann, Christian, and Jens Boysen-Hogrefe. 2011. *Determinants of Government Bond Spreads in the Euro Area—in Good Times as in Bad.* Kiel, Germany: Kiel Institute for the World Economy.

Begg, David. 2009. *The Consequences of the UK Saying No to the Euro.* London: Britain in Europe Foundation.

Begg, I., ed. 2002. *Running EMU: The Challenges of Policy Coordination.* London: Federal Trust.

Beirne, John, Lars Dalitz, Jacob Ejsing, Magdalena Grothe, Simone Manganelli, Fernando Monar, Benjamin Sahel, Matjaž Sušec, Jens Tapking, and Tana Vong. 2011. *The Impact of the Eurosystem's Covered Bond Purchase Program on the Primary and Secondary Markets.* Occasional Paper Series 122. Frankfurt: European Central Bank.

Blanchard, Olivier, and Francesco Giavazzi. 2003. Macroeconomic Effects of Regulation and Deregulation in Goods and Labor Markets. *Quarterly Journal of Economics* 118, no. 3: 879-907.

171

Blanchard, Olivier, and Pedro Portugal. 2006. What Hides Behind an Unemployment Rate: Comparing Portuguese and U.S. Labor Markets. *American Economic Review* 91, no. 1: 187–207.

Brück, Tilman, and Andreas Stephan. 2006. Do Eurozone Countries Cheat with Their Budget Deficit Forecasts? *Kyklos* 59, no. 1 (February): 3–15.

Buti, Marco, Daniele Franco, and Hedwig Ongena. 1998. Fiscal Discipline and Flexibility in EMU: The Implementation of the Stability and Growth Pact. *Oxford Review of Economic Policy* 14, no. 3: 81–97.

Calomiris, Charles. 1999. The Impending Collapse of the European Monetary Union. *Cato Journal* 18, no. 3 (January): 445–52.

Chintrakarn, Pandej. 2008. Estimating the Euro Effects on Trade with Propensity Score Matching. *Review of International Economics* 16, no. 1 (February): 186–98.

Claessens, Stijn, Ashoka Mody, and Shahin Vallée. 2012. *Paths to Eurobonds*. Bruegel Working Paper 2012/10. Brussels: Bruegel.

Debrun, Xavier, Laurent Moulin, Alessandro Turrini, Joaquim Ayuso-i-Casals, and Manmohan Kumar. 2008. Tied to the Mast? National Fiscal Rules in the European Union. *Economic Policy* 23, no. 54 (April): 297–362.

Delplas Jacques, and Jakob von Weizsäcker. 2011. *Eurobonds: The Blue Bond Concept and Its Implications*. Bruegel Policy Contribution (March). Brussels: Bruegel.

Djankov, Simeon, Caralee McLiesh, Tatiana Nenova, and Andrei Shleifer. 2003. Who Owns the Media? *Journal of Law and Economics* 46, no. 2: 341–81.

Djankov, Simeon, Neil Gregory, Michael Klein, and Facundo Martin. 2009. *The Road to 2020: Scenarios for a World in Crisis*. Washington: World Bank.

Dushko, Josheski, Ljubica Cikarska, and Cane Koteski. 2011. *The Macroeconomic Implication of Exchange Rate Regimes*. MPRA Paper 32926. University of Munich.

Eichengreen, Barry. 2010. The Break-up of the Euro Area. In *Europe and the Euro*, ed. Alberto Alesina and Francesco Giavazzi. Chicago: University of Chicago Press.

Eijffinger, Sylvester, and Lex Hoogduin. 2012. *The European Central Bank in (the) Crisis*. CESifo DICE Report. Brussels.

Ellsberg, Daniel. 1972. *Papers on the War*. New York: Simon and Schuster.

European Commission. 2013a. *Blueprint for a Deep and Genuine Economic and Monetary Union*. Brussels.

European Commission. 2013b. *Annual Growth Survey 2013*. Brussels.

European Council. 2011. *Towards a Genuine Economic and Monetary Union Interim Report*. Brussels.

Favero, Carlo, and Alessandro Missale. 2011. Sovereign Spreads in the Euro Area: Which Prospects for a Eurobond? Paper presented at the Fifty-fourth Panel Meeting Hosted by the National Bank of Poland, Warsaw, October 27–28.

Ferreira do Amaral, João. 2013. *Porque Devemos Sair do Euro*. Lisbon: Lua de Papel (April).

Frankel, Jeffery. 2009. *The Estimated Trade Effects of the Euro: Why Are They Below Those from Historical Monetary Unions Among Smaller Countries?* Working Paper 2009-0008. Cambridge, MA: Weatherhead Center for International Affairs, Harvard University.

Frankel, Jeffery, and Jesse Schreger. 2013. Over-optimistic Official Forecasts and Fiscal Rules in the Eurozone. *Review of World Economics (Weltwirtschaftliches Archiv)* 149, no. 2.

Goretti, Chiara, and Lucio Landi. 2012. Walking on the Edge: How Italy Rescued Italy in 2012. *Intereconomics* 48 (January/February).

Gros, Daniel, and Thomas Mayer. 2010. *Towards a Euro(Pean) Monetary Fund*. CEPS Policy Brief 202. Brussels: Centre for European Policy Studies.

Heipertz, Martin, and Amy Verdun. 2004. *The Dog that Would Never Bite? What We Can Learn from the Origins of the Stability and Growth Pact.* CGPE Working Paper 04-06 (January). Vancouver: Centre for Global Political Economy.

Issing, Otmar. 2008. *The Birth of the Euro.* Cambridge: Cambridge University Press.

Jonung, Lars, and Eoin Drea. 2010. The Euro: It Can't Happen, It's a Bad Idea, It Won't Last. U.S. Economists on the EMU, 1989–2002. *Economics in Practice* 7, no. 1 (January): 4–52.

Kenen, Peter. 1969. The Theory of Optimum Currency Areas: An Eclectic View. In *Monetary Problems of the International Economy*, ed. R. Mundell and A. Swoboda. Chicago: University of Chicago Press.

Kenen, Peter. 1995. *Economic and Monetary Union in Europe: Moving Beyond Maastricht.* Cambridge: Cambridge University Press.

Lourtie, Pedro. 2011. Understanding Portugal in the Context of the Euro Crisis. Paper prepared for Resolving the European Debt Crisis, a conference hosted by the Peterson Institute for International Economics and Bruegel, Chantilly, France, September 13–14.

Ludlow, Peter. 1982. *The Making of the EMS.* London: Butterworth.

Mayer, Thomas. 2012. *Europe's Unfinished Currency: The Political Economy of the Euro.* London: Anthem Press.

McKinsey & Company. 2012. *The Future of the Euro: An Economic Perspective on the Eurozone Crisis* (January). Frankfurt.

Mundell, Robert. 1960. The Monetary Dynamics of International Adjustment under Fixed and Flexible Exchange Rates. *Quarterly Journal of Economics* 84, no. 2 (May): 227–57.

Mundell, Robert. 1961a. Flexible Exchange Rates and Employment Policy. *Canadian Journal of Economics and Political Science* 24, no. 4 (November): 509–17.

Mundell, Robert. 1961b. The International Disequilibrium System. *Kyklos* 14, no. 2: 154–72.

Mundell, Robert. 1961c. A Theory of Optimum Currency Areas. *American Economic Review* 51, no. 4 (November): 509–17.

Mundell, Robert. 1968. The Collapse of the Gold Standard. *American Journal of Agricultural Economics* (December).

Richter, Franziska, and Peter Wahl. 2011. *The Role of the European Central Bank in the Financial Crash and the Crisis of the Euro-Zone Report.* Berlin: Environment and Development Association.

Rose, Andrew. 2000. One Money, One Market: Estimating the Effect of Common Currencies on Trade. *Economic Policy* 30: 9–45.

Shambaugh, Jay. 2012. The Euro's Three Crises. *Brookings Papers on Economic Activity* (Spring). Washington: Brookings Institution.

Strauch, Rolf, Mark Hallerberg, and Jurgen von Hagen. 2009. How Forms of Fiscal Governance Affect Fiscal Performance. In *Fiscal Governance in Europe*, ed. Mark Hallerberg, Rolf Strauch, and Jurgen von Hagen. Cambridge: Cambridge University Press.

van Overtveldt, Johan. 2011. *The End of the Euro: The Uneasy Future of the EU.* Chicago: Agate Imprint.

Véron, Nicolas. 2013. *A Realistic Bridge towards European Banking Union.* Policy Brief 13-17. Washington: Peterson Institute for International Economics.

World Bank. 2013. *Doing Business 2013: Smarter Regulations for Small and Medium-Size Enterprises.* Washington.

Chronology of Events

Date	Event
2009, Onset of the Crisis	
October 23, 2009	**Greek prime minister Georgios Papandreou announces revised Greek deficit numbers of 12.5 percent of GDP—over twice the previous estimate.**
December 8–22, 2009	Greece's debt reaches €300 billion ($415 billion)—the highest in its modern history. Downgrades from all three ratings agencies ensue.
2010, Transmission of the Crisis	
April 23, 2010	Greek finance minister George Papaconstantinou asks the European Union (EU) for a €45 billion ($62 billion) bailout package for Greece.
April 27, 2010	Standard and Poor's (S&P) downgrades Greek debt to junk and Portuguese debt to A– as market worries over sovereign debt solvency spread to other countries.

Tipping points are highlighted in bold. The external sources used in constructing this timeline include "The Euro Crisis Timeline Prolegomenon" from Bruegel; "Timeline: The Unfolding of the Euro Crisis" from BBC News; "Tracking Europe's Debt Crisis" from CBA News; and "Timeline of a Crisis: How Greece's Tragedy Unfolded" by the *Telegraph*.

May 2, 2010	The European Union and the International Monetary Fund (IMF) agree to a €110 billion ($152 billion) bailout package for Greece, which in turn commits Greece to lower its budget deficit from 14 to 3 percent by 2014.
May 3, 2010	The European Central Bank (ECB) announces it will indefinitely accept Greek collateral, regardless of the country's credit rating.
May 9–10, 2010	EU finance ministers agree on a temporary €440 billion ($609 billion) bailout fund, the European Financial Stability Facility (EFSF).
September 30, 2010	The Irish government nationalizes Allied Irish Bank and injects more capital into the Anglo Irish Bank, which it had taken over in 2009.
October 6, 2010	Fitch downgrades Ireland's sovereign credit rating. Moody's and S&P follow with downgrades as well in December.
October 18, 2010	**German chancellor Angela Merkel and French president Nicolas Sarkozy meet in Deauville, France, and announce a crisis management system to replace the EFSF.**
October 28–29, 2010	EU leaders agree on a new management system, the European Stability Mechanism (ESM), to safeguard financial stability in the eurozone.
November 28, 2010	Ireland applies for and receives an €85 billion ($117 billion) bailout.

2011, Escalation of the Crisis

January 20, 2011	Irish prime minister Brian Cowen calls for new elections in March 2011 and resigns two days later.
March 23, 2011	Portuguese prime minister José Sócrates resigns after the parliament rejects his austerity plans. His Socialist Party loses the parliamentary elections on June 5, paving the way for a new center-right coalition government led by Pedro Passos Coelho.
May 17, 2011	EU finance ministers approve Portugal's €78 billion ($108 billion) bailout.

June 5, 2011	Moody's downgrades Portugal's sovereign rating to junk status, citing the possibility of private sector involvement in debt restructuring and the unlikelihood of Portugal meeting its deficit targets.
June 13, 2011	S&P downgrades Greek debt to CCC, its lowest rating for any country in the world.
July 21, 2011	An EU summit agrees to a second Greek bailout of €109 billion ($151 billion). Commercial banks accept a cut on the net present value of their Greek bonds.
August 7, 2011	The ECB announces it will buy Italian and Spanish sovereign bonds in secondary markets as part of its Securities Markets Programme.
August 17, 2011	Chancellor Merkel and President Sarkozy call for strengthening conomic governance and economic policy coordination in the eurozone. Both leaders reject eurobonds as a short-term solution.
September 19, 2011	S&P downgrades Italy's sovereign rating because of its lower growth prospects and fragile political environment. The downgrade occurs despite the Italian Parliament's approval of its austerity package one month earlier.
September 20, 2011	The European Council, European Commission, and European Parliament agree on "six pack" legislation: six legislative proposals aimed at reforming economic governance within the European Union and strengthening its framework for preventing excessive imbalances and deficits.
October 4–18, 2011	Spain and Italy face a series of downgrades from all three rating agencies because of weak growth expectations, the intensification of the euro crisis, and political uncertainty in Italy.
October 13, 2011	**Slovakia becomes the 17th and final country to approve the expansion of the eurozone's rescue fund.**
October 27, 2011	European leaders agree on a new bailout plan for Greece, which includes a 50 percent private sector writedown. EU leaders also strengthen their tools against the euro crisis via increased EFSF leverage options and stronger eurozone budgetary rules.

October 31, 2011	Greek Prime Minister Papandreou announces plans for a referendum on the new bailout plan.
November 4, 2011	Mario Draghi becomes president of the ECB and within a few days announces a steep cut in the bank's benchmark rate from 1.5 to 1.25 percent.
November 6, 2011	Greek prime minister Papandreou resigns. A national unity government led by former ECB vice president Lucas Papademos takes over.
November 12, 2011	Italian prime minister Silvio Berlusconi resigns after parliamentary approval of a package of debt reduction measures. Mario Monti takes over as Italy's prime minister.
November 20, 2011	Mariano Rajoy's People's Party wins the general elections in Spain, as well as the largest majority in the Spanish Parliament in 29 years.
November 23, 2011	The European Commission proposes "two pack" legislation that would strengthen budgetary surveillance and monitoring, complementing the six measures ("six pack" legislation) agreed on in September.
December 21, 2011	The ECB's first 36-month long-term refinancing operation (LTRO) takes place; 523 banks borrow €489.2 billion ($677.7 billion).
December 30, 2011	Within two weeks of taking office, Prime Minister Rajoy announces that Spain's deficit for 2011 will be 8 percent of GDP, exceeding its target of 6 percent. The government then adopts more than €15 billion ($21 billion) in new budget cuts.

2012, Containment of the Crisis

January 15, 2012	S&P downgrades the sovereign debt of nine eurozone countries. The EFSF is also downgraded to AA+.
January 30, 2012	EU countries (except the Czech Republic and the United Kingdom) agree to a German-led Fiscal Compact that caps the annual structural deficits of EU member states at 0.5 percent of their respective GDPs.

February 28, 2012	A second LTRO round by the ECB proceeds, with 800 banks borrowing €529.5 billion ($733.1 billion).
March 9, 2012	The second Greek rescue package is approved following the high private sector involvement (PSI) participation rate announced by the Greek finance ministry and a positive Troika report on the implementation of Greek reforms.
March 13, 2012	Moody's downgrades the credit rating of Cyprus to junk status. Fitch's downgrade one month later compels the Cypriot government to request a bailout from the EFSF/ESM.
March 30, 2012	The ceiling for EFSF/ESM lending is increased to €700 billion ($970 billion).
April 30, 2012	S&P downgrades 16 Spanish banks, as well as Spain's sovereign credit rating the previous week because of banking sector risks.
May 7–12, 2012	The Spanish government nationalizes Bankia, a conglomerate of Spain's fourth largest bank and several regional banks. The Spanish government also adopts a series of comprehensive measures to strengthen the country's banking sector.
May 15, 2012	New elections are announced after Antonis Samaras of New Democracy and Alexis Tsipras of Syriza each fail to form a coalition government.
June 9, 2012	Eurozone finance ministers agree to a €100 billion ($136 billion) bailout of Spanish banks. With this rescue, the European Union and the IMF have committed €500 billion ($693 billion) thus far to finance European bailouts.
June 15, 2012	ECB president Mario Draghi announces continued support for solvent European banks via the ECB's LTRO funding program.
June 17–20, 2012	New elections are held in Greece, with New Democracy winning 30 percent of the votes. Antonis Samaras is sworn in as prime minister after his party forms a coalition government with the socialist PASOK and the Democratic left. Samaras and his team are expected to renegotiate the terms of Greece's €130 billion ($180 billion) bailout.

June 25, 2012	Cyprus requests financial assistance from the European Union and the IMF.
June 29, 2012	After a 14-hour meeting in Brussels, EU leaders agree to allow the ESM rescue fund to recapitalize Spanish banks and to directly buy Italian sovereign bonds.
July 10, 2012	Eurozone finance ministers agree to a €30 billion ($41 billion) bailout of Spain's troubled banks. Ministers also extend by one year, until 2014, the country's deadline to achieve a budget deficit of 3 percent of GDP.
July 11, 2012	Spanish prime minister Mariano Rajoy maintains his government's commitment to the deficit targets for 2013 and 2014 with a new €65 billion ($90 billion) austerity package.
July 26, 2012	**ECB president Mario Draghi announces that the ECB will do "whatever it takes to preserve the euro." Markets rally around his announcement.**
September 6, 2012	The ECB provides details on its new secondary market bond purchasing program, Outright Monetary Transactions (OMT).
September 12, 2012	The German Constitutional Court in Karlsruhe allows the ESM and the Fiscal Compact to be ratified, clearing the way for implementation of the eurozone's permanent rescue mechanism.
October 8, 2012	The ESM is declared operational in Luxembourg.
October 9, 2012	After its growth prospects are revised downward, Portugal has until 2014 to correct its excessive government deficit.
October 18–19, 2012	EU leaders in the European Council discuss the completion of the Economic and Monetary Union (EMU) on the basis of an interim report presented by Herman Van Rompuy, president of the Council, and agree on a timetable to have the single banking supervisory mechanism in place by January 1, 2013.
November 7, 2012	The European Commission forecasts GDP growth for the EU economy in 2013, as well as a large improvement in the budgetary situation of many member states.

December 14, 2012	The Economic and Financial Affairs Council of the European Union (Ecofin, composed of the economic and finance ministers of the member states) decides on a single banking supervisor, the ECB.

2013, Remaining Risks and Lessons of the Crisis

March 25, 2013	**The Eurogroup, European Commission, ECB, and IMF agree to a €10 billion ($14 billion) bailout for Cyprus, including heavy losses for uninsured depositors and the closure of the Cyprus Popular Bank (Laiki Bank), Cyprus's second largest bank.**
April 2, 2013	The Cypriot finance minister, Michalis Sarris, resigns.
April 18, 2013	Slovenian central bank governor Marko Kranjec announces that bad loans held by Slovenian banks amount to approximately 10 percent of GDP.
April 30, 2013	The Cypriot Parliament accepts the terms of the bailout, including the closure of Laiki, recapitalization of the Bank of Cyprus, fiscal consolidation, and structural reforms.
May 2, 2013	Moody's downgrades Slovenia's credit rating to junk status because of banking system turmoil and the risk of government recapitalization.
December 10, 2013	Independent stress tests on the Slovenian banking system indicate a potential capital shortfall of €4.8 billion ($6.7 billion) under adverse scenarios. Banking and sovereign risks remain.

Who's Who in the Euro Crisis

Almunia, Joaquín (b. 1948) Spanish politician; European Commissioner for Competition, 2010– ; European Commissioner for Economic and Financial Affairs, 2004–10; member of the Socialist Workers' Party.

Anastasiades, Nicos (b. 1946) Cypriot politician; president of Cyprus, 2013– .

Asmussen, Jörg (b. 1966) German economist; deputy social minister of Germany, 2013– ; member of Executive Board, European Central Bank, 2012–13; deputy finance minister of Germany, 2008–11; member of Social Democratic Party.

Balcerowicz, Leszek (b. 1947) Polish economist; deputy prime minister of Poland, 1989–1991, 1997–2000; finance minister, 1989–91, 1997–2000; president, National Bank of Poland, 2001–07.

Barnier, Michel (b. 1951) French politician; European Commissioner for Internal Market and Services, 2010– ; vice president, European People's Party, 2006– ; member of Union for a Popular Movement (UMP).

Barroso, Manuel José (b. 1956) Portuguese politician; president, European Commission, 2004– ; prime minister of Portugal, 2002–04; member of Social Democratic Party and European People's Party.

Berlusconi, Silvio (b. 1936) Italian politician; prime minister of Italy, 1994–95, 2001–06, 2008–11; leader of Forza Italia.

Borg, Anders (b. 1968) Swedish economist and politician; finance minister of Sweden, 2006– ; member of Moderate Party.

Borisov, Boyko (b. 1959) Bulgarian politician; prime minister of Bulgaria, 2009–13; leader, Citizens for European Development of Bulgaria (GERB).

Bratušek, Alenka (b. 1970) Slovenian politician; prime minister of Slovenia, 2013–14; leader of Positive Slovenia, 2013–14.

Claessens, Stijn (b. 1959) Dutch economist; assistant director, Research Department, International Monetary Fund, 2007– ; previously held senior positions at the World Bank.

Coelho, Pedro Passos (b. 1964) Portuguese politician; prime minister of Portugal, 2011– ; president of the Social Democratic Party, 2010– .

Cowen, Brian (b. 1960) Irish politician; Taoiseach (prime minister) of Ireland, 2008–11.

de Guindos, Luis (b. 1960) Spanish politician; minister of economy and competitiveness of Spain, 2011– ; member of the Spanish People's Party.

Dijsselbloem, Jeroen (b. 1966) Dutch politician and economist; finance minister of the Netherlands, 2012– ; president, Eurogroup, 2013– ; president, Board of Governors of the European Stability Mechanism, 2013– ; member of Labour Party.

Draghi, Mario (b. 1947) Italian economist; president, European Central Bank, 2011– ; governor, Bank of Italy, 2006–11.

Fekter, Maria (b. 1956) Austrian politician; finance minister of Austria, 2011–13; federal minister for the interior, 2008–11; member of Austrian People's Party (ÖVP).

Frieden, Luc (b. 1963) Luxembourgian economist and politician; finance minister of Luxembourg, 2009–13; member of Christian Social People's Party (CSV).

Grilli, Vittorio (b. 1957) Italian economist; minister of economy and finance of Luxembourg, 2012–13; chairman, Economic and Financial Committee of the European Union, 2011–12; deputy minister of economy and finance, 2011–12.

Hollande, François (b. 1954) French politician; president of France, 2012– ; member of Socialist Party.

Jager, Jan Kees de (b. 1969) Dutch economist; finance minister of the Netherlands, 2010–12; member of Christian Democratic Appeal (CDA).

Janša, Janez (b. 1958) Slovenian politician; prime minister of Slovenia, 2012–13, 2004–08; minister of defense, 1990–94; leader of the Slovenian Democratic Party, 1993– .

Juncker, Jean-Claude (b. 1954) Luxembourgian politician; prime minister of Luxembourg, 1995–2013; finance minister, 1989–2009; president, Eurogroup, 2005–13.

Karamanlis, Konstantinos (b. 1966) Greek politician; prime minister of Greece, 2004–09; member of New Democracy Party.

Katainen, Jyrki (b. 1971) Finnish politician; prime minister of Finland, 2011– ; deputy prime minister and finance minister, 2007–11.

Kranjec, Marko (b. 1940) Slovenian economist; governor, Bank of Slovenia, 2007–13; finance minister and ambassador to European Union, 1997–2002.

Lagarde, Christine (b. 1956) French economist; managing director, International Monetary Fund, 2011– ; finance minister of France, 2007–11.

Lenihan, Brian (b. 1959, d. 2011) Irish politician; finance minister of Ireland, 2008–11.

Lewandowski, Janusz (b. 1951) Polish economist and politician; European Commissioner for Financial Programming and the Budget, 2010– ; member of Civic Platform party in Poland and European People's Party.

Ligi, Jürgen (b. 1959) Estonian politician; finance minister of Estonia, 2009– ; member of Estonian Reform Party.

Merkel, Angela (b. 1954) German politician; chancellor of Germany, 2005– ; member of Christian Democratic Union.

Monti, Mario (b. 1943) Italian politician; prime minister of Italy, 2011–13; European Commissioner for Internal Market, Services, Customs and Taxation, 1995–2004; member of Civic Choice Party.

Moscovici, Pierre (b. 1957) French economist; finance minister of France, 2012– ; minister for European affairs, 1997–2002; vice president, European Parliament, 2003 and 2007; member of French Socialist Party.

Orbán, Viktor (b. 1963) Hungarian politician; prime minister of Hungary, 2010; member of Fidesz.

Osborne, George (b. 1971) British politician; Chancellor of the Exchequer (finance minister) of the United Kingdom, 2010– ; member of British Conservative Party.

Papaconstantinou, George (b. 1961) Greek economist and politician; finance minister of Greece, 2009–11.

Papademos, Lucas (b. 1947) Greek economist; prime minister of Greece, 2011–12; vice president, European Central Bank, 2002–10; governor, Bank of Greece, 1994–2002.

Papandreou, Georgios (b. 1952) Greek politician; prime minister of Greece, 2009–11; leader of Panhellenic Socialist Movement (PASOK), 2004–12.

Radičová, Iveta (b. 1956) Slovakian politician; prime minister of Slovakia, 2010–12; member of Slovak Democratic and Christian Union–Democratic Party (SDKÚ-DS).

Rajoy, Mariano (b. 1955) Spanish politician; prime minister of Spain, 2011– ; leader of People's Party, 2004– .

Regling, Klaus (b. 1950) German economist; chief executive officer of the European Financial Stability Facility, 2010– ; managing director of the European Stability Mechanism, 2010– ; director general for European and international financial relations of the German Ministry of Finance, 1995–98.

Rehn, Olli (b. 1962) Finnish politician; European Commissioner for Economic and Monetary Affairs and the Euro, 2010– ; vice president, European Commission 2010– ; member of Center Party.

Samaras, Antonis (b. 1951) Greek politician; prime minister of Greece, 2012– ; leader of New Democracy Party, 2009– .

Sarkozy, Nicolas (b. 1955) French politician; president of France, 2007–12; member of Union for a Popular Movement (UMP).

Sarris, Michalis (b. 1946) Cypriot economist and politician; finance minister of Cyprus, February–April 2013.

Schäuble, Wolfgang (b. 1942) German politician; finance minister of Germany, 2009– ; member of Christian Democratic Union (CDU) Party.

Šemeta, Algirdas (b. 1962) Lithuanian economist; European Commissioner for Taxation and Customs Union, Audit and Anti-Fraud, 2010– ; member of Homeland Union–Christian Democrats and European People's Party.

Sigurðardóttir, Jóhanna (b. 1942) Icelandic politician; prime minister of Iceland, 2009–13; member of Social Democratic Party.

Sócrates, José (b. 1957) Portuguese politician; prime minister of Portugal, 2005–11; president, European Council, 2007–08.

Stark, Jürgen (b. 1948) German economist; member of the Executive Board, European Central Bank, 2006–11.

Strauss-Kahn, Dominique (b. 1949) French economist; managing director, International Monetary Fund, 2007–11; finance minister of France, 1997–99.

Šušteršič, Janez (b. 1966) Slovenian economist and professor; finance minister of Republic of Slovenia, 2012–13; member of Gregor Virant's Civic List Party.

Teixeira dos Santos, Fernando (b. 1951) Portuguese economist and professor; finance minister of Portugal, 2005–11.

Tremonti, Giulio (b. 1947) Italian politician; finance minister of Italy, 1994–95, 2001–04, 2005–06, 2008–11.

Trichet, Jean-Claude (b. 1942) French civil servant; president, European Central Bank, 2003–11.

Urpilainen, Jutta (b. 1975) Finnish politician; deputy prime minister of Finland, 2011– ; minister of finance of Finland, 2011– ; leader of the Social Democratic Party, 2008–14.

Van Rompuy, Herman (b. 1947) Belgian politician; president, European Council, 2009– ; prime minister of Belgium, 2008–09; member of Christian Democratic and Flemish Party (CD&V) and European People's Party.

Venizelos, Evangelos (b. 1957) Greek politician; deputy prime minister and minister of foreign affairs of Greece, 2013– ; deputy prime minister and finance minister, 2011–12, member of Panhellenic Socialist Movement (PASOK).

Vincent-Rostowski, Jan (b. 1951) Polish and British economist; finance minister of Poland, 2007–13; deputy prime minister, 2013; member of Conservative Party in Britain and Civic Platform Party in Poland.

Vlădescu, Sebastian (b. 1958) Romanian economist and politician; finance minister of Romania, 2005–07 and 2009–10; member of National Liberal Party (PNL).

Waigel, Theo (b. 1939) German politician; finance minister of Germany, 1989–98; member of Christian Social Union Party.

Weber, Axel A. (b. 1957) German economist; president, Bundesbank, 2004–11; member of Governing Council, European Central Bank, 2004–11.

Weidmann, Jens (b. 1968) German economist; president, Bundesbank, 2011– .

Wieser, Thomas (b. 1954) president, Economic and Financial Committee of the European Union, 2009– ; president, Eurogroup Working Group, October 2011– .

Zapatero, José Luis Rodríguez (b. 1960) Spanish politician; prime minister of Spain, 2004–11; member of Spanish Socialist Workers' Party (PSOE).

Glossary

Alert Mechanism Report. The initial screening device of the macroeconomic imbalance procedure. The report is used to determine whether an in-depth review of a member state is necessary to decide whether an imbalance that needs immediate policy attention exists.

Bundesbank. The central bank of the Federal Republic of Germany and a part of the European System of Central Banks.

Council of Ministers. Formally known as the Council of the European Union and informally as the EU Council, one of the seven institutions governed by Article 13 of the Treaty on European Union. The council is part of the European Union's bicameral legislature and consists of 28 national ministers (one for each member state), along with a six-month rotating council presidency. This is where national ministers meet to adopt laws and coordinate policies. (Not to be confused with the **European Council**.)

currency board. A monetary policy objective with three distinct characteristics: the maintenance of a fixed exchange rate with a foreign "anchor" currency, automatic convertibility to exchange domestic currency at this fixed rate, and a long-term commitment by a country's monetary authority to this exchange system.

Economic and Financial Affairs Council (Ecofin). A configuration of the Council of Ministers consisting of the economics and finance ministers of all 28 member states. Ecofin legislates in specific EU economic and financial areas such as economic policy coordination and surveillance, the euro, and monitoring of the budgetary and public finance policy matters of member states.

eurobond. A proposed financial instrument to deal with the sovereign debt crisis facing the southern rim countries. Sovereign bonds jointly issued by the eurozone, eurobonds would provide indebted states access to otherwise unavailable credit because the sovereign rating of crisis and noncrisis member countries would both be taken account. However, questions about the immediate need for structural reforms and the eurozone's lack of a central financial authority to issue and guarantee them rendered the proposal unlikely.

Eurogroup. A group composed of eurozone finance ministers. As representatives of member states that have adopted the euro, they exercise control over the economic governance of the euro and agreements affecting the monetary union. (Not to be confused with the Eurogroup Working Group, which provides assistance to the Eurogroup and its president in preparing ministers' discussions.)

European Banking Authority (EBA). The banking regulatory authority of the European Union whose activities include conducting European bank stress tests and identifying banks' capital structure weaknesses. The EBA is one of the three new European Supervisory Authorities to improve the European Union's financial supervisory architecture. See also **European Insurance and Occupational Pensions Authority** and **European Securities and Markets Authority**.

European Central Bank (ECB). The central bank for the euro. It administers the monetary policy of the eurozone's 18 member states, and its governing mandate is to maintain price stability within the eurozone.

European Commission. The executive arm of the European Union, whose functions are to implement EU decisions, uphold its treaties, and propose legislation. The Commission consists of 28 commissioners, from which the European Commission president is chosen by the European Council and elected by the European Parliament, the European Union's bicameral legislature.

European Council. An official EU institution that defines the general political direction and priorities of the European Union. It does not exercise legislative functions. With the entry into force of the Treaty of Lisbon on December 1, 2009, the council became one of the seven institutions of the union. It consists of the heads of state or government of the member states, together with its president and the president of the European Commission. (Not to be confused with the **Council of Ministers**, formally known as Council of the European Union.)

European Court of Justice (ECJ). Also called the Court of Justice, the highest court in the European Union on matters of EU law. The court was established in 1952 through the Treaty of Paris as a part of the original European Coal and Steel Community, the predecessor of the current European Union.

European Economic Community (EEC). The supranational organization established by the Treaty of Rome in 1957 that was a precursor of the current European Union. The EEC aimed to create a common market and greater economic integration among its six founding members: Belgium, France, Italy, Luxembourg, the Netherlands, and West Germany.

European Financial Stability Facility (EFSF). Created and financed by euro-zone member states on May 9, 2010, as a special-purpose vehicle mandated to safeguard Europe's financial stability by providing financial assistance to euro-zone states facing immediate economic difficulty. The EFSF was created as a temporary rescue mechanism and was replaced by the permanent European Stability Mechanism (ESM) on October 8, 2012.

European Insurance and Occupational Pensions Authority (EIOPA). A European financial regulatory institution established on January 1, 2011, to act as an independent advisory board to the European Commission, Council of the European Union, and European Parliament. EIOPA supports financial stability and transparency as well as protects insurance policy holders, pension scheme members, and their beneficiaries. EIOPA is one of the three new European Supervisory Authorities to improve the EU's financial supervisory architecture, along with the **European Banking Authority** and **European Securities and Markets Authority**.

European People's Party (EPP). A liberal center-right European political party founded in 1976. The EPP is the largest party in the European Parliament, the European Council, and the current European Commission. The EPP consists of major Christian Democratic and liberal national parties such as Germany's Christian Democratic Union (CDU), France's Union for a Popular Movement (UMP), and Spain's People's Party (PP). The party Citizens for European Development of Bulgaria (GERB) is an EPP member as well.

European Redemption Fund (ERF). A proposed solution to the sovereign debt problems of eurozone countries in which countries with excessive debt (above the 60 percent of GDP required by the Maastricht Treaty) would have their debt collectively converted into eurobonds, which would then be paid off over 25 years. The incentives for going deeper into debt rather than mini-mizing it prevented serious consideration of the ERF proposal.

European Securities and Markets Authority (ESMA). A European finan-cial regulatory institution responsible for overseeing securities legislation and regulation, strengthening investor protection, and fostering cooperation among national authorities. ESMA is one of the three new European Supervisory Authorities intended to improve the European Union's financial supervisory architecture, along with the **European Banking Authority** and the **European Insurance and Occupational Pensions Authority**.

European semester. An annual economic policy coordination cycle set up by the European Commission in which member states undergo a detailed analysis of their economic and structural reforms. On this basis, the European Commission gives its assessment and recommendations for the next 12 to 18 months.

European Stability Mechanism (ESM). A mechanism established as a permanent safeguard in the eurozone against the financial difficulties of member states and as a firewall against financial contagion. The ESM, which replaced two previous funding programs, the European Financial Stability Facility (EFSF) and the European Financial Stabilization Mechanism (EFSM), has a total lending capacity of €500 billion ($693 billion).

European Structural Funds. Along with the cohesion funds, financial tools that are a part of the European Union's regional policy aimed at accelerating economic convergence and reducing the income disparities between Europe's richer and poorer regions.

European Union. The economic and political union of 28 states located in Europe. The major institutions of the European Union are the European Commission, Council of the European Union, European Council, European Court of Justice, European Central Bank, European Court of Auditors, and European Parliament.

Euro Plus Pact. Also known as the Competitiveness Pact, implemented in 2011 by eurozone governments in order to commit to political reforms that lead to higher levels of competitiveness, employment, and fiscal sustainability. The pact is viewed as a stronger version of the Stability and Growth Pact, which had been widely criticized for its inconsistent implementation.

eurozone. The Economic and Monetary Union of the 18 EU member states that have adopted the euro as their official currency: Austria, Belgium, Cyprus, Estonia, Finland, France, Germany, Greece, Ireland, Italy, Latvia, Luxembourg, Malta, the Netherlands, Portugal, Slovakia, Slovenia, and Spain.

excess deficit procedure (EDP). An action implemented by the European Commission if, as obligated by the Stability and Growth Pact, the budget deficit of a member state exceeds the threshold of 3 percent of GDP or its public debt exceeds the threshold of 60 percent of GDP. Several steps are then undertaken by the European Commission to encourage the member state to minimize its budget deficit, possibly culminating in sanctions if the member state's public finances continue to pose a risk to the proper functioning of the Economic and Monetary Union.

Exchange Rate Mechanism II (ERM II). Exchange rate criteria applied to the euro and participating national currencies to maintain exchange rate stability and avoid excessive exchange rate fluctuations in the single market. The mechanism is also intended to help noneurozone countries become members of the eurozone.

Fiscal Compact (Treaty on Stability, Coordination and Governance in the Economic and Monetary Union). Signed on March 2, 2012, by all member states of the European Union (except the Czech Republic and United Kingdom), a stricter version of the Stability and Growth Pact requiring signatories to enact into national law a self-correcting budgetary mechanism. The Fiscal Compact complements the EU "six pack" measures by enforcing budgetary discipline and independent fiscal monitoring, but it remains an intergovernmental treaty rather than EU law.

full allotment. Unlimited access. In reference to the "fixed-rate full allotment" procedure of the ECB, banks under financial stress that can provide adequate collateral have unlimited access to ECB liquidity at a fixed rate.

Governing Council of the ECB. The main decision-making body of the ECB, composed of six members of the Executive Board and a governor from each of the 18 members of the European System of Central Banks.

Greek Loan Facility. The €52.9 billion ($73.3 billion) loan package for Greece consisting of bilateral loans between Greece and 14 eurozone countries coordinated, disbursed, and monitored by the European Commission. The undisbursed amounts of the Greek Loan Facility were added to Greece's second bailout program on March 14, 2012, which was financed through the European Financial Stability Facility rather than bilateral loans.

joint and several guarantee. A legal guarantee undertaken by multiple people in which any one guarantor can be held fully responsible for repaying the whole of the debt despite each guarantor only being partially responsible for that debt.

long-term refinancing operation (LTRO). The process by which the ECB provides financing to eurozone banks. The purpose of LTROs is to provide an adequate capital cushion to eurozone banks holding illiquid assets so that interbank lending will not be interrupted and a liquidity crunch will be prevented.

Maastricht criteria. Also known as the euro convergence criteria, criteria that must be met by all EU member states that want to adopt the euro as their national currency. The five criteria are meant to maintain price stability and fiscal responsibility in the eurozone: (1) Harmonized Index of Consumer Prices (HICP) inflation no higher than 1.5 percent; (2) a budget deficit no higher than 3 percent from the previous fiscal year; (3) a debt-to-GDP ratio no higher than 60 percent; (4) adoption of ERM II for at least two years with an exchange rate band no higher than 15 percent; and (5) long-term interest rates no higher than 2 percent.

Maastricht Treaty. Also known as the Treaty on European Union, a treaty signed on February 7, 1992, establishing the institutional pillars of the EU system and the basic criteria for adopting the future common currency, the euro.

macroeconomic imbalance procedure. Established in 2011 as a part of the larger "six pack" legislation, a protocol undertaken by the European Union to detect, correct, and prevent macroeconomic imbalances among the EU member states. See **Alert Mechanism Report**.

northern euro. A common currency proposed for a dual-speed eurozone to resolve the euro crisis. The northern euro would be the common currency for the "core" eurozone countries—Austria, Belgium, France, Germany, the Netherlands, and Luxembourg—distinct and independent from the weaker **southern euro**. The impracticality of how it could implemented without reversing the tide of European integration prevented the dual-speed solution from gaining serious traction.

Outright Monetary Transactions (OMT). A secondary sovereign bond buying program of the European Central Bank that aims to safeguard effective monetary policy transmission and ensure the ECB's ability to guide price stability in the medium term. Although OMT share the objectives of the Securities Markets Programme, three differences exist: (1) OMT require "strict and effective conditionality" tied to the appropriate EFSF and ESM programs so that national governments have the incentive to undertake fiscal and structural reforms; (2) they are ex ante unlimited in one- to three-year sovereign bond markets; and (3) the ECB receives equal treatment for its holdings as private or other creditors.

real economy. The part of the economy in which real goods and services are produced, as opposed to the part of the economy in which financial securities are bought and sold.

Securities Markets Programme (SMP). An ECB bond-buying program in specific dysfunctional public and private debt securities markets in order to ensure adequate depth and liquidity in those market segments. The objective of the SMP is to ensure the proper functioning of the ECB's monetary policy transmission mechanism so that monetary policy can effectively guide price stability in the medium term.

"six pack" legislation. A set of measures agreed on in March 2011 by Ecofin and implemented in December 13, 2011. The legislation aimed to strengthen the Stability and Growth Pact by enforcing public deficit reduction and introducing macroeconomic surveillance measures.

southern euro. A common currency proposed for a dual-speed eurozone to resolve the euro crisis. The southern euro would be the common currency for the southern rim eurozone countries—Italy, Portugal, and Spain—distinct and independent from the stronger **northern euro**. The impracticality of how it could be implemented without reversing the tide of European integration prevented the dual-speed solution from gaining serious traction.

Stability and Growth Pact. An agreement signed by the 28 member states of the European Union and enacted through two separate resolutions on July 1, 1998, and January 1, 1999, with the goal of maintaining and enhancing stability within the Economic and Monetary Union. Because the pact's fiscal discipline rules were considered insufficient and selectively unenforceable, additional reform measures were adopted to rectify its ineffectiveness.

Target2. The real-time gross settlement system owned and operated by the Eurosystem. Target stands for Trans-European Automated Real-time Gross Settlement Express Transfer system.

Troika. A nickname for the European Central Bank, the European Commission, and the International Monetary Fund, in reference to their collective actions, decisions, and presence in financially distressed countries during the euro crisis.

"two pack" legislation. Two regulations being negotiated in the European Union to strengthen the surveillance mechanism of the eurozone. The regulations aim to complement recently approved measures such as the "six pack" legislation and the Fiscal Compact by monitoring and assessing the draft budgetary plans of eurozone states, lowering their excessive budget deficits, and enhancing the surveillance of states currently experiencing financial difficulties.

Treaty on European Union. See Maastricht Treaty.

Abbreviations

CDS	credit default swap
EBA	European Banking Authority
EC	European Commission
ECB	European Central Bank
ECJ	European Court of Justice
Ecofin	Economic and Financial Affairs Council of the European Union
EDP	excess deficit procedure
EEC	European Economic Community
EFSF	European Financial Stability Facility
EFSM	European Financial Stabilization Mechanism
EIOPA	European Insurance and Occupational Pensions Authority
EMU	Economic and Monetary Union
EPP	European People's Party
ERF	European Redemption Fund
ERM II	Exchange Rate Mechanism II
ESM	European Stability Mechanism
ESMA	European Securities and Markets Authority
EU	European Union
GDP	gross domestic product
GERB	Citizens for European Development of Bulgaria
GLF	Greek Loan Facility
HICP	Harmonized Index of Consumer Prices
IMF	International Monetary Fund
LTRO	long-term refinancing operation
NBER	National Bureau of Economic Research

OECD	Organization for Economic Cooperation and Development
OMT	Outright Monetary Transactions
PSI	private sector involvement
S&P	Standard and Poor's
SMP	Securities Markets Programme

Index

Other Publications from the
Peterson Institute for International Economics

103 **Economic Normalization with Cuba: A Roadmap for US Policymakers**
Gary Clyde Hufbauer, Barbara Kotschwar, assisted by Cathleen Cimino and Julia Muir
April 2014   ISBN 978-0-88132-682-6

BOOKS

IMF Conditionality*   John Williamson, ed.
1983   ISBN 0-88132-006-4
Trade Policy in the 1980s*   William R. Cline, ed.
1983   ISBN 0-88132-031-5
Subsidies in International Trade*   Gary Clyde Hufbauer and Joanna Shelton Erb
1984   ISBN 0-88132-004-8
International Debt: Systemic Risk and Policy Response*   William R. Cline
1984   ISBN 0-88132-015-3
Trade Protection in the United States: 31 Case Studies*   Gary Clyde Hufbauer, Diane E. Berliner, and Kimberly Ann Elliott
1986   ISBN 0-88132-040-4
Toward Renewed Economic Growth in Latin America*   Bela Balassa, Gerardo M. Bueno, Pedro Pablo Kuczynski, and Mario Henrique Simonsen
1986   ISBN 0-88132-045-5
Capital Flight and Third World Debt*
Donald R. Lessard and John Williamson, eds.
1987   ISBN 0-88132-053-6
The Canada-United States Free Trade Agreement: The Global Impact*   Jeffrey J. Schott and Murray G. Smith, eds.
1988   ISBN 0-88132-073-0
World Agricultural Trade: Building a Consensus*   William M. Miner and Dale E. Hathaway, eds.
1988   ISBN 0-88132-071-3
Japan in the World Economy*   Bela Balassa and Marcus Noland
1988   ISBN 0-88132-041-2
America in the World Economy: A Strategy for the 1990s*   C. Fred Bergsten
1988   ISBN 0-88132-089-7
Managing the Dollar: From the Plaza to the Louvre*   Yoichi Funabashi
1988, 2d ed. 1989   ISBN 0-88132-097-8
United States External Adjustment and the World Economy*   William R. Cline
May 1989   ISBN 0-88132-048-X
Free Trade Areas and U.S. Trade Policy*
Jeffrey J. Schott, ed.
May 1989   ISBN 0-88132-094-3
Dollar Politics: Exchange Rate Policymaking in the United States*   I. M. Destler and C. Randall Henning
September 1989   ISBN 0-88132-079-X
Latin American Adjustment: How Much Has Happened?*   John Williamson, ed.
April 1990   ISBN 0-88132-125-7
The Future of World Trade in Textiles and Apparel*   William R. Cline
1987, 2d ed. June 1999   ISBN 0-88132-110-9
Completing the Uruguay Round: A Results-Oriented Approach to the GATT Trade Negotiations*   Jeffrey J. Schott, ed.
September 1990   ISBN 0-88132-130-3

Economic Sanctions Reconsidered (2 volumes)
Economic Sanctions Reconsidered: Supplemental Case Histories   Gary Clyde Hufbauer, Jeffrey J. Schott, and Kimberly Ann Elliott
1985, 2d ed. Dec. 1990   ISBN cloth 0-88132-115-X/ paper 0-88132-105-2
Economic Sanctions Reconsidered: History and Current Policy   Gary C. Hufbauer, Jeffrey J. Schott, and Kimberly Ann Elliott
December 1990   ISBN cloth 0-88132-140-0
      ISBN paper 0-88132-136-2
Pacific Basin Developing Countries: Prospects for the Future*   Marcus Noland
January 1991   ISBN cloth 0-88132-141-9
      ISBN paper 0-88132-081-1
Currency Convertibility in Eastern Europe*
John Williamson, ed.
October 1991   ISBN 0-88132-128-1
International Adjustment and Financing: The Lessons of 1985-1991*   C. Fred Bergsten, ed.
January 1992   ISBN 0-88132-112-5
North American Free Trade: Issues and Recommendations*   Gary Clyde Hufbauer and Jeffrey J. Schott
April 1992   ISBN 0-88132-120-6
Narrowing the U.S. Current Account Deficit*
Alan J. Lenz
June 1992   ISBN 0-88132-103-6
The Economics of Global Warming
William R. Cline
June 1992   ISBN 0-88132-132-X
US Taxation of International Income: Blueprint for Reform   Gary Clyde Hufbauer, assisted by Joanna M. van Rooij
October 1992   ISBN 0-88132-134-6
Who's Bashing Whom? Trade Conflict in High-Technology Industries   Laura D'Andrea Tyson
November 1992   ISBN 0-88132-106-0
Korea in the World Economy*   Il SaKong
January 1993   ISBN 0-88132-183-4
Pacific Dynamism and the International Economic System*   C. Fred Bergsten and Marcus Noland, eds.
May 1993   ISBN 0-88132-196-6
Economic Consequences of Soviet Disintegration*   John Williamson, ed.
May 1993   ISBN 0-88132-190-7
Reconcilable Differences? United States-Japan Economic Conflict*   C. Fred Bergsten and Marcus Noland
June 1993   ISBN 0-88132-129-X
Does Foreign Exchange Intervention Work?
Kathryn M. Dominguez and Jeffrey A. Frankel
September 1993   ISBN 0-88132-104-4
Sizing Up U.S. Export Disincentives*
J. David Richardson
September 1993   ISBN 0-88132-107-9
NAFTA: An Assessment   Gary Clyde Hufbauer and Jeffrey J. Schott, *rev. ed.*
October 1993   ISBN 0-88132-199-0
Adjusting to Volatile Energy Prices
Philip K. Verleger, Jr.
November 1993   ISBN 0-88132-069-2
The Political Economy of Policy Reform
John Williamson, ed.
January 1994   ISBN 0-88132-195-8

Measuring the Costs of Protection in the United States   Gary Clyde Hufbauer and Kimberly Ann Elliott
January 1994   ISBN 0-88132-108-7
The Dynamics of Korean Economic Development*   Cho Soon
March 1994   ISBN 0-88132-162-1
Reviving the European Union*
C. Randall Henning, Eduard Hochreiter, and Gary Clyde Hufbauer, eds.
April 1994   ISBN 0-88132-208-3
China in the World Economy   Nicholas R. Lardy
April 1994   ISBN 0-88132-200-8
Greening the GATT: Trade, Environment, and the Future   Daniel C. Esty
July 1994   ISBN 0-88132-205-9
Western Hemisphere Economic Integration*
Gary Clyde Hufbauer and Jeffrey J. Schott
July 1994   ISBN 0-88132-159-1
Currencies and Politics in the United States, Germany, and Japan   C. Randall Henning
September 1994   ISBN 0-88132-127-3
Estimating Equilibrium Exchange Rates
John Williamson, ed.
September 1994   ISBN 0-88132-076-5
Managing the World Economy: Fifty Years after Bretton Woods   Peter B. Kenen, ed.
September 1994   ISBN 0-88132-212-1
Reciprocity and Retaliation in U.S. Trade Policy
Thomas O. Bayard and Kimberly Ann Elliott
September 1994   ISBN 0-88132-084-6
The Uruguay Round: An Assessment*   Jeffrey J. Schott, assisted by Johanna Buurman
November 1994   ISBN 0-88132-206-7
Measuring the Costs of Protection in Japan*
Yoko Sazanami, Shujiro Urata, and Hiroki Kawai
January 1995   ISBN 0-88132-211-3
Foreign Direct Investment in the United States, 3d ed.   Edward M. Graham and Paul R. Krugman
January 1995   ISBN 0-88132-204-0
The Political Economy of Korea-United States Cooperation*   C. Fred Bergsten and Il SaKong, eds.
February 1995   ISBN 0-88132-213-X
International Debt Reexamined*
William R. Cline
February 1995   ISBN 0-88132-083-8
American Trade Politics, 3d ed.   I. M. Destler
April 1995   ISBN 0-88132-215-6
Managing Official Export Credits: The Quest for a Global Regime*   John E. Ray
July 1995   ISBN 0-88132-207-5
Asia Pacific Fusion: Japan's Role in APEC*
Yoichi Funabashi
October 1995   ISBN 0-88132-224-5
Korea-United States Cooperation in the New World Order*   C. Fred Bergsten and Il SaKong, eds.
February 1996   ISBN 0-88132-226-1
Why Exports Really Matter!*
          ISBN 0-88132-221-0
Why Exports Matter More!*   ISBN 0-88132-229-6
J. David Richardson and Karin Rindal
July 1995; February 1996

Global Corporations and National Governments
Edward M. Graham
May 1996   ISBN 0-88132-111-7
Global Economic Leadership and the Group of Seven   C. Fred Bergsten and C. Randall Henning
May 1996   ISBN 0-88132-218-0
The Trading System after the Uruguay Round*
John Whalley and Colleen Hamilton
July 1996   ISBN 0-88132-131-1
Private Capital Flows to Emerging Markets after the Mexican Crisis*   Guillermo A. Calvo, Morris Goldstein, and Eduard Hochreiter
September 1996   ISBN 0-88132-232-6
The Crawling Band as an Exchange Rate Regime: Lessons from Chile, Colombia, and Israel   John Williamson
September 1996   ISBN 0-88132-231-8
Flying High: Liberalizing Civil Aviation in the Asia Pacific*   Gary Clyde Hufbauer and Christopher Findlay
November 1996   ISBN 0-88132-227-X
Measuring the Costs of Visible Protection in Korea*   Namdoo Kim
November 1996   ISBN 0-88132-236-9
The World Trading System: Challenges Ahead
Jeffrey J. Schott
December 1996   ISBN 0-88132-235-0
Has Globalization Gone Too Far?   Dani Rodrik
March 1997   ISBN paper 0-88132-241-5
Korea-United States Economic Relationship*
C. Fred Bergsten and Il SaKong, eds.
March 1997   ISBN 0-88132-240-7
Summitry in the Americas: A Progress Report
Richard E. Feinberg
April 1997   ISBN 0-88132-242-3
Corruption and the Global Economy
Kimberly Ann Elliott
June 1997   ISBN 0-88132-233-4
Regional Trading Blocs in the World Economic System   Jeffrey A. Frankel
October 1997   ISBN 0-88132-202-4
Sustaining the Asia Pacific Miracle: Environmental Protection and Economic Integration   Andre Dua and Daniel C. Esty
October 1997   ISBN 0-88132-250-4
Trade and Income Distribution
William R. Cline
November 1997   ISBN 0-88132-216-4
Global Competition Policy   Edward M. Graham and J. David Richardson
December 1997   ISBN 0-88132-166-4
Unfinished Business: Telecommunications after the Uruguay Round   Gary Clyde Hufbauer and Erika Wada
December 1997   ISBN 0-88132-257-1
Financial Services Liberalization in the WTO
Wendy Dobson and Pierre Jacquet
June 1998   ISBN 0-88132-254-7
Restoring Japan's Economic Growth
Adam S. Posen
September 1998   ISBN 0-88132-262-8
Measuring the Costs of Protection in China
Zhang Shuguang, Zhang Yansheng, and Wan Zhongxin
November 1998   ISBN 0-88132-247-4

Foreign Direct Investment and Development: The New Policy Agenda for Developing Countries and Economies in Transition
Theodore H. Moran
December 1998   ISBN 0-88132-258-X
Behind the Open Door: Foreign Enterprises in the Chinese Marketplace   Daniel H. Rosen
January 1999   ISBN 0-88132-263-6
Toward A New International Financial Architecture: A Practical Post-Asia Agenda
Barry Eichengreen
February 1999   ISBN 0-88132-270-9
Is the U.S. Trade Deficit Sustainable?
Catherine L. Mann
September 1999   ISBN 0-88132-265-2
Safeguarding Prosperity in a Global Financial System: The Future International Financial Architecture, Independent Task Force Report Sponsored by the Council on Foreign Relations
Morris Goldstein, Project Director
October 1999   ISBN 0-88132-287-3
Avoiding the Apocalypse: The Future of the Two Koreas   Marcus Noland
June 2000   ISBN 0-88132-278-4
Assessing Financial Vulnerability: An Early Warning System for Emerging Markets
Morris Goldstein, Graciela Kaminsky, and Carmen Reinhart
June 2000   ISBN 0-88132-237-7
Global Electronic Commerce: A Policy Primer
Catherine L. Mann, Sue E. Eckert, and Sarah Cleeland Knight
July 2000   ISBN 0-88132-274-1
The WTO after Seattle   Jeffrey J. Schott, ed.
July 2000   ISBN 0-88132-290-3
Intellectual Property Rights in the Global Economy   Keith E. Maskus
August 2000   ISBN 0-88132-282-2
The Political Economy of the Asian Financial Crisis   Stephan Haggard
August 2000   ISBN 0-88132-283-0
Transforming Foreign Aid: United States Assistance in the 21st Century   Carol Lancaster
August 2000   ISBN 0-88132-291-1
Fighting the Wrong Enemy: Antiglobal Activists and Multinational Enterprises
Edward M. Graham
September 2000   ISBN 0-88132-272-5
Globalization and the Perceptions of American Workers   Kenneth Scheve and Matthew J. Slaughter
March 2001   ISBN 0-88132-295-4
World Capital Markets: Challenge to the G-10
Wendy Dobson and Gary Clyde Hufbauer, assisted by Hyun Koo Cho
May 2001   ISBN 0-88132-301-2
Prospects for Free Trade in the Americas
Jeffrey J. Schott
August 2001   ISBN 0-88132-275-X
Toward a North American Community: Lessons from the Old World for the New
Robert A. Pastor
August 2001   ISBN 0-88132-328-4

Measuring the Costs of Protection in Europe: European Commercial Policy in the 2000s
Patrick A. Messerlin
September 2001   ISBN 0-88132-273-3
Job Loss from Imports: Measuring the Costs
Lori G. Kletzer
September 2001   ISBN 0-88132-296-2
No More Bashing: Building a New Japan– United States Economic Relationship   C. Fred Bergsten, Takatoshi Ito, and Marcus Noland
October 2001   ISBN 0-88132-286-5
Why Global Commitment Really Matters!
Howard Lewis III and J. David Richardson
October 2001   ISBN 0-88132-298-9
Leadership Selection in the Major Multilaterals
Miles Kahler
November 2001   ISBN 0-88132-335-7
The International Financial Architecture: What's New? What's Missing?   Peter B. Kenen
November 2001   ISBN 0-88132-297-0
Delivering on Debt Relief: From IMF Gold to a New Aid Architecture   John Williamson and Nancy Birdsall, with Brian Deese
April 2002   ISBN 0-88132-331-4
Imagine There's No Country: Poverty, Inequality, and Growth in the Era of Globalization   Surjit S. Bhalla
September 2002   ISBN 0-88132-348-9
Reforming Korea's Industrial Conglomerates
Edward M. Graham
January 2003   ISBN 0-88132-337-3
Industrial Policy in an Era of Globalization: Lessons from Asia   Marcus Noland and Howard Pack
March 2003   ISBN 0-88132-350-0
Reintegrating India with the World Economy
T. N. Srinivasan and Suresh D. Tendulkar
March 2003   ISBN 0-88132-280-6
After the Washington Consensus: Restarting Growth and Reform in Latin America   Pedro-Pablo Kuczynski and John Williamson, eds.
March 2003   ISBN 0-88132-347-0
The Decline of US Labor Unions and the Role of Trade   Robert E. Baldwin
June 2003   ISBN 0-88132-341-1
Can Labor Standards Improve under Globalization?   Kimberly Ann Elliott and Richard B. Freeman
June 2003   ISBN 0-88132-332-2
Crimes and Punishments? Retaliation under the WTO   Robert Z. Lawrence
October 2003   ISBN 0-88132-359-4
Inflation Targeting in the World Economy
Edwin M. Truman
October 2003   ISBN 0-88132-345-4
Foreign Direct Investment and Tax Competition
John H. Mutti
November 2003   ISBN 0-88132-352-7
Has Globalization Gone Far Enough? The Costs of Fragmented Markets   Scott C. Bradford and Robert Z. Lawrence
February 2004   ISBN 0-88132-349-7
Food Regulation and Trade: Toward a Safe and Open Global System   Tim Josling, Donna Roberts, and David Orden
March 2004   ISBN 0-88132-346-2

Controlling Currency Mismatches in Emerging
Markets   Morris Goldstein and Philip Turner
April 2004   ISBN 0-88132-360-8
Free Trade Agreements: US Strategies and
Priorities   Jeffrey J. Schott, ed.
April 2004   ISBN 0-88132-361-6
Trade Policy and Global Poverty
William R. Cline
June 2004   ISBN 0-88132-365-9
Bailouts or Bail-ins? Responding to Financial
Crises in Emerging Economies   Nouriel Roubini
and Brad Setser
August 2004   ISBN 0-88132-371-3
Transforming the European Economy   Martin
Neil Baily and Jacob Funk Kirkegaard
September 2004   ISBN 0-88132-343-8
Chasing Dirty Money: The Fight Against
Money Laundering   Peter Reuter and
Edwin M. Truman
November 2004   ISBN 0-88132-370-5
The United States and the World Economy:
Foreign Economic Policy for the Next Decade
C. Fred Bergsten
January 2005   ISBN 0-88132-380-2
Does Foreign Direct Investment Promote
Development?   Theodore H. Moran, Edward M.
Graham, and Magnus Blomström, eds.
April 2005   ISBN 0-88132-381-0
American Trade Politics, 4th ed.   I. M. Destler
June 2005   ISBN 0-88132-382-9
Why Does Immigration Divide America? Public
Finance and Political Opposition to Open
Borders   Gordon H. Hanson
August 2005   ISBN 0-88132-400-0
Reforming the US Corporate Tax   Gary Clyde
Hufbauer and Paul L. E. Grieco
September 2005   ISBN 0-88132-384-5
The United States as a Debtor Nation
William R. Cline
September 2005   ISBN 0-88132-399-3
NAFTA Revisited: Achievements and
Challenges   Gary Clyde Hufbauer and
Jeffrey J. Schott, assisted by Paul L. E. Grieco and
Yee Wong
October 2005   ISBN 0-88132-334-9
US National Security and Foreign Direct
Investment   Edward M. Graham and
David M. Marchick
May 2006   ISBN 978-0-88132-391-7
Accelerating the Globalization of America: The
Role for Information Technology   Catherine L.
Mann, assisted by Jacob Funk Kirkegaard
June 2006   ISBN 978-0-88132-390-0
Delivering on Doha: Farm Trade and the Poor
Kimberly Ann Elliott
July 2006   ISBN 978-0-88132-392-4
Case Studies in US Trade Negotiation, Vol. 1:
Making the Rules   Charan Devereaux, Robert Z.
Lawrence, and Michael Watkins
September 2006   ISBN 978-0-88132-362-7
Case Studies in US Trade Negotiation, Vol. 2:
Resolving Disputes   Charan Devereaux, Robert
Z. Lawrence, and Michael Watkins
September 2006   ISBN 978-0-88132-363-2

C. Fred Bergsten and the World Economy
Michael Mussa, ed.
December 2006   ISBN 978-0-88132-397-9
Working Papers, Volume I   Peterson Institute
December 2006   ISBN 978-0-88132-388-7
The Arab Economies in a Changing World
Marcus Noland and Howard Pack
April 2007   ISBN 978-0-88132-393-1
Working Papers, Volume II   Peterson Institute
April 2007   ISBN 978-0-88132-404-4
Global Warming and Agriculture: Impact
Estimates by Country   William R. Cline
July 2007   ISBN 978-0-88132-403-7
US Taxation of Foreign Income   Gary Clyde
Hufbauer and Ariel Assa
October 2007   ISBN 978-0-88132-405-1
Russia's Capitalist Revolution: Why Market
Reform Succeeded and Democracy Failed
Anders Åslund
October 2007   ISBN 978-0-88132-409-9
Economic Sanctions Reconsidered, 3d ed.
Gary Clyde Hufbauer, Jeffrey J. Schott, Kimberly
Ann Elliott, and Barbara Oegg
November 2007
              ISBN hardcover 978-0-88132-407-5
     ISBN hardcover/CD-ROM 978-0-88132-408-2
Debating China's Exchange Rate Policy
Morris Goldstein and Nicholas R. Lardy, eds.
April 2008   ISBN 978-0-88132-415-0
Leveling the Carbon Playing Field: International
Competition and US Climate Policy Design
Trevor Houser, Rob Bradley, Britt Childs, Jacob
Werksman, and Robert Heilmayr
May 2008   ISBN 978-0-88132-420-4
Accountability and Oversight of US Exchange
Rate Policy   C. Randall Henning
June 2008   ISBN 978-0-88132-419-8
Challenges of Globalization: Imbalances and
Growth   Anders Åslund and
Marek Dabrowski, eds.
July 2008   ISBN 978-0-88132-418-1
China's Rise: Challenges and Opportunities
C. Fred Bergsten, Charles Freeman, Nicholas R.
Lardy, and Derek J. Mitchell
September 2008   ISBN 978-0-88132-417-4
Banking on Basel: The Future of International
Financial Regulation   Daniel K. Tarullo
September 2008   ISBN 978-0-88132-423-5
US Pension Reform: Lessons from Other
Countries   Martin Neil Baily and
Jacob Funk Kirkegaard
February 2009   ISBN 978-0-88132-425-9
How Ukraine Became a Market Economy and
Democracy   Anders Åslund
March 2009   ISBN 978-0-88132-427-3
Global Warming and the World Trading System
Gary Clyde Hufbauer, Steve Charnovitz, and
Jisun Kim
March 2009   ISBN 978-0-88132-428-0
The Russia Balance Sheet   Anders Åslund and
Andrew Kuchins
March 2009   ISBN 978-0-88132-424-2
The Euro at Ten: The Next Global Currency?
Jean Pisani-Ferry and Adam S. Posen, eds.
July 2009   ISBN 978-0-88132-430-3

Financial Globalization, Economic Growth, and the Crisis of 2007–09   William R. Cline
May 2010   ISBN 978-0-88132-4990-0
Russia after the Global Economic Crisis
Anders Åslund, Sergei Guriev, and Andrew Kuchins, eds.
June 2010   ISBN 978-0-88132-497-6
Sovereign Wealth Funds: Threat or Salvation?
Edwin M. Truman
September 2010   ISBN 978-0-88132-498-3
The Last Shall Be the First: The East European Financial Crisis, 2008–10   Anders Åslund
October 2010   ISBN 978-0-88132-521-8
Witness to Transformation: Refugee Insights into North Korea   Stephan Haggard and Marcus Noland
January 2011   ISBN 978-0-88132-438-9
Foreign Direct Investment and Development: Launching a Second Generation of Policy Research, Avoiding the Mistakes of the First, Reevaluating Policies for Developed and Developing Countries   Theodore H. Moran
April 2011   ISBN 978-0-88132-600-0
How Latvia Came through the Financial Crisis
Anders Åslund and Valdis Dombrovskis
May 2011   ISBN 978-0-88132-602-4
Global Trade in Services: Fear, Facts, and Offshoring   J. Bradford Jensen
August 2011   ISBN 978-0-88132-601-7
NAFTA and Climate Change   Meera Fickling and Jeffrey J. Schott
September 2011   ISBN 978-0-88132-436-5
Eclipse: Living in the Shadow of China's Economic Dominance   Arvind Subramanian
September 2011   ISBN 978-0-88132-606-2
Flexible Exchange Rates for a Stable World Economy   Joseph E. Gagnon with Marc Hinterschweiger
September 2011   ISBN 978-0-88132-627-7
The Arab Economies in a Changing World, 2d ed.   Marcus Noland and Howard Pack
November 2011   ISBN 978-0-88132-628-4
Sustaining China's Economic Growth After the Global Financial Crisis   Nicholas R. Lardy
January 2012   ISBN 978-0-88132-626-0
Who Needs to Open the Capital Account?
Olivier Jeanne, Arvind Subramanian, and John Williamson
April 2012   ISBN 978-0-88132-511-9
Devaluing to Prosperity: Misaligned Currencies and Their Growth Consequences   Surjit S. Bhalla
August 2012   ISBN 978-0-88132-623-9
Private Rights and Public Problems: The Global Economics of Intellectual Property in the 21st Century   Keith E. Maskus
September 2012   ISBN 978-0-88132-507-2
Global Economics in Extraordinary Times: Essays in Honor of John Williamson
C. Fred Bergsten and C. Randall Henning, eds.
November 2012   ISBN 978-0-88132-662-8
Rising Tide: Is Growth in Emerging Economies Good for the United States?   Lawrence Edwards and Robert Z. Lawrence
February 2013   ISBN 978-0-88132-500-3

Responding to Financial Crisis: Lessons from Asia Then, the United States and Europe Now
Changyong Rhee and Adam S. Posen, eds
October 2013   ISBN 978-0-88132-674-1
Fueling Up: The Economic Implications of America's Oil and Gas Boom
Trevor Houser and Shashank Mohan
January 2014   ISBN 978-0-88132-656-7
How Latin America Weathered the Global Financial Crisis   José De Gregorio
January 2014   ISBN 978-0-88132-678-9
Confronting the Curse: The Economics and Geopolitics of Natural Resource Governance
Cullen S. Hendrix and Marcus Noland
May 2014   ISBN 978-0-88132-676-5
Inside the Euro Crisis: An Eyewitness Account
Simeon Djankov
June 2014   ISBN 978-0-88132-685-7

SPECIAL REPORTS

1   Promoting World Recovery: A Statement on Global Economic Strategy*
by 26 Economists from Fourteen Countries
December 1982   ISBN 0-88132-013-7
2   Prospects for Adjustment in Argentina, Brazil, and Mexico: Responding to the Debt Crisis*   John Williamson, ed.
June 1983   ISBN 0-88132-016-1
3   Inflation and Indexation: Argentina, Brazil, and Israel*   John Williamson, ed.
March 1985   ISBN 0-88132-037-4
4   Global Economic Imb alances*
C. Fred Bergsten, ed.
March 1986   ISBN 0-88132-042-0
5   African Debt and Financing*   Carol Lancaster and John Williamson, eds.
May 1986   ISBN 0-88132-044-7
6   Resolving the Global Economic Crisis: After Wall Street*   by Thirty-three Economists from Thirteen Countries
December 1987   ISBN 0-88132-070-6
7   World Economic Problems*   Kimberly Ann Elliott and John Williamson, eds.
April 1988   ISBN 0-88132-055-2
Reforming World Agricultural Trade*
by Twenty-nine Professionals from Seventeen Countries
1988   ISBN 0-88132-088-9
8   Economic Relations Between the United States and Korea: Conflict or Cooperation?*
Thomas O. Bayard and Soogil Young, eds.
January 1989   ISBN 0-88132-068-4
9   Whither APEC? The Progress to Date and Agenda for the Future*   C. Fred Bergsten, ed.
October 1997   ISBN 0-88132-248-2
10   Economic Integration of the Korean Peninsula   Marcus Noland, ed.
January 1998   ISBN 0-88132-255-5
11   Restarting Fast Track*   Jeffrey J. Schott, ed.
April 1998   ISBN 0-88132-259-8
12   Launching New Global Trade Talks: An Action Agenda   Jeffrey J. Schott, ed.
September 1998   ISBN 0-88132-266-0

WORKS IN PROGRESS

Managing the Euro Area Debt Crisis
William R. Cline
**Markets over Mao: The Rise of the Private
Sector in China**   Nicholas R. Lardy
**From Wariness to Partnership: Integrating the
Economies of India and the United States**
C. Fred Bergsten and Arvind Subramanian
**Bridging the Pacific: Toward Free Trade and
Investment Between China and the United
States**   C. Fred Bergsten and
Gary Clyde Hufbauer

DISTRIBUTORS OUTSIDE THE UNITED STATES

**Australia, New Zealand,
and Papua New Guinea**
Co Info Pty Ltd
648 Whitehorse Road Mitcham VIC 3132
Australia
Tel: +61 3 9210 77567
Fax: +61 3 9210 7788
Email: babadilla@coinfo.com.au
www.coinfo.com.au

India, Bangladesh, Nepal, and Sri Lanka
Viva Books Private Limited
Mr. Vinod Vasishtha
4737/23 Ansari Road
Daryaganj, New Delhi 110002
India
Tel: 91-11-4224-2200
Fax: 91-11-4224-2240
Email: viva@vivagroupindia.net
www.vivagroupindia.com

**Mexico, Central America, South America,
and Puerto Rico**
US PubRep, Inc.
311 Dean Drive
Rockville, MD 20851
Tel: 301-838-9276
Fax: 301-838-9278
Email: c.falk@ieee.org

**Asia (*Brunei, Burma, Cambodia, China,
Hong Kong, Indonesia, Korea, Laos, Malaysia,
Philippines, Singapore, Taiwan, Thailand,
and Vietnam*)**
East-West Export Books (EWEB)
University of Hawaii Press
2840 Kolowalu Street
Honolulu, Hawaii 96822-1888
Tel: 808-956-8830
Fax: 808-988-6052
Email: eweb@hawaii.edu

Canada
Renouf Bookstore
5369 Canotek Road, Unit 1
Ottawa, Ontario KlJ 9J3, Canada
Tel: 613-745-2665
Fax: 613-745-7660
www.renoufbooks.com

Japan
United Publishers Services Ltd.
1-32-5, Higashi-shinagawa
Shinagawa-ku, Tokyo 140-0002
Japan
Tel: 81-3-5479-7251
Fax: 81-3-5479-7307
Email: purchasing@ups.co.jp
*For trade accounts only. Individuals will find
Institute books in leading Tokyo bookstores.*

Middle East
MERIC
2 Bahgat Ali Street, El Masry Towers
Tower D, Apt. 24
Zamalek, Cairo
Egypt
Tel. 20-2-7633824
Fax: 20-2-7369355
Email: mahmoud_fouda@mericonline.com
www.mericonline.com

**United Kingdom, Europe
(*including Russia and Turkey*), Africa,
and Israel**
The Eurospan Group
c/o Turpin Distribution
Pegasus Drive
Stratton Business Park
Biggleswade, Bedfordshire
SG18 8TQ
United Kingdom
Tel: 44 (0) 1767-604972
Fax: 44 (0) 1767-601640
Email: eurospan@turpin-distribution.com
www.eurospangroup.com/bookstore

Visit our website at:
www.piie.com
E-mail orders to:
petersonmail@presswarehouse.com